GROWING WINGS

THE SUMMERS CHRONICLE   BOOK TWO

PHILLIP ROSEWARNE

Published in Australia by Sid Harta Books & Print Pty Ltd,
ABN: 34632585293
23 Stirling Crescent, Glen Waverley, Victoria 3150 Australia
Telephone: +61 3 9560 9920, Facsimile: +61 3 9545 1742
E-mail: author@sidharta.com.au

First published in Australia 2022
This edition published 2022
Copyright © Phillip Rosewarne 2022
Cover design, typesetting: WorkingType (www.workingtype.com.au)

The right of Phillip Rosewarne to be identified as the Author of the Work
has been asserted in accordance with the Copyright, Designs and Patents Act 1988.

This book is a work of fiction. Any similarities to that of people living
or dead are purely coincidental.

All rights reserved. No part of this publication may be reproduced,
stored in a retrieval system, or transmitted, in any form or by any means without the prior written permission of the publisher, nor be otherwise circulated in any form of binding or cover other than that in which it is published and without a similar condition being imposed on the subsequent purchaser.

Phillip Rosewarne
Growing Wings
Book Two
ISBN: 978-0-6484916-9-9 (pbk)
978-0-6456825-8-8 (ebook)
pp322

ABOUT THE AUTHOR

Phillip Rosewarne has lived and worked in various places on the east coast of Australia, his first job being for a shipping company. After working in New Guinea, Phillip was a project clerk for the Australian government in Canberra and the Northern  Territory, where he worked in Katherine and Darwin, initially for the Commonwealth Department of Works, and then for three years as head storeman for Woolworths in the Darwin area, two years either side of Cyclone Tracy. Phillip bought a cattle property in Queensland, which he operated for four years.

After returning to Canberra, he spent the next twenty-five years at the Commonwealth Department of Primary Industries, as it was then known. During that time, he worked in a science bureau within several primary industry sections. He gained a Certificate of Horticulture from the Tafe College and an Applied Science Degree from the University of Canberra.

Phillip always had a desire to write novels as opposed to scientific papers. He began writing shortly after leaving school, and the passion to write never left him. It was only later in life that he had the opportunity to write fiction on a more permanent basis.

Phillip is currently retired, and lives in the Northern Beaches region of Sydney.

This book is the second of a trilogy of vast disparity
and apparent disconnection, but coming together
in the third book.
The trilogy is dedicated to my wife Patricia, who inspired
so much of what has been written.

CHAPTER 1

This was the third day Don had seen the little girl wandering about the markets. He did not take much notice at first, but then it began to strike him as unusual to see such a young child roaming about apparently unaccompanied. Furthermore, she stood out, particularly with her brilliant crop of short, pure blonde hair, big blue eyes and pale skin. This contrasted hugely with the usual urchins that frequented the markets because most of the stallholders were either Greek, Italian or Slavonic and, apart from their swarthy appearance and dark hair, under no circumstances did they usually allow their children to roam freely for too long without regular checking.

Don noticed that she seemed to be wearing the same clothes, which were especially filthy, and she continually snacked on any available fruit she could remove from unguarded boxes.

She had passed him once, peering at him coldly and not smiling, but he had not attempted to communicate, as he had no idea how to treat a small child; it was way beyond his understanding. However, when he had heard one or two of the less likeable Italians making unsavoury remarks about this small blonde child wandering about, he kept a keener eye on her.

She was removing an apple from one of the lower cases within his earshot and the subsequent disturbance from the owner attracted his gaze. He turned in time to see a large and cranky Mediterranean waving demonstrably and shouting at her in broken English to depart. This she did so with some aplomb, and with the offending apple encased in her tiny hand. She scampered away from him and in the direction of Don's market site, contentedly munching on the forbidden fruit. She approached him as he sat on his fold-up chair.

'Hello sweetie, and what's your name?'

Don noticed her expressionless face and staring eyes. She was sporting small bruises on both her arms and legs and small welts along one arm. She also had some minor facial injuries, he thought, but was not sure what was bruising and what was just plain dirt. She stared up at him, seemingly mute to his question; she just stood quietly, with an ominous presage, her tiny body not moving. After what seemed an eternity, she answered, lowering the stolen apple behind her back, 'My name is Chessabel,' she replied in a soft apologetic voice, reeking with innocence and guilt mixed into a wispy kind of sigh. Don was quite taken aback by the angelic emanation wrapped in the earthy surrounds of the all-too human figure. He hesitated for a minute, then continued, a little more nervously than he had anticipated, 'That's a pretty name, isn't it?' There was another small delay on her part.

'No,' she announced, still staring up at him, this time with a little more defiance.

'Oh, and why not then?' he asked her, becoming slightly more puzzled. There was another deliberate pause before she was able to continue, and she blinked several times at him.

'Because I am evil,' she said, still looking up at him, and speaking in a very slow and deliberate manner, as if emphasising the point.

'And why would that be?' he asked, half expecting to be told she was in minor parental trouble for some trivial misdemeanour.

'Because I are a child of the Devil.'

'What?' said Don, slightly bewildered. 'And why would that be?'

'I just are,' she said matter-of-factly, as if everybody knew.

'And how old are you?' he continued. She was on more confident ground now and answered with less of a delay than previously.

'I'm five!' she announced proudly, holding up five dirty fingers of her free hand, the other still behind her back with the pilfered fruit.

'Where do you live then?' he asked, dreading the reply. There was a slight delay, suggestive of either confusion or deceit.

'Oh, I've run away,' she announced. 'I used to live at the big place but they keep hitting me and shouting at me.'

'Why?' he asked. Her demeanour changed to an even deeper gloom at the prospect of having to answer that query. She was unflinchingly and rather unsettlingly still staring directly at him with big blue eyes and downcast mouth.

'Because I can't write with my proper hand,' she said, very softly, almost as if she were ashamed. She thrust out her left hand disparagingly. He could see it was covered in small bruises and weals and signs of restraint marks left by rope. It disturbed him.

Don could see that this confusing conversation might drag on interminably, with little result. From what he was able to glean from the child, he believed that she was from the Catholic orphanage further up the hill. It was often referred to as the big place because it was so ornate and gloomy rather than particularly large. He decided to telephone the sisters and ask if they had a missing child.

There was a telephone box further down the street for the use of all the market licensees that allowed him to also keep an eye on his produce. He looked up the number of the orphanage and spoke to somebody there who happened to answer the telephone. There was a long and curious conversation, but indeed they did have a missing child fitting the description of Chessabel. One of the nuns would be right down to collect her from the markets.

Don did not want to get involved in any of this so declined to give his name, but said she was wandering about the market site and could not be missed if they came down. This they promptly did, two nuns arriving shortly after on foot. They searched the site, asking occasionally of different sellers if they had seen the girl. As most of the replies were either in broken English or in no English, the nuns gravitated to Donald's holding. They could see he was Australian by his nameplate that was painted over the cage, so they stopped to ask him about her. Don took the opportunity to try to learn a bit more about her.

One of the nuns was quite elderly. The younger one did all the talking in a raspy and shrill voice that quite offended Don's sensibilities. He did learn from her, however, some more details about Chessabel as the nun related what little of the story that she was prepared to tell a complete stranger.

It seemed to Don that the little girl was dumped on their doorstep about five years ago. They had no idea who her parents were. From the beginning, she had been a burden to them both physically and spiritually. The latter was because she was obviously born out of wedlock, a dire sin in the eyes of the nuns. This offence was compounded by her Jezebel-like features and appearance; blonde hair, blue eyes and very pretty face; features sent by the Devil to haunt and tempt men. However, worst of all, Chessabel insisted on trying to perform all her tasks left-handed; a sure sign of evil and the hand of the Devil as listed in Scripture.

'A wise man's heart is at his right hand; but a fool's heart is at his left,' declared the older nun in a disdainful and contemptuous tone, to no one in particular as they were talking.

'Is that so?' commented Don.

'Yes, indeed.' She continued, 'This is the word of the Lord.'

Don had no answer to that.

The younger nun continued with her story, relating how the child was intractable, unable to be corrected, and that she resisted all attempts at redemption. Don was horrified at this dilemma but could only agree with them and sent them in the direction he had last seen the child wander.

This conversation was disturbing for Don. Their description of the child as spawn of the Devil simply because she was pretty was, he thought, a trifle severe. He had never known any left-handers, but on reflection, could see that life would be difficult for anybody with that affliction. He began to contemplate all the normal activities that being left-handed would impose special difficulties. All in all, he began to agree with the nuns' approach – that it needed correction; and the sooner the better. He had also never had anything to do with nuns. He was not a Catholic; indeed, he was not anything, but he began to appreciate the service they provided to the abandoned.

Don felt a tinge of righteousness swell within him, something he rarely felt, at being instrumental in assisting in this tiny drama of life. He turned deliberately to gaze at the windblown and water-stained calendar that hung on the post under the awning. He noted the date. It was October 1972. He made a mental note of that date to recall his rare good deed.

Don gave no more thought to the episode, except to congratulate himself on its ultimate success of returning a lost sheep to the good shepherds in the form of the obliging nuns. However, he was totally stunned when, three days later, the small child was again back in the area and wandering the markets.

It was unusual for Don to frequent the market holding so often. He was primarily a car man, amongst other professions, but became involved with the market outlet through a partnership he had with an Irish ne'er-do-well who held a permit authorising him to trade as a wholesaler of fruit and vegetables at the Flemington markets. This was an immensely beneficial and useful asset for those wishing to engage in clandestine sidelines and illicit activities that could be conducted under the cover of legitimate business.

Paddy, as Don called him, was not a serious criminal, but walked a fine line between honesty and shady dealing. Paddy was real bog-Irish and what Don called a 'Mick on the make'. He certainly wanted to go places and Don thought that if he could ride Paddy's coat-tails, some of the shine might rub off on him. Don did not ask too many questions about what went on at the stall but found it useful to assist his friend.

Don knew Paddy by virtue of also being his neighbour in adjoining businesses, Paddy owning the small mixed business next to his workshop in Newtown. He was away for three weeks and had asked his trusted partner to man the holding during his absence.

Don dreaded another encounter with this strange and mysterious child: well, all children were strange and mysterious to him; she just more so. He also feared the worst.

She was doing the same procedures as before in taking fruit from unguarded stalls or from conveniently positioned cases when the wholesaler was not watching. This time he reluctantly called her over. She was much cleaner this time, so she must have just arrived. He asked her who was with her and she responded, after an annoying little pause, accompanied by that unsettling stare, that no one accompanied her. He scrutinised her tiny body.

She's quite thin and weedy, probably under fed by the cash-strapped nuns making her small for her age of five, he thought, but disturbingly, she was still covered in bruises and some were obviously new.

He interrogated her at length feigning friendship in an attempt to learn of her latest experiences. She basically repeated the former story in all its gruesome details, alluding again to her intrinsic evilness for so existing. Don invited her to remain in the security of the back packing area while he thought about it all.

The little girl stayed with Don for most of the day, happily amusing herself, playing with wooden fruit boxes behind the rear wall. Occasionally he would peer around the corner of the packing room to see if she were all right. She would cease her activity and gaze at him interminably, not moving a muscle; not smiling. When he departed, she would return to her activities as if nothing had happened. She was indeed peculiar, at least within Don's bounds of understanding. He could easily see why the nuns were unnerved by her. He even wondered if she were all there sometimes. He was, however, touched by her plight, but what was he to do with her?

Several times he prepared to ring the orphanage again, but each time was pulled up short by the thought of the welts and the determination presented by this tiny personality, steadfastly refusing even to attempt to forgo her natural endowment for an imposed deviant and abnormal one. The problem for Don now was three-fold. He could walk away and leave her to her fate, or arrange to return her to the orphanage, or he could take her home. None of these was particularly palatable to him. The first exposed her to all the dangers of unsavoury inner-city life; the second to further abuse or worse; and the third would expose him to impossible difficulties at home.

Don's home was not the normal habitation that was usually encased in that label of 'home'. His domicile consisted of small living quarters located upstairs above the mechanical workshop that was the main basis of his life. He had several sidelines, the markets being only one of them. His main income, however, and occupation, revolved around his workshop where he concentrated on mechanical and panelbeating repairs to motor vehicles.

The problem was that he did not live alone. He had Werner, the mechanical engineer who carried the qualifications required for his business, Don having no formal training or qualifications himself. Don was what was called a bush mechanic, but very good at it. More importantly though, there was Dawn. She lived with Don but was not his wife, nor was she really his *de facto*; she was not even a girlfriend any more. She really just lived there now more out of convenience and an inability to make the effort to move on in life on both their accounts. How could he explain to her bringing home an abandoned child?

Don stayed at the stall until as late as he could to ensure that most of the others had departed. It was after dark by the time he summoned up the courage to shut up his grills and put some items into his van. Jessie, as he called her, for he refused to call her Jezebel, no matter how evil the nuns thought she was, played contentedly all afternoon in the back part of the work area, not disturbing him at all. He was finally ready to leave when he looked down at her and asked if she would like to spend the night at his house. She agreed readily and appeared happy at that prospect. Together they walked to his van outside the enclosed and locked holding.

She sat quietly in the front passenger's side as he drove home in a mild daze, wondering all the time whether he knew what he was really doing in this mess.

Don pulled into his workshop in Newtown and unloaded a few items from the back while Jessie looked on. He gathered her by the hand and with considerable trepidation began the awkward climb up the stairs into the living area where he knew trouble would await. He was not wrong. Werner quickly dismissed himself from the room and proceeded back down to the workshop to work on some cars. Dawn could not believe her eyes at the sight.

'You can't just bring home a kid like a stray dog, idiot!' she exclaimed in a raucous, high-pitched voice on seeing the girl and being informed of her plight. 'That's kidnapping, fool,' she continued, becoming slightly hysterical. 'You've done some pretty dumb things in your day but this takes the cake.'

'What could I do?' was all he could say.

Jessie cringed behind Don's legs, peeking out at the horrible ogre that reminded her for all the world of the dragons in black she had so desperately tried to escape.

'Can you get her something to eat, she's probably starving. She hasn't eaten all day, except some fruit. Is there anything she can have while I think what to do?'

'What's her name then?' asked Dawn.

'Jessie. Jessie,' replied Don, deliberately avoiding any reference to Jezebel.

Dawn peered down at the cowering child with a look of disdain on her gnarled face and sighed in resignation, beaten for the moment by the circumstances presented. She determined to remove this problem at first light, however.

Dawn was a plain, short woman, very thin and scrawny, and in her late forties, with sallow wrinkled skin from a life spent in the sun. Her crooked yellowish teeth were the result of many years of smoking. She had been married a couple of times, but her assertive and slightly aggressive personality drove men away, and her bossy and unco-operative nature grated with everybody. She was a capable cook, though not very imaginative and, while she possessed natural guile and cunning, was not highly educated; a condition that tended to encourage her opinionated temperament to exert itself at every opportunity and on any and every subject. Dawn also possessed a raspy and grating voice caused possibly from years of smoking and working at her only pastime, a barmaid at one of the close-by hotels. Here she mixed it with the rest of the ruffians and could swear like a trooper with the best of them. She had lived with Don for about five years as he tolerated her ways and knew it could be difficult for a single woman to secure accommodation.

Don was pragmatic and normally prudent, but had a latent tendency to act impulsively on the rare occasion. However, he had never brought home a wandering child before. This caused considerable and justified consternation within the jumbled household that constituted Don's immediate acquaintances. He did not have a 'family' as he had never been married. He lived a strange bachelor existence in this dilapidated part of Newtown, which was strictly working class and rather shabby and drab.

Dawn finally agreed to overcome her objections to attend to Jessie while they collectively decided what to do with her. Even Dawn had to acknowledge the bruises and welts covering the child's slightly emaciated body. It aroused long-denied maternal instincts she thought she lacked, but only momentarily, and she soon brushed them aside. Dawn could quickly see why the nuns would think her a child of the Devil and rapidly began to dislike Jessie herself the more she was around her.

Jessie possessed absolutely everything Dawn lacked, from the locks of pure blonde hair and the biggest blue eyes to a flawless white skin, except for the human damage inflicted by the nuns. Jessie had a beautiful set of white shining teeth that emphasised her generous pink mouth and cute button nose. Dawn could quickly grow to dislike Jessie if she were not careful. Jessie would have to go, and soon.

The other occupant in the group was Werner. He had come into Don's life about ten years earlier when, as a young travelling backpacker from Germany, he had overstayed his visa but really wanted to remain in Australia. Don effectively vouched for him and went guarantor in order to keep him on as his mechanic. Don had no qualifications at all but Werner was a qualified mechanical engineer with talents that could take him anywhere within Australia, so Don valued him enormously.

Werner so loved his carefree existence in the sunshine that he had abandoned all ambition and contentedly pottered in Don's mechanical workshop on the strange assortment of vehicles that came through his hands. Werner did not ask questions, just repaired the cars as requested and pursued his real love, photography. He spoke fluent English and was popular with the few clients with whom he had any direct dealings.

The first few days were a novelty for Don as Jessie occupied hours of his time. He was able to relieve the squabbles with Dawn by leaving before sunrise to attend to the market stall for the first few days while Paddy was still away on business. He enjoyed the girl's company and began to conceive the hint of seemingly paternal stirrings within him. He had never married and did not particularly like children, more from unfamiliarity than from detestation. He could not but notice lately how the brusque and gruff market men treated their offspring with so much love and attention. He would often watch, sometimes with the slightest tinge of envy, as they interacted with their small children who seemed ubiquitous around the markets.

What if I could arrange to keep her for a while? he mused. *Werner would be no trouble; Dawn would be the only difficulty.* He thought about it carefully. *No harm in dreaming.*

Jessie was attentive as she followed Don around the workshop, incessantly asking questions and helping him with his chores. She was just like a faithful puppy and no trouble at all. She even shared his slight distaste for Dawn, a feeling that had been slowly growing within him over the last few years as they drifted completely apart.

Before Don knew it, a week had elapsed. Jess had settled in admirably and there was no mention of any missing children on any of the news services. But Don rang the orphanage after eight days. He was put through to the mother superior and he asked casually how the little girl that was found in the markets was faring. To his amazement, he was told that she had been removed by some recently discovered family members and taken back to their house in the western suburbs. He asked her if he could get their name but that was refused. Could he obtain their name if he involved the police? There was a long silence on the telephone followed by a stuttering reply indicating that the information was confidential. When Don asked if the nuns would take her back if she proved difficult at

Chapter 1

pioneer of the 1880s overland droving days into the last untouched expanse of northern Australia. He came out from Scotland as a wiry eighteen-year-old to escape the Sassenachs and their interminable incursions and resettlements of the defeated Scots in the 1860s and drifted up to the Kimberley as most of the other good country closer in had been taken by then. He married one of the neighbouring station manager's daughters as soon as he arrived in the northwest while overlanding to the Kimberley. Don's father was born on the run in 1893 and died there in 1958.

Don learnt all the skills of an outback stockman, but excelled at motor engine mechanics in particular. Don was no fool and he could see the writing on the wall. He decided early on that the harsh life of outback struggle was not for him. He left the run in 1960 to be managed and developed by Stuart, who was a different kettle of fish altogether from Donald. He was steadier than Don, more serious and much more enamoured of the outback life. Don left without ceremony and unannounced, and never regretted the decision for one minute. Don eventually drifted to Sydney where a young man with no suitable qualifications and training could find work of some kind with little trouble.

By 1971, he had been in Sydney for over ten years. In that time, he had amassed several sidelines. Don had a half share in the market franchise licence with Paddy, who diversified into some, shall we say, less honourable sidelines; mostly dealing drugs and illicit cigarettes using the legitimate produce as a ruse to pass on other items. Paddy also owned the small mixed business in Australia Street, Newtown, next door to Don's workshop: that is how they met. Here he was also able to augment his legitimate income by a drug disposal sideline and gain pecuniary advantage through various forms of deception. Whenever Paddy had items for sale other than the usual groceries he purported to retail, he would put out his advertising board reading 'assot groc'.

Paddy had his fingers in a couple of other small shady dealings as well, but Don was not involved. Don's biggest source of income was generated by his extremely successful mechanical workshop. Here he was able to convert wrecked vehicles purchased from auctions into saleable cars at a handsome profit. This was due entirely to the expert assistance of Werner on the mechanics and Antoine on the panelbeating. Neither of these two really understood what was going on and did not want to know, as long as Don paid well and provided them with safe accommodation, and kept them safe from the immigration people.

Australia Street was a rather long, narrow and grimy inner-city road that consisted of mostly street-front small shops of every description plus several hotels, some housing and more than one school. Don's workshop fronted Australia Street but also had a very narrow lane running up the side of it as well. This gave him access to the back and allowed ingress for vehicles via this laneway, which was much less busy than Australia Street. It also allowed easier access to the adjoining mixed business's backyard where all the deliverables were stored.

Chapter 1

All the premises in the street were at least two storeys, most possessing living quarters above the shops where their respective operators lived. Thus, Don had access to two sets of living spaces, one above the workshop and one above the grocery store because Paddy lived a few streets away, not above his shop. Antoine and his girlfriend Micheline lived above that shop and Don, Dawn, Werner and now Jessie lived above the workshop. It was Antoine's lovely young French girlfriend, Micheline, whom he had brought out with him on his travels, who took to Jess as a sister and ensured she was well cared for. Micheline attended to Jessie's needs initially, while Dawn fiddled about trying to avoid her. This had the added benefit of increasing Jessie's exposure to French.

The rooms were all small and pokey and usually possessed only small, if any, windows. Right at the back of the upper level of the workshop was an even smaller room that was accessed by going down three narrow steps and into a dingy, rather dusty, room that was really no more than a glorified attic. It was here that Don had cleared out the rubbish and given Jessie a room of her own. She was ecstatic as she had never known the luxury of sleeping alone, having to sleep in a dormitory arrangement in the orphanage. The upper second floor also possessed a narrow railing that permitted access to viewing any activities that were occurring down in the workshop, a facility that enabled Don to monitor goings-on after hours.

Jessie really loved living in these exciting surroundings. The only drawback was Dawn. Jessie began to seriously dislike her because she continually threatened her newfound freedom with warnings to expose her existence. Furthermore, Dawn represented everything distasteful in Jessie's short life; the black-garbed ugly dragons who had made her life a misery with their continuous beatings and haranguing of her because of her 'afflictions'. But here, Jessie was never scolded for using her preferred left hand and never reminded that she was the Devil's daughter; besides she was being continuously educated in languages and mechanics and now going to 'big school'. All this was under threat from the one source of discontent in her life: Dawn. This was compounded by Jessie's unknowing and misunderstood dislike of older women, consequent on her suffering at the nuns' hands.

Jessie had been with Don one year. He had nominated a birth date for her and she was growing slowly but was still smaller than her peers. He figured she was born in 1967, so in 1973 she must have been about six. She was becoming fluent in German and French as well as picking up quickly the simpler aspects of motor mechanics. She was excelling at primary school. Dawn had reluctantly accepted that Jessie was going to be part of this life, at least for the moment.

When Jessie was seven, she returned home one afternoon from school with lacerations on her arm and face. Don enquired as to the cause of the cuts and was told that some of the bigger girls were picking on her because of her achievements, and genteel and classic demeanour. Don was annoyed and announced that, starting immediately, Jess would be attending the local academy of martial arts that had a small gymnasium setup only five doors down the street.

The next morning, he wandered down to the premises and enquired if he could enrol his daughter. The owner agreed and Jessie could commence training that week. Jessie enjoyed the classes and showed such aptitude that she was soon able to train every afternoon. This was particularly convenient as she only lived five doors up. It wasn't long before Jessie graduated to the advanced classes for her age.

Don was very pleased with himself over this decision. Jessie was not especially enamoured of physical activities at the school, mostly because she was relatively shorter and more delicately boned than most of her peers, many of whom were of 'New Australian' stock, thus often more robust and bigger children. While she excelled academically, she was less enthusiastic at any, especially communal, physical activity. This problem was immediately solved by her enrolment in martial arts, plus it also had the advantage of improving her self esteem.

Over the next few years, Jessie became a very successful exponent of self-defence and the head trainer of the academy was keen for her to advance to representative combat. This she would eventually decline, but was nevertheless exceptionally proficient at this sport. It had the added bonus of making her very fit and highly supple as well.

Jessie was a loner and spent most of her free time either studying or working in the workshop where she became proficient at motor mechanics. She enjoyed the martial arts activity because she could train alone and exercise incessantly for as long as she pleased. The instructor got to know the MacIntyres very well and allowed her to train most evenings alone or with older more advanced exponents over time.

The chief instructor informed Don that Jess was admirably suited to this form of activity because of her smaller build. Shorter people had faster and more rapidly responsive muscular structures that allowed them to react and respond quicker than their taller or heavier opponents. He also noted that Jess had a mindset that matched her physical ability. She was focused, sharp, and possessed a certain type of killer instinct. What he liked about her was that her personality did not lead her to be aggressive; only reactive. He suggested to Don that she could go far in this sport if she so chose.

As time went by, the atmosphere between Don and Dawn slowly deteriorated to the point where it was becoming obvious that something would have to be done. The catalyst arose when, after a particularly torrid exchange, Dawn made the fatal threat to expose Don and his pseudo-daughter to the police. She had made veiled threats on a couple of occasions when they had disagreements but nothing too dangerous. This time, however, Don was seriously annoyed and finally demanded she depart from her room and seek accommodation elsewhere.

They departed under acrimonious, spiteful and bitter circumstances, with Don warning her that she faced serious danger if she attempted to interfere with his arrangements. He was so enraged, that Dawn, for once in their long relationship, could see that he really meant it. She knew one thing about Don, and that was that she feared he was more than capable of carrying out his threats. She prudently decided that she was not going to tempt fate on this matter.

Dawn departed that afternoon and managed initially to obtain accommodation in the hotel where she worked as a barmaid. Don frequented that establishment but from then on simply moved patronage to the one further up the street. Dawn ended up staying there for many years but avoided seeing any of them. Jessie was not sorry to see her nemesis and rival for Don's attention depart her life. She was, however, slightly disturbed at the thought that she was the source that precipitated the rupture. Even as a child, she could discern the anguish she had caused to her so-admired benefactor and regretted that aspect of it enormously.

When Jess was ten, she was asked to complete some assignments for school projects that required her to purchase special paper. This triggered in Don's mind the recollection that somewhere within the building he had stashed away some very old accounting books and other stationery items that she might find useful. He hunted around the upper floor rooms and finally found where he had hidden them years ago. He offered Jess the cardboard box full of stationery to use as she wished.

The contents were not particularly noteworthy for a ten-year-old child, except for two items. The bulk consisted of mostly foolscap notebooks, accounting journals and reams of foolscap paper, something she could utilise for scrap.

However, within the contents of the box were two large, cloth-covered journals of over three hundred pages each. They were obviously very expensive and rather extravagantly bound, and covered in a soft velvety material with fine leather corners.

Jessie was enthralled by this find. She had never before in her life seen such extravagance and elegance in so humble an artefact. They were by far and away the nicest objects she had ever been given. They were so extraordinary that she decided they needed to be reserved for special use. She carefully put them aside in her room and hid them just in case Don saw them and decided to change his mind and request their return.

After some serious thought, Jess decided that she would utilise these two lovely books to keep a daily diary of her life. Commencing immediately, she would detail all the events that occurred throughout the years until they were full. Every evening she would dutifully record the day's events and then secrete the volume away in her special hiding place under the bed.

Paddy was expanding his enterprises, mostly unknown to Don, and was also becoming better known to the police. Nothing too serious, but nevertheless his activities were noted. On one of the increasing visits to Paddy's grocery shop, one of the detectives paid a visit to Don. This was a development that was definitely not welcomed. While Don was not entirely honest, he drew the line at out-and-out criminal activity. He was aware that Paddy had less scruples than himself, but he always thought Paddy was basically reliable and honourable.

The detective introduced himself as Inspector Ian Knuckey. He was looking for Mr McGuiness who supposedly lived at the address next door. Don was unaware of Paddy's whereabouts but asked what he desired of his neighbour. Ian Knuckey was not forthcoming, but did intimate that there was some unlawful activity occurring in the street related to drug dealing and car theft. This worried Don as he was well aware that Paddy sailed close to the wind. His own business was legitimate, but also would not stand too much scrutiny as he often obtained wrecked vehicles that had a dodgy background. Don was also troubled by the attention the police had been paying to the market outlet, which Paddy had increasingly been seconding Don into attending as Paddy's affairs seemed to be taking him away more frequently.

A few weeks after this incident, Don received another visit from Detective Knuckey. He came armed with a search warrant, and politely and rather deferentially requested if he could examine a couple of the cars to which Werner and Antoine were attending at that time. Detective Knuckey spent some time examining the vehicles and then departed without saying a word. Don was perplexed but satisfied all was well. Don duly passed on the cars to the pre-arranged purchasers and thought no more about it.

A few days later, Detective Knuckey returned. It seemed he was on the trail of some possibly corrupt police officers who may be involved in a car scam that entailed stealing cars and re-assembling them; possibly at Don's place. Don was horrified, not so much at the fraud, which was bad enough, but at the thought of the police doing such unspeakable crimes. It simply never occurred to him that such things would happen in Sydney. Little did Don know that that story was a ruse to conceal an even worse offence.

Knuckey reappeared several more times over the next few months and then disappeared completely for quite some time. Then about six months later, he again entered Don's workshop with another request. This time he was chasing more serious criminals and would appreciate Don's assistance. Don was not impressed with all this police attention. Firstly, he was mindful of the circumstances surrounding Jessie, who was now approaching eleven. Secondly, association with the police did not auger well for his business clientele or his reputation as a bit of a lad.

Detective Ian Knuckey was an unusual man, especially for a cop. He was rather weedy and slight of statue. He was also mildly hunched and smoked incessantly, usually roll-your-owns. He always had a harassed appearance about him and dressed in a dishevelled, almost unkempt manner. His hair was grey and longish, though short at the back and sides. His manner was almost apologetic and he spoke rather softly in a deferential way that Don surmised did not inspire awe, let alone much respect from the criminal classes. Yet here he was, still at it, and apparently meeting with some success.

Knuckey wanted to arrange a sting in an attempt to catch some alleged crooked cops operating a clandestine drug ring and money laundering scheme along with stand-over tactics that amounted to protection rackets. Would Don be interested and willing to assist? Don was indeed not very happy about this or interested in it either.

However, over time, Don was convinced, more out of sympathy for the down-at-heel air about Knuckey rather than any persuasive impact of his arguments. The upshot was that apparently the operation went according to plan though Don was not fully aware of which vehicles and purchasers were the offenders.

This operation had the unexpected and long-term consequence of endearing Detective Knuckey to Don and they struck up a casual and lasting friendship fostered by the fact that they both drank at the same pub, consequent on Don's moving further up the street after his fall-out with Dawn. This had totally unintended and unforeseeable outcomes on Don's life, impacts that would reverberate for decades.

By the time Jess was approaching thirteen years old, she had established a pleasant routine for herself. Jess was a gentle, caring soul. She was also developing into a refined young girl. Don was a rough diamond and had never been exposed to anything approaching elegance and class, but he was astute enough to recognise in Jess the foundations of something indefinable. She was not what he would call beautiful, but she was nonetheless attractive in her own way. She had grown into a shapely young teenager through all the training she constantly did, and had befriended several of the neighbouring families who attended the local school and lived nearby.

Jess, for her part, was introverted and shy. She was still small for her age but had filled out more through all the exercise. She excelled at academic pursuits and was obviously very intelligent. She thoroughly mastered German from Werner and was passably good at French, which she still utilised regularly with Antione. She was now so competent at mechanics that she was able to disassemble and reassemble small engines and make them work. She was not in the slightest interested in pursuing any mechanical vocation, but instead aspired to academia.

She had by now become very friendly with the owner of the martial arts school, which had grown into quite a successful business. Much to the constant frustration of the instructors, Jess refused to be drawn into serious competition; instead, she followed her own level of attainment and received immense satisfaction from knowing that she was proficient enough to protect herself.

Jess had few friends. The few she did have tended to be of 'New Australian' descent, often mistreated by the locals and they tended to gather within their own communities. One of the girls whom she did befriend resulted from the disparaging remarks that Don had made about her family. He had called her father an 'Icky Mo' and cast aspersions on the family's ability to fit in. Jess found that kind of attitude tended to arouse within her feelings of sympathy and empathy for the accused, possibly because she had commenced life as an outcast. She had then observed the gaunt and somewhat plain child of the family passing her own house on her way to the local school. Jess found herself drawn to underdogs and those cast in poor circumstances, a trait that widened her knowledge of humanity considerably. She found the different mixes of nationalities strange, and their culinary habits most interesting.

The other item that occupied her attention was the now extensive diary that she had religiously maintained since being given the diaries by Don. Every evening she would sit at her small desk and write assiduously about the day's events and the things that impacted on her life. It was a serious outlet for her newly acquired and growing desire to create and to accurately record.

Over the next few years, Don slowly increased the frequency and quality of the villains with whom he had interactions, which were instigated at the behest of Ian Knuckey. However, one unintended consequence of this assistance was that, independent of Ian Knuckey, other police, and worse, some members of the judiciary became involved in what amounted to straight out criminal graft. Don would probably have been unaware of their real backgrounds except for Ian's advising. Don could see that this could escalate out of control, especially if anything ever happened to Ian.

Because the upper level of the workshop had a small internal balcony that allowed full viewing of activities in certain parts of the downstairs area as well as concealment from view, Don began to get Werner to take secret photographs of meetings that were being increasingly arranged at Don's. Unfortunately, Don was getting the reputation for being a safe haven for clandestine gatherings where unlawful activities could be securely planned. His only course of action for protection was to ensure Werner documented all meetings and that details of names, times and dates were scrupulously recorded. Don then guaranteed his protection by securely hiding the notes and photographs in a solid concrete pigeon-hole located in one of the main pillars supporting the building.

All this activity began to impact on everybody in the household. Werner was regularly requested to spy on, and photograph, the irregular meetings, and then develop and protect the negatives that resulted. They were also having an increasing impact on Jessie. She was forbidden to go anywhere near the workshop on some evenings when these meetings were occurring and she was to remain completely out of sight and quiet during these happenings. This intrigued her and she sometimes disobeyed Don and snuck out to join Werner in his operations. She had no interest in either the goings-on or the attendees, but was concerned about her activities having to be curtailed occasionally.

Not many people knew that Jessie was living with Don, but the few who did, thought she was Don's daughter. Most never saw her, and those who knew of her were told that she was much older than she really was. He usually informed people that she was well into her twenties. This was partially to protect her identity if anything went wrong, but also to keep prying eyes away. Because she kept a secret diary, she also occasionally noted down that a meeting had happened and even sometimes who attended. This she did because of the impact it had on her life, not because the meetings had any interest to her. She was aware of the calibre of those attending these planning nights. Apart from some crooked cops, there also appeared to be solicitors and even an occasional judge. This instilled in Jessie a deep-seated loathing and disrespect for the entire legal system; indeed, any form of authority, especially when she recalled her formative years at the orphanage.

The gatherings grew to be a regular occurrence and over time Ian seemed to slowly disappear. But after an absence of many months, he suddenly approached Don in their old pub. He was about to expose some serious corruption at senior levels of the police force but wanted some final concrete evidence for his case. He requested that two new men be admitted to the next evening's gathering to familiarise themselves with the details and gather more evidence for his case. They would be specially selected and very experienced and reliable policemen who were working directly under him. Don reluctantly agreed and duly the two officers turned up for their first meeting.

Don was warned that they would be reappearing at the next meeting, but Ian Knuckey advised he hoped this would be the last as he would then be able to move. The meeting was planned for after eight on an August night. The weather was bitter, especially for Sydney, but not unusual. Werner was in place as usual to take some pictures and Jess had been down to the gym a few doors along the street. She would return about ten, silently ascend the back stairs, and then remain out of sight. That night the alignment of influences in the cosmos was inauspicious for all those in attendance at that address in Australia Street.

Ian Knuckey was unaware that his careful planning and methodical execution of this investigation had been discovered by his superiors and perpetrators of some of the criminal activity and that steps were being taken that evening to silence him.

Just after ten o'clock that evening, Jessie departed the martial arts gym and quietly walked up the back ally that led to the rear door of the workshop. She slowly opened the heavy wooden door and silently entered the building. Then everything happened so quickly. She could hear the muffled whispers of two men in the dark of the narrow hall that led to the workshop where the meeting was being held. Suddenly the back door opened again and two large, heavy-set men noisily and clumsily staggered into the darkened hall. They both had torches and were shining them around in the darkness.

The two men further down the hall turned to confront the two new intruders. Flashlights were beaming around the confined space of the hallway, finally resting on the two original men. There was a lot of chatter, both in English and, surprisingly to Jess, also in German, both from the original two and the intruders. Suddenly, two muffled handgun shots pierced the maelstrom and the two original men fell to the ground motionless. One of the intruders walked straight up to them in the torch light and Jessie watched as the intruder fired another shot into the head of one of the fallen men. She let out a muffled gasp and scampered towards the door through which she had just entered, terrified for her life and shocked beyond belief at what she had just witnessed. As she reached the door, however, one of the intruders turned and fired again, this time at her. Two torches had swung around to the door and momentarily lit up the exit. Two shots rang out, both hitting the doorjamb quite close to her head.

There were police sirens wailing in the distance and she assumed they were headed this way. She waited momentarily not far from the doorway, then saw the two assassins run from the building and around the corner. She rushed back inside and Don was standing by the two dead men in the now lit-up hallway.

She quickly stammered, 'Two men did this! And they shot at me as well!' She told Don that she had recognised one of the intruders.

Don stood silently for a minute. Then he said in a commanding but calm voice, 'Go upstairs immediately and grab a few things. I'm gonna send you off to my brother's place in the Kimberley for a while. Just till this blows over.'

'What will I get?' she asked, totally confused and frightened.

'Just a few clothes and good shoes. Oh … and you better grab a hat. Quick about it now.'

Jessie rushed upstairs to her tiny room. She grabbed a couple of shirts and a pair of jeans. She put on her best pair of sandshoes and rummaged about for a hat. She was about to depart when she stopped and turned for a second.

What about my diaries? she thought. She hesitated then rushed back to their hiding place and retrieved the two large volumes, stuffing them into the back of the small knapsack she was carrying. They barely fitted, but she wanted them to be safely with her in case she was away for some time. She raced back downstairs to find Don waiting at the back door with the van running outside. They quickly got into the car and he drove off recklessly into the alley and out the other end of the lane into the darkened cold streets. He headed towards the airport.

CHAPTER TWO

Don drove mostly in silence all the way to Mascot Airport. He tried to reassure the trembling teenager that he would arrange everything for her, but he spent most of the time staring straight ahead, deep in thought. Don told Jess that he would contact his brother Stuart before she arrived at his place and he would be waiting to pick her up at the airport. They drove into the deepening night and about four miles from the airport, he pulled up along the waterfront facing Botany Bay and said that they would wait there until daylight and then he would take her to the aerodrome.

Jess was still in some of her gear that she had worn to and from the gymnasium. She also had not had time to clean herself up much after her workout. She wanted a shower, but there was little chance of that just yet. It was also very cold waiting in the confines of the delivery van, parked by the dark and forbidding waters of the large and open bay.

As the sun began to slowly and weakly rouse itself from behind the misty, cloud-enshrouded horizon, Don checked that Jess was still okay and started up the van. That at least would give them some modicum of heating. He drove to the airport, which by this time of day was stirring, as many passengers had early flights both in and out of Sydney. He parked the van and together they rushed into the terminus. It was fairly quiet at the booking counter at this hour of the morning as Don rushed up to the attendant with Jess in tow. Jessie could hear the conversation but was not clearly concentrating following her harrowing experience. She only caught bits of the conversation as Don spoke for some time to the booking attendant and finally arranged for a flight from Sydney to Perth and then connecting on to Derby.

'What name, sir?' asked the woman.

Don was stumped for a minute. He glanced around the terminus building without making it too obvious and Jess saw him looking at the advertising boards scattered about the room.

'Jane,' he said, rather unconvincingly. 'Jane Ransom.'

Under normal circumstances, Jess might have been amused at Don's antics, but not this time. She was also staring at the advertisements and acknowledged his genius. One said, 'Be a Tarzan to your Jane' and another said, 'Why pay a king's ransom – use Kings Hire Cars'.

Jess was now Jane Ransom, a rather not unpleasant name,

she thought.

Don took her over to the waiting area and spoke to her lovingly. He advised her that he would contact his brother Stuart and tell him she was on the way.

'When will I see you again?' she asked softly.

'Soon. Soon,' he said nervously. 'I'll be in touch as soon as I can. Now listen to me carefully, Jess. Don't tell anyone what you've seen. Promise?'

Jess nodded silently.

'And make sure you tell Stuey you're my daughter. Is that clear? Listen sweetie, I must go back now. Will you be all right?'

'Yes, I think so,' she said sadly and very softly.

'Don't lose your tickets. Oh … I almost forgot. Look, here's some money. It's all I've got. It should get you to Derby but—'

With that, Don handed her all he had in his pocket, which was about five hundred dollars. Jess was used to seeing large sums of cash in Don's hands so thought little of the amount. He leaned over and gave her a loving and long hug, rubbing her back and hoping this would not be the last he saw of the young woman he had grown to love so much. Jess watched as he hurriedly walked towards the exit doors, not even turning to take one last look at her. She was suddenly very alone.

Jessie sat silently and in fits of occasional shivers as she awaited the boarding call for the flight to Perth. Don had told the hostess that Jess was his daughter going to visit her uncle in Derby. He lied about her age too, telling them that she was sixteen. She had grown quite a bit in the last few years, especially since she had been taking so much time at the gymnasium and training at the martial arts school. She was still only a short child for her age, though she had thickened up quite a bit. Physically she would not normally pass for sixteen, but her face and bearing suggested a much older and more sophisticated young woman.

Jess possessed a soft and refined voice, and she spoke in an elegant and educated manner. This was her saving grace, as the flight attendant could see that she was indeed mature in conversation if not entirely in appearance.

The call finally came and Jess boarded the flight with little trouble, carrying her treasured possessions. The flight departed from Mascot mid-morning, but as it was at least a six-hour flight to Perth it would not arrive until the afternoon, though she would pick up two hours more because of the difference in Western Australian time.

Derby was a long way from Perth and in an isolated part of a sparsely populated and enormous state. There was only one flight a day to the northwest, operated by a small but imposing little jet with the strange livery of MMA painted on its side and the now familiar Ansett star beside it. MacRobertson Miller Airlines serviced the whole of the distant north and did not arrive in Derby until late in the afternoon. MMA was an unfortunate acronym, as it allowed the locals to refer to it rather disparagingly as Mickey Mouse Airlines; something it really was not.

In any case, as Jess later learned, it was a far more polite reference when compared to the rather unfortunate other outback Territory airline that was canary yellow and branded with a far worse epithet. It was going to be a long and tiring day for the young teenager. There was a short time in Perth between flights, so Jess had time to buy a few small supplies to tide her over until she arrived at Stuart's.

Derby was a small outback coastal tourist centre that also serviced the remote cattle stations that dotted the sparsely populated and rugged west Kimberley district. As she flew in, Jess could see the immense jetty stretching hundreds of metres out into King Sound. She also noticed there were many well-sealed roads leading off into the dismal surroundings comprising uninviting coastal mud and tidal flats that stretched eternally in all directions.

Jess got off the small aeroplane and wandered over to the unimposing low-set wooden structure that was the airport terminus. She was immediately struck by the warmer weather and the strange noises of the local bird population preparing itself for the evening to come. She was also struck by the cosmopolitan nature of the people who seemed to be loitering about the lounge. Jess gazed about for someone who might be looking for her but no one came forward. She decided to sit in the lounge and wait.

Evening descended rather quickly and there were now few people remaining in the airport. Jess decided to make her own arrangements or somebody would get suspicious. She wandered out to the road and surveyed her options. She managed to hitch a ride with one of the cargo vans that was heading back into town and she was dropped off near the centre. She found a cheap backpackers' hostel in Loch Street where she spent the night.

Next morning, she enquired of the desk the best way to get to Milbark Station out on the Gibb River Road. She did not have much information, just a mud map that Don had drawn for her on the back of some brochure, and the name of the station out in the Kimberley. The attendant, a young woman of pleasing appearance but untailored and careless attire, had never heard of Milbark Station. However, she was familiar with the track that had become a beef development road called Gibb River Road. She helpfully suggested to Jess several possibilities including perhaps hitching a ride with one of the fuel transports that frequently delivered fuel to the properties along that road.

That appealed to Jess, so she found the fuel depot and approached a couple of the drivers. She was informed that it was against company policy to accept passengers. However, one of the drivers told her that if she went along the road and he saw her there he would pick her up as he was going on to the next property along the road with a big delivery and he could drop her at the entrance to Milbark. Jess hitched another ride out to the Gibb River Road turnoff and began slowly walking along it waiting for traffic to arrive. About half an hour later, the road train tanker came along the narrow bitumen road.

It was a long way to Milbark, time and distance concepts that were totally foreign to city-bred Jessie. She assumed the station was reasonably close to town and that she would be there in an hour or two. This was to be her first lesson in Kimberley living. It took all day just to arrive at the turnoff that was the crude entrance road to Stuart's cattle run. The driver, a solid, shortish man in a blue singlet, was surprisingly talkative, which Jess found confusing as she assumed he would be used to lonely travel and value his silence. Not so; he chatted the whole time in a strong and deep voice on any and all subjects. Jess found it difficult to join the conversation as she possessed a soft voice and found it hard to converse in the noisy cab above the sound of the huge engine whining away out front and with the wind pouring in through the windows, except by shouting. This she found exhausting so in the end decided it was simpler to allow the driver to hog the conversation and air all his ideas to the ready listener. She concluded that, contrary to what she had thought, he obviously had untold time on his hands to think about all manner of topics and so rarely found an outlet to espouse his thoughts, and when he did find one, it was all go for him.

The road quickly turned into gravel not far out of Derby. It meandered gently through the drab khaki-coloured countryside, avoiding any of the stark and sudden ragged hills that appeared irregularly dotted on the dry plain.

The driver made a couple of deliveries along the way that caused delays in her travel and he also stopped at a scenic, though hot and dry, spot along the track to partake of a lavish lunch that he informed her his good wife prepared for him every trip. He did spend some time listening to his surroundings and occasionally pulled the huge vehicle up in the middle of the road to check on some extraneous noise he heard, usually, he advised her, a tyre blowing out, the curse of the bush truckies. According to the truckie, it was a difficult and dirty job to change a tyre on the road, especially if it was an inner.

Finally, they arrived at an isolated and deserted gravel turn-off that had a wide well-used open area where many trucks had manoeuvred in the past. Here the driver stopped the truck ready to drop her off.

'You sure you'll be all right?'

'Yes,' Jess assured him, hoping her uncle would be along any minute.

'Well, if you're sure. The homestead is about thirty kilometres down there,' he said, pointing in the direction of the disappearing track that headed off into the untamed bush. 'About two kilometres in you'll come to the river, then it's about another twenty-eight-odd Ks.'

'Thank you so much for the lift,' she said to him, as she climbed out of the cabin and onto the dry hard gravel that was now the road. She waved and watched as he slowly waded up through the gears, disappearing in an increasing haze of dust and distance. She could hear the huge road train negotiating the dusty gravel road for many minutes in the deep brooding silence that was the Australian bush late in the afternoon.

The air was filled with strange and peculiar sounds from the many birds that flitted about noisily in the sparse vegetation, which itself gave off weird aromas after the heat of the day. There was also the unmistakable smell of bushfires burning somewhere in the hazy distance.

What to do? Her thoughts turned to Don and the life she had just left behind. A feeling of mild fear overcame her momentarily at the prospect of where she was and how to cope.

Again, there was no one to meet her. *Nothing for it*, she thought, *but to start walking down the gravel track that led to the homestead.*

She hitched the rucksack up onto her back and began to walk down the track in the direction of the river. It was getting quite late now and there were many strange and unfamiliar sights, animals and birds beginning to stir in the cooling evening light. After about twenty minutes she came to the river. She could hear its babbling for some time before she actually got to it. It was a wide, waist-deep, gently surging mass where the road crossed it, but Jess could see the flood debris high up in the spindly misshapen trees that were scattered about in the large, boulder-strewn and gravelly riverbed that extended for many hundreds of metres either side of the actual water itself.

It must flood something shocking, she thought to herself.

Jess removed her shoes, socks and dusty jeans, and waded across the stream, which she found to be surprisingly cold. Then she put on her shoes and jeans once she reached the rough gravelly bank on the other side.

Jess walked on for about an hour when she realised that she was not going to get to the house before it was completely dark. She decided she had better prepare to stop for the night and find somewhere to sleep. As she got older, Jess needed much less sleep than the rest of her peers and often worked well into the night at home, even after physical exercise either at the gym or working on motors. It was far too early for her to be going to sleep in the early dark. The night was also getting surprisingly cool after such a warm day. She hoped she had enough clothes. Jess also began to notice there were many insects buzzing around her, especially mosquitos. Then there were all the strange noises emanating from the surrounding darkening bush. Unfortunately, Jess had no means of starting a fire. It was going to be a scary sort of night.

Next morning, well before dawn and after a fitful and uncomfortable night, Jess was awakened by the rustling of animals and the cacophony of birdcalls that seemed to fill the whole scene with strange and often startlingly raucous calls. It was barely light with a cold chill in the heavy air scented with unfamiliar smells from the spindly and sparse bushy vegetation. She aroused herself and gazed around at the weird scenery that comprised her new world. She could hear the faint gurgling of the river that paralleled the track, but at some distance away through the long grass and bush. She decided to make for that and have a clean-up. Luckily, she still had one apple and a banana left over from her purchases in Derby.

She stumbled through the long, cutting grass, picking her way as best she could in the direction of the river. Colourful and unfamiliar small birds chirped and chirruped in noisy protest at the intruder walking past every spindly bush.

She could often see them and certainly heard them. As she approached the river, she heard a loud splash coming from the far side of the sandy bed, but took little notice of it. She walked across the wide expanse of sandy gravel and to the water's edge. She disturbed all manner of small sand-dwelling animals and quick-running dotterels as she picked her way through the warming coarse gravel.

Here she was able to wash herself as best she could and ventured a few mouthfuls of the clear cool water. She sat down on the sand and contemplated her situation. *Best stick to the original plan of following the road to the homestead.*

She wondered why no one met her at the airport or even at the road junction. She was deep in these thoughts and warming herself in the now-risen and bright sunlight when she heard another loud splash nearby and shot a glance in that direction. She was horrified to see an enormous reptile slithering violently into the stream from the far bank and finally realised that it was actually a crocodile. In a moment of fearful panic, she grabbed her sack and bolted through the long grass and back to the road.

It took Jess another four and a half hours to walk the track that would finally lead her to the homestead. The country she traversed was a grey-green and brown drab landscape of sameness that seemed to stretch interminably in all directions, ending in distant bluish and red hills shrouded in the faint hint of blue from the smoke of the bushfires that were burning somewhere nearby. These hills inspired no enthusiasm in her at all. They were very craggy and sparsely treed.

The track was a rough, gravel affair that she could see had been graded recently and followed the flatter country, avoiding any hills or rises. It meandered through the brown savannah, which was dotted with grotesquely bent trees interspersed with the oddly shaped boabs with their bulbous grey trunks and almost leafless stick headdress. The smaller birds seemed to reduce their protesting as the day warmed up, only to be replaced by much larger birds flying listlessly in the hazy, slightly smoky air. Their piercing screeches and mournful moaning gave her a sensation of foreboding and alienation as she trudged on in this totally unfamiliar landscape.

She plodded on until, in the hazy shimmer that was the focus at the ever-moving end of the track, the house began to emerge from between the scattered trees and tall grass. The homestead also did not inspire any enthusiasm in her. It was unkempt, rather dilapidated, and rambling in a slightly crooked fashion. She hoped someone would be there to greet her but her hopes were not very high, as there did not appear to be any life at all about it. She could not help thinking of Don again and how he was faring after those terrible events of the last few days. Maybe there will be some news of him when she arrived.

Jessie approached the farmhouse door and called out. Nobody replied. She called a couple of times and wandered around the building. Finally, with tiredness creeping over her she entered the house through the unlocked front door. The rooms were shabbily and sparsely furnished, many of the items damaged or even broken. She sauntered through to the kitchen, still calling out occasionally to anybody who might be there. The place seemed entirely deserted. She removed her pack and placed it on the large, solid, wooden table and sat down with a flop on one of the hard wooden chairs. She looked about, trying to take in the strange and peculiar surroundings in which she so unexpectedly found herself.

Jess waited for a while, hoping somebody might come along about dark. There was a light switch, but strangely, there was no light when switched on. She tried a few others with the same result.

Strange, she thought, *there must be no electricity.*

In the corner was a large cream-coloured refrigerator. It was making audible gurgling and rattling noises so she assumed it was on and must have power. She went over to investigate. It was an ancient artefact with faded paintwork and a few minor dints. She noted the name. It read Silent Knight. She had never heard of a refrigerator of that make. She thought she could smell something strange around it, such as petrol or methylated spirits or something but could not discern from where it emanated. She opened the door to discover a fridge stocked with beers and a few other bottles and some margarine and other small items.

There were plenty of cupboards in the rather large room so she began to explore them. Most were moderately full with packets, tins and boxes of food. She tried the tap over the dirty and slightly rusting sink. It did work and emitted clean water but it only came out in a slow dribble. There was a huge stove and it seemed to be gas, which was a blessing, for at least she knew how to use gas in the workshop in Newtown.

She walked about while there was still the faintest daylight left and discovered a few candles in bottles on the outside washroom shelves. She grabbed a couple of them and a box of matches that sat beside them. At least she would have some light. By ten o'clock, it was obvious nobody was coming there that night. She hunted around in the cupboards and the fridge and gathered together a few items to prepare herself some tea.

After tea she searched the entire house for a bedroom and found several, all with beds and most noticeably all covered with a fine netting hanging from the wooden ceiling. She surmised that this was to keep the insects at bay. *Brilliant*, she thought.

Jess found a small bed that appeared unused and lay down on it in all her dirty clothing. This was unusual for her as she hated dirt, but finally, the events of the last few days were starting to take their toll on her strength. She slept the best she had done in about three nights.

She awoke quite late for her, disturbed by the same unfamiliar cacophony as the previous morning. Still nobody seemed to be around. She prepared a breakfast and finally washed herself in the room where all the candles had been located. She then prepared to wait again for the arrival of somebody ... anybody.

By mid-morning, it was obvious that no one was going to appear. Jess decided to explore the surroundings of the homestead. There were several buildings scattered about, mostly galvanised iron and all in differing states of repair. There was a huge tin shed that was obviously the workshop, as it had two large iron doors that were propped open by drums and Jess could see inside even from the house that it was filled with mechanical items.

There were several other buildings that contained various things, but it all looked shabbily untidy. One thing was for sure, however, and that was that the whole place looked thoroughly utilised so somebody must be coming and going, and often, she surmised. The ground was very dry and dusty and the vegetation looked as if it were really suffering from lack of rain. The day quickly warmed up and the cloudless sky was pale blue with almost no breeze.

Nearly lunch time and still no one. Jess sat at the table and rummaged in her rucksack and pulled out her diary. She wanted to write down all that had happened to her over the last few days. She went to the office and found a pen that worked and returned to the table and began to write. It proved quite cathartic for her, and as she got underway, she found herself warming to the task of furiously trying to express all her emotions from the recent occurrences. This occupied her for over two hours. She prepared some lunch and headed back outside.

In the hazy heat of the afternoon stillness, Jess could faintly hear, muffled in the distance, the low continuous din that sounded as if it were the rumbling of bellowing cattle. There was a slight hint of dust rising in that direction as well.

Every now and then, she could distinctly hear the familiar hum of big truck engines straining under heavy loads and the recognisable sound of gears being constantly changed. There was certainly some activity in that direction.

If nobody comes today, I'll walk over there tomorrow.

Jess sat on the veranda facing the activity to wait and survey this strange world. Late in the afternoon she finally heard the distinct sound of a motor that was getting closer to her.

At last, she thought, *someone is coming.*

An old, battered Land Cruiser finally emerged from the scrubby bush and hurtled into the yard with a cloud of dust and hard braking causing the vehicle to slide slightly along the dirt.

It had the battle scars of many encounters with objects that gave it a ramshackle appearance. The mudguards were dented, the spotlights were in various states of operation and the massive bull bar was skew-whiff and bent in several places. A smallish thin rake of a young man dressed in filthy moleskins and khaki shirt, and sporting a battered hat, emerged from the vehicle. He was unshaven, with a cigarette in his lips.

He strode around to the back tray and noisily retrieved a stout wooden crate. He was about to enter the house when he spied Jess standing on the veranda.

'Hoo the 'ell are you?' he asked, startled to see someone there.

'I'm Jessie,' she replied. 'I'm Don's daughter. Weren't you expecting me?'

'I know noffin' 'bout that.'

He brushed past Jess and went into the house, fossicking about in the cupboards and the fridge and packing some items into the box. He looked up at her a couple of times then continued on with his packing. He picked up the weighty box and began to stride back out to the Cruiser, straining noticeably under the burden.

'You better come wiv me,' he commanded, rushing out the door and throwing the laden box back into the tray with a thudding slide. Jess grabbed her rucksack and followed him out to the vehicle. She peered into the back of the tray and disdainfully decided it was far too filthy for her rucksack so she clutched it tightly in her right arm as she tried to negotiate the difficult manoeuvre of entering the dusty and grimy cabin, which was high off the ground, especially for her.

The trip was short and very rough. The man drove like a bull at a gate and treated the vehicle with absolutely no respect. He drew to a rough halt after about fifteen minutes at a complete melee of activity.

Jess was mesmerised momentarily. There was a huge set of rough cattle yards constructed of a mixture of wooden logs and metal of varying sizes. There were many holding yards filled with a motley collection of mostly reddish or whitish exotic-looking cattle of all ages and horses standing about or being ridden in the yards. She could see through the dust several men working in a jumble of movement, sorting cattle into different yards and loading some into long trailers.

The man got out of the car and left her there, saying, 'The

boss's over there,' as he pointed in the general direction of the largest and highest cattle yard.

Jess was not only confused but a bit apprehensive as well. She sat for quite a while drinking in this hellish activity and movement, all accompanied by a constant low din of moving animals mixed with the sound of engines. Finally, she managed to place her sack on the seat and climb out of the cabin. She stood there in total confusion and nervous anxiousness as she tried to think how to approach Stuart, and indeed, which one he was. Eventually, she walked over to a man and asked if he were Stuart. The man looked at her in a startled manner and responded that he was not and that Stuart was over there, pointing to another man standing near the race watching as cattle were being loaded into the trucks. Jess did not like the unwelcome scowling peer he gave her as he stared out under his hat.

Jess knew she would have difficulty being heard in these noisy circumstances. She approached Stuart from behind, but when he saw her at close range he suddenly stopped and stared at her in disbelief. Jess tried to speak but the noise drowned out her soft voice. Stuart passed the clipboard he was holding to another man standing near to him and came over to her.

'Can I help you?' he asked with a puzzled look on his face.

'I'm Jessie,' she announced again. 'Why aren't you expecting me?' she asked in total exasperation.

'And who the hell is Jessie? And why would I be expecting you?' he asked in an unhelpful tone.

'I'm Don's daughter. Didn't he contact you?'

'Bloody Don. I might've known. The bloody good-for-nothin' bastard.'

'Sorry?' asked Jess, totally confused and very offended.

'I didn't even know he 'ad a daughter. I 'aven't heard from 'im for years.'

Jess looked at him in dismay. *How can I be in this position: unknown and apparently unwelcome.*

Stuart waved her away with an air of annoyance and told her to wait by the car and he would be with her shortly. Jess returned to the vehicle, sadly, and with a feeling of remorse for the life and comforts she had so recently and unwillingly jettisoned. She sat dejectedly watching the maelstrom of activity in a slight daze. She missed her comforts and especially the presence of Donald.

Stuart finally returned to her late in the afternoon and started the car. He drove back to the house in silence as the noise of the vehicle, the rough road, and the softness of Jessie's voice made conversation impossible. Back in the kitchen, he began to interrogate her with rapid-fire questions.

Stuart was a solid man in his fifties. He was wearing the same sort of dirty clothes that the other man was wearing and had a few days' growth on his face. He was tanned and muscular, though slightly shorter than Don, but still of medium height. It turned out that Don had never contacted Stuart by either telephone or letter. Stuart was obviously very annoyed.

'How old are you?' he finally asked.

'I'm nearly sixteen,' she said, lying to him as Don had suggested.

'You don't look it.'

But Stuart thought to himself, *What would I know about kids, I rarely see any – well, white ones anyway.*

They spoke some more then Stuart told her to wait while he tried to contact George. She watched as he walked over to the telephone hanging on the wall and carried out some fancy manoeuvres to get it to operate.

So that is how you do it, she thought. *No wonder I could not get it to work.*

She heard Stuart talking on the hand piece, but could also hear the other person.

Strange, she thought.

'George. Are you there? Where are you, George? Over.'

A crackly voice was heard coming through from the other end. It was a foreign voice with a heavy accent, but she could understand him.

'I'm at Five Mile Jump Up. Vot is matter?'

'George, we've got a problem. Can you come in immediately? Over.'

'Can't it vait? I nearly finished here. Von't two days do?'

'No George. Can you come in now? Be here by lunch. I'll see you then. Over and out.'

'Okay Stuey. See you 'morrow. Over,' said the fading voice on the other end.

Stuart hung up the receiver and came back to Jess. 'Where did you sleep last night?'

Chapter Two

'In there,' she said, pointing to the small room where she had set herself up.

'Can you doss down there again?' he asked. 'I'll go an' get some...' He suddenly stopped, turning to face her again. 'Hey, how did you get out here anyway?'

'I walked.'

'Come off it,' he scoffed. 'You can't walk all the way out here.'

'Well, I got a lift to the turn-off then walked in from there.'

'But it's twenty miles.'

'So?' she responded, knitting her brow in almost derisorily fashion, as much as to say, 'Do you think I'm incapable of that?'

'You mean to say you walked out from the Gibb. Where did you sleep?'

'On the road,' she said, in a tone of slight anger.

Stuart was staggered.

He ensured she was alright, told her to make herself at home, and he would return about lunchtime the next day.

Stuart left and she settled into the same routine as the previous night, entering her misgivings and the details of that first inauspicious meeting in her diary as a last act before retiring.

Next morning, about ten-thirty, Jess could hear the unmistakable sound of an approaching machine. She went to the veranda again and watched down the same track that she had walked along. Out of the sepia vista, there slowly emerged the dull yellow of the looming machine. As it drew nearer, Jess began to make out the shape of a grader that was rapidly motoring along, kicking up a cloud of fine dust that trailed behind, hanging in the air long after the machine had passed, the engine revving noisily as it bounced and bounded along the road.

She watched as it sped past the house and over to the huge workshop shed, pulling up outside the building next to the bowser. This adorned the left front of the shed accompanied by a huge tank placed atop a heavy set of log posts in order to give it height for gravity.

Jess watched as a man alighted from the partially glassed-in cab and walked around to the bowser and began to fiddle with the diesel tank on the machine. She could hear a lot of banging and clanking going on in the shed but decided to remain in the house this time, considering the unenthusiastic greetings from the previous day.

About an hour later, she heard the now-familiar sound of the approaching Land Cruiser. Stuart parked the car over near the grader and she could see the two men talking and waving their arms as each pointed in various directions, obviously discussing work matters relating to the grader operations.

After a short interlude, she could see them both turn and head for the house. Jess felt a tinge of apprehension as she went back into the kitchen and waited at the table. The two men entered the room and Stuart, pointing and looking at Jessie said, 'George, this is Don's daughter Jessie.'

'Yessie, hello,' was the gruff and rather deep voice that

Jess detected could really bellow if the owner so desired. The accent, if not the owner, was uncannily familiar to her, as it instantly smacked to her of Teutonic origin.

'Hi George,' said Jess softly, looking him in the face but not smiling.

'George, I need you to mind her for me for a few days while we finish loading the cattle,' said Stuart.

'Vot you mean? … mind.'

'Look George, please just look after her until we finish with the stock.'

'You mean for me to take vit me on dozer?' He always called it a dozer for some reason, not a grader. 'I not babysitter Stuey. Cannot be done. She is girlie anyway.'

'There's plenty of room in the cab. Just keep her with you for a few days.'

'No. Not good Stuey.'

Stuart insisted and then asked him to prepare the grader to go out tomorrow and to take her with him for a few days. George protested vigorously, but was cut short by a quickly angering Stuart.

'Just do it!' he finally said in exasperation. 'Please, just for a few days while I sort something out.'

Stuart looked at Jess and asked her to stay with George and he would catch up with her later in the week. Then he departed in a rather foul state of mind to return to the stock yards, muttering as he left the room, 'This is all I need right now.'

George had already departed the room and was walking

back to the workshop and his grader. Jessie got up from the table and followed Stuart out of the house. She watched as he got into the vehicle and drove off back to the yards. Then Jess proceeded to follow George over to the huge building that was the workshop.

George continued on with the maintenance work he had already started and was noisily and rather dramatically banging and crashing things displaying his discontent. He continually mumbled away, sometimes audibly about the whole situation. Jess tried to follow him about, more out of interest in what he was doing as she was starting to become intrigued by the work he systematically assembled into neat heaps. He climbed in under the grader and began to grease the blade with a large grease gun, still mumbling away and muttering constantly.

George was obviously annoyed and after one particularly odious outburst she finally responded in German, 'Ich bin nicht der chef's Nichte, und ich bin nicht ein kind. Ich brauche keine mutter (I am not the boss's niece, and I am not a child. I do not need a mother).'

George suddenly stopped what he was doing and partially sat up in silence. He shook his head then continued on with his job.

'Haben sie mich hören (Did you hear me)?' she asked again severely in German, this time trying to shout a little at him to ensure he heard. He slithered out from under the grader and stood up staring at her incredulously, rubbing his grimy hands up and down on his already filthy overalls.

'Sie deutsch sprechen,' he asked with an enormous grin over his formerly severe countenance. 'Wie kommt das? (But how come)?'

Jessie looked at him quizzically and replied, 'Ja, Ich spreche natürlich Deutsch, mein Herr. Natürlich,' as if it were common knowledge. George was suddenly transformed into a jocular and garrulous person, the antithesis of his former self. He suddenly found his manners and they began to strike up a camaraderie that Jess found totally incongruous.

George was a solid, roly-poly sort of a man of slightly below average height and in his sixties. He wore grease-covered grey overalls and heavy black boots. He had a mostly shaven, round and tanned face, with eyes that were close together and rather smallish for his large head. His hair was a grey-black colour and matted from years of minimal care. He was, however, excited to be able to speak his native tongue to another human.

Apart from his shortwave radio, a couple of magazines and a few books, the only German he spoke was to himself. Now, here was this new young person speaking to him in near-perfect German, who also appeared to share his other talent; working on machinery. The friendship was sealed for eternity on both their sides; his for the opportunity to converse in his own language and hers because of the genuine friendship he showed her once this smoothed the way. Together they chattered away in German until well into the evening. Jess even showed George the courtesy of pronouncing his name correctly, something that had not occurred for decades.

George showed her how to service the grader and work on the small motors lying about on the benches. More importantly, he showed her how to fire up the generator that would provide power to the homestead for the time they remained there. He also revealed the mysteries associated with the kerosene refrigerator, a concept that was up until then totally foreign to Jess. It was George's ability with all things mechanical that enabled this isolated cattle property to retain such an ancient relic in any kind of working order. It was one of his duties to ensure the kerosene was correctly and regularly administered, the others being totally unreliable in that arena.

When Stuart briefly returned next morning, he expected a cold reception and a lecture from George, who had all night to prepare a defence. He half expected George to have departed without Jessie. Stuart could not understand the apparent change of heart and the rather chummy *bon homme* he found instead. In fact, they both were chipper and preparing the grader for a bush stay, which would keep them both away camping for about five days. He wasn't worried, as long as she was out of his way for a while.

Jess, for her part, gave no thought to the strange turn of events whereby, through a peculiar and unique occurrence, she had inadvertently been taught to speak a language that had now set her on her way to a lasting and meaningful relationship with a complete stranger. She did, momentarily, allow her mind to drift back to Werner, who began teaching her German, initially as an amusement, but now the key to her future.

Strange, she thought, *that Werner also taught me the rudiments of the other asset I have in common with George – mechanics.*

CHAPTER THREE

George loaded up the grader and allocated a portion of the box for Jessie to stow her small amount of gear. He warned her that they would be camping and she would need to bring everything she needed for the week, including her toothbrush and all her clothes. After he checked the machine carefully, he started the engine and let it idle for a while. Then they headed off back into the dry and brown bush for George to continue his road maintenance before the onset of the Wet. He was finalising preparations for the oncoming watery onslaught that always resulted from the arrival of the Wet season when unpredictable but always heavy rains scudded in from the north to inundate the countryside, extensively covering the flood plains and isolating properties for months.

Jess was fascinated by the novelty of all this strange new

scenery. This time, however, she felt more secure with George, who was a capable and knowledgeable guardian familiar with these surroundings. He drove briskly, bouncing along the gravel track for over two hours before slowing down and arriving at his campsite.

George possessed a deep and resonating voice that allowed him to engage in conversation above the noise of the whining grader, but Jess, with her soft voice found it more difficult. In the end, he did most of the talking.

He pulled into a large and well-used graded flat area where Jess could see an awkward-looking, enormous four-wheeled trailer completely occupied by a metal tank that contained diesel fuel. Attached at the back was a much smaller trailer that George used to carry all his tools, spares and personal things, including a couple of large metal tucker boxes.

They spent five days up to fifty kilometres from the homestead, working from mid-morning until about an hour before dark. This gave George time to see to the grader and prepare for the evening in daylight. All this time, Jess was learning rapidly about the nuances of machinery and grader operations.

George was quite a student of the tropical Australian bush and its vagaries. He enthused volubly about its attractions, and slowly and imperceptibly he was passing on to Jessie all the knowledge he had accumulated over many years. Jess also was learning some of the history of this remarkable man. George was a private and introverted character, but he found the company of this young girl, who was so familiar with his long-deserted culture, deepening the usually hidden feelings and loss of his home. As he grew older, he found his thoughts would more and more drift back to the happier times before the war when, as a young man in his native Austria he would wander the mountains in awe of the creation laid out for him to explore.

His background was of peasant stock, rural people who tilled the difficult terrain and tended their few animals for a meagre but wholesome survival. George was one of four children and, as the youngest, had been apprenticed to the fast-growing motor mechanic trade in the largest nearby town. At the outbreak of the war, which was preceded by the Anschluss in March 1938, he was conscripted into the transport corps driving lorries over the mountains to supply the German troops fighting in southern Europe. He lost both his brothers in the war and his broken-hearted parents lost the will to struggle. Eventually, only his sister and himself were left. When she married and moved to West Germany to avoid the Russians, he decided to get as far away as possible from the traumas and suffering as he could.

George had been a keen student of his country's glorious past. His father hankered in deep nostalgia for the past grandeur of the Hapsburgs and the Austro-Hungarian Empire and had detested the French with great fervour because of Napoleon and the devastation he had wrought on both the Holy Roman Empire and the Austro-Hungarian Empire. His father had at first been supportive of the Nazi Party before their true destructive powers and aims became clearer to all the Germans.

After the war, Austria was divided into four allied zones for administration but unfortunately for George, his home had been in the Burgenland Province in the extreme east of the country and fell under the Russian zone. He lived relatively close to Vienna but that too had been divided into four zones and one of those was Russian. It was not until the mid-nineteen-fifties that Austria was finally reunited as one nation, but by then George was well away from his war-torn homeland.

He recounted to Jess terrible tales of Russian atrocities perpetrated on the citizenry of the zone under their control and he still hated them with as much fervour as his father had hated the French. George, who was partial to schnapps and vodka, and could drink substantial amounts without becoming inebriated, boasted to Jess that it was the Austrians' ability to handle their drink that finally freed them from Russian control. According to George, the Austrians drank the Russians under the table and in the end, they did not know what they were signing, thus Austria was reunited and freed from the despised Russians. Eventually, though, George departed Europe as a refugee bound for as distant a place as he could muster, and that ended up being Australia.

He was initially bound for the Barossa Valley where he heard many Germans had been settling for decades. However, George first landed in Perth and after a short stay realised that he would not settle there very well because of his nationality and his lack of English. With his trade, he found he was able to find work in the isolated outback stations where his poor English skills were less of a drawback. Thus, he ended up in Broome and struck up a conversation with a neighbour of Stuart's, who suggested that he might get work as a station mechanic out in the Kimberley.

George had a sombre demeanour, a product of both his race and his experiences. Being of eastern Austrian stock, he was a mixture of Slavonic, Magyar, Italian, Baltic and Aryan races and this was all reflected in his sallow, tanned complexion and stocky physique. He found the lonely, isolated existence manageable.

George took solace in the wonders of his adopted country's untouched natural attractions and contented himself with infrequent contacts with his background by reading rare magazines and listening to his shortwave radio. The only tangible items he brought with him from his past were a few books and two ancient coins that his father had so cherished, plus a gold ring with the most exquisite and unusual design on its black carapace: a relic from an ancient age.

Jessie was also of quiet disposition. She was naturally a sombre character, almost glum. She never determined, even years later, whether this was the result of her genetics or her traumatic early life experiences. After years of being told one was born in sin, and of sin, the impression never quite left her. Compounding these epithets was the added disadvantage of being assigned a left-handed preference. Together they dominated her formative years. She could do nothing about the first but, she was determined not to be denied the second.

Chapter Three

It was the one aspect of her make-up to which she clung tenaciously and which she steadfastly refused to alter.

Jess rarely smiled and never joked. Life for her was serious and fraught with imminent trauma. The company of such a similar character in the isolation of the all-pervading Australian outback gave her an unusually comforting inner peace that she had never really experienced before. She felt she could grow to really like this man and maybe this country too.

George had been on the station for many years and had made a hobby of learning all he could about the bush from observing, and from the local Indigenous people, with whom he had a good relationship. George thoroughly empathised with them because he was astute enough to understand that they were as he was—displaced. He thought of them as the dying remnants of the childhood of humanity: simple yet complex, wise yet befuddled, living in a world peopled by spirits most of whom were evil.

George's interests and knowledge were awakening in Jess a desire to understand more about her surroundings and the people that inhabited it. Her initial detestation of her situation was diminishing as she slowly began to understand it more and replace abhorrence with mild adoration.

George also taught Jess another important lesson. Just because they were camping in the bush did not mean they deprived themselves of all possible comforts. He was a marvellous cook and rustled up gourmet repasts from what he brought with him and from the surrounding larder in the well-stocked Kimberley bush. He taught Jess throughout the years how and where to catch many of the gourmand dishes that existed all around in the living world. She loved the way he always called her 'Yessie'.

After five days, they returned to the homestead. Stuart was able to maintain contact with the grader through short-range radio so he knew how Jess was going. On their return, George again attended to the grader preparatory to going out again in a few days while the weather lasted, as once the Wet set in there would be little or no road work to do. However, before he could resume his road works, he had a chore to do that rolled around on the first working day of each month during the Dry season. He needed to completely empty what was left in the fuel trailer into the tank by the bowser and then proceed with the empty trailer back out onto the Gibb River Road to meet the fuel tanker from the Derby depot.

This entailed waiting around at the junction where Jess had first been dropped off and filling up the trailer from the road train, which continued on to a couple of the stations further out before returning to Derby. It cost George a full day in waiting and transferring fuel and returning back to the homestead. He often did not return until very late in the evening. Stuart asked Jess if she wished to accompany him and she leapt at the opportunity.

This event set a rhythm for George that he had to accommodate or the station would run out of diesel, gas and kerosene. The only tricky bit was negotiating the long, gravelly river crossing two kilometres in from the Gibb, but otherwise it was straightforward. George had to use the grader as the river crossing, even in the late Dry was still difficult for a normal vehicle.

Stuart had given a lot of thought to Jessie while she was away. He still had not heard from Donald, nor was he able to contact him by radio telephone. Stuart was in no position to be looking after a city child in these primitive and dangerous surroundings. They adjourned to his office where he sat her down to plan their next move.

'Why did Don send you here?' he began.

After an uncomfortable pause, she answered, 'Something happened and I had to leave in a hurry.' That was all she said, remembering Don's advice to remain silent.

'What sort of thing?'

There was another long delay while she thought how to reply. Then she continued, 'Something serious but Don would fix it up and I can go home.'

'How old are you really?'

'I'm nearly sixteen,' she said, lying again just as Don had advised.

'I don't believe you. You look too young to be sixteen.'

'Well, I am,' she stated defiantly, staring at him unflinchingly with her big blue eyes. Stuart could see that she had character.

Jess was relieved that she would at least be able to remain for the short term, at least it was safer here than back in Sydney. She was not, however, looking forward to meeting the rest of the crew as Stuart called them, especially if that first man she met was any indication of their type. It was now getting late in the Dry, and as nearly all the cattle that were to be sent off had now gone, the station could settle down to preparing for the isolation and disruption of the Wet. This meant that most of the men would now be about the homestead more often and interacting with her, so she wanted to meet a few of them.

Stuart warned her that the blokes were a bit rough and not used to females being about the house. When they returned to the kitchen there were three men sitting there. Stuart introduced them as Norm Woods, Peter Taylor and Josh.

Norm was a greying, rather elegant, man with fine features and a surprisingly refined manner. He was thin and wiry, fair-skinned but lightly tanned from years in the sun. He greeted her with a quiet remoteness accompanied by an indifferent air that exuded disinterest. Jess was slightly embarrassed by the totally non-effusive response and pursed her lips slightly, reacting as best she could in the difficult atmosphere.

Peter was a little more pleasant. He was a much older man. Again, wiry and tanned, unshaven and dishevelled, but he proffered a powerful and gnarled hand while remaining seated accompanied by the hint of a respectful smile and a soft, 'G'day Jess.'

Josh grunted through his beer and acknowledged her with nothing else. He was the man she first encountered at the house. He was quite young and rough-looking in his dirty clothes.

Jess acknowledged each in turn as they were introduced, but gained no inspiration from this first encounter. There was an awkward silence for a few minutes, then Norm got up and mumbling something about things to do, excused himself from the gathering. The other two fiddled with their beers on the table then Josh also departed. Old Peter looked at Jess and began to ask her a few questions to pass some time and then he too departed for the quarters.

Jess spent more and more time with George, speaking to him in German, listening to his shortwave from West Germany and reading his magazines and the few German books he had. Once it was common knowledge that Jess spoke German, and following a period of teasing and raising of eyebrows, it became acceptable to all that those two would converse for hours in German. It was strange for the others to see George so animated as he was normally reticent and retiring and very taciturn. This turn of events seemed to soften Norm over time, as he thought anybody who could rouse George must have some admirable qualities. Finally, Norm began to loosen his reticence and reserve and at least acknowledge that Jess was now present in the boss's house.

Jess always went to bed quite late at night and woke very early. She seemed to need little sleep and engaged herself in books, mechanics and her love of the martial arts, all things she could do after hours. It was, however, much more difficult in the bush as lighting was dependent on generators and these were often turned off quite early in the evening. She had to make her own arrangements for lighting to work at night. She also missed her exercises at the gym so continued on by herself trying to retain her suppleness and fitness.

She began to discover that there was a lot of activity at night in the bush. She often wandered out into the night air on the veranda and encountered all sorts of activity. The most enthralling to her, however, emanated from what Stuart disparagingly called the 'Black's camp'. Jess was discouraged from fraternising with them, as their ways might be a little indelicate for someone so young and city-bred. This was not the message she received from George, who admired them in many ways. This only intrigued her more, so she secretly wished to spy on the activities of their camp. It was located over three miles away from the house on the banks of a huge tree-lined billabong, which resounded to the sounds of wildlife of every description.

Jess had been at the house for a couple of months when one evening she was standing on the veranda in the cooling air. The Wet was now not very far off and the slowly increasing humidity and more frequent thunderstorms were beginning to affect the station work. In the mysterious and total darkness that was the bush at night, she could hear the low rhythmic drone of didgeridoos and bullroarers, and the piercing incessant beat of the clicking sticks from the lagoon. She had heard it occasionally before and had spied out the lay of the land in that direction in the daylight. She decided to venture a clandestine trip through the darkness along the track she had reconnoitred to investigate the corroboree.

She grabbed a particularly big torch and a small knife, and set off in the direction of the rhythmic drone. She tried to walk quietly down the track but did not make the best effort.

As she approached the lagoon, she could hear the wailing and steady beat of the gathered group and smell the gum leaves that they used to smoke away the spirits and to illuminate the otherwise pitch-black night.

She was a little afraid of them and the unknown so she hesitated at some distance to watch. She could clearly see the men dancing around in their inimitable and staccato style, thumping the ground with bare feet and almost naked as they whirled and mimicked and performed; their white-painted faces were ghost-like through the shimmering heat of the large fires that were strategically placed all around them in the corroboree ground. She was fascinated. She stayed for hours enthralled by the heady mix of exotic humans, intoxicating primitive rhythmic music, and the familiar fragrant smell of the Australian bush when it burns, all accompanied by the mystery that was the deep dark night. She began to feel that something of great consequence was occurring and that she was exceedingly privileged to be illicitly viewing it.

Finally, Jess could stand in the darkness no longer and reluctantly she had to withdraw back to the house. She was in a mild state of euphoria from witnessing such a sacred event and spent hours contemplating its significance. She noticed that the corroboree continued long into the small hours of the morning.

She did not mention it to anyone. However, over the next few days Jessie noticed that several Aboriginal women were seen about the homestead on the pretence of foraging, but seemingly intent on seeking out the 'small white spirit that wanders the night'. Both George and Norm were well known to the small clan that camped by the billabong and George knew all their names and ages. The women remarked that someone with a ghostly white appearance was seen observing the secret corroboree that night.

Jess decided to wander near to their camp during the day and was finally invited over amid much giggling and amusement at her pale and unusual features. Over the next few days, she increasingly ventured to the camp and began to accumulate small articles and mementoes of her sojourns. These she laid out neatly on a small table in her room. One of these objects caught the eye of Stuart with a startled turn. It was a secret object that was for the young girls only and at only one special time in their lives. It disturbed him somewhat.

The Wet was beginning to rumble in more seriously now and soon all cattle work would have to cease. This was the time to attend to maintenance of the machinery and repairs to equipment that could be done at the homestead. With the onset of the Wet, the cattle would now all be able to disperse as water and green feed became more plentiful and the movement of men more difficult.

Stuart thought that this might be a good time to attend to the problem Jessie had brought to his attention with the secret artefact from the Aboriginal camp. A plan had begun to hatch in Stuart's mind to counter the issue and he would now try to implement it. He went to the radiotelephone and called his most valued neighbour, the Conistons, who ran a very successful tourist accommodation sideline to their cattle business on the property adjoining his and further up the Gibb River Road. As the Wet was imminent, their patronage would now be almost nil so it was doubly convenient for the task at hand. He wanted to speak to Edna, the wife of the owner, and luckily, she answered. Stuart began by asking how things were going.

Then, 'Edna, I don't know exactly how to say this but I'm wondering if you could do me a big favour?' There was a slight pause. 'Well, my niece is here, you know Donald my brother, his daughter. Look she tells me she's sixteen but I don't believe her. I think she's a bit younger. She hasn't been here more than a few months and the other day she came home with a jacdat. You know what that means. I wonder, as there are no women here and she doesn't appear to have had a mother anywhere, could I send her over to you to have a talk to her, you know about … well things that ladies need to discuss at this age. You sure? Oh, thanks Edna. I wouldn't want her to be getting led up the garden path with such matters, if you know what I mean. It's such a relief. How can I get her to you? You sure? Tomorrow would be perfect. Many thanks again Edna. See you later then.' He hung up the handset and sat down to contemplate events. He must tell Jess straight away.

Jess was a little perplexed when informed by Stuart that he had arranged for her to visit the neighbours for a few days. He failed to advise her of the real reason, but concocted a story about her needing to familiarise herself with the surroundings before the onset of the Wet.

Next morning about eleven, the helicopter from Ravymoota Station arrived in a whirl of debris and noise and landed in the open area near the homestead. It had arrived to pick up Jess and take her back to Edna's for a week or so. The flight was very short, only about ten minutes over rugged and exotic country sprinkled with rivers and creeks overflowing, and billabongs quickly filling with water, all surrounded by a riot of greening vegetation.

The helicopter landed at Ravymoota and they waited for the rotors to slow before alighting. Jess had her rucksack with a few possessions including her quickly filling diary. She was ushered to the rather imposing and extensive homestead to be greeted at the door under the enormous veranda by a middle-aged slightly plump and exuberant woman wearing a brightly coloured dress and neat shoes. Jess thought it was so strange to see a dress out here of all places. Edna Coniston demonstratively welcomed her and attempted a generous hug, but she was a little taken aback by the frigid reserve of the demure young teenager in front of her, but put it down to shyness.

'Hello, my dear,' she enthused.

'Hello Mrs Coniston,' replied Jess in a soft almost inaudible voice. Edna was so struck by the reserve and self-effacing demeanour of her guest that she was for a moment perplexed. This was not at all what she expected of a child of the city. She cordially led Jess into the cool and airy homestead and showed her to a large and colourful room full of ample and decorative furniture.

'Come and have some lunch with us, Jess.'

Chapter Three

'Thank you.'

After being shown to a bedroom where she could stash her things, Jess was shown the bathrooms and then asked to join them in the magnificent dining room set in an understated but functional manner that could normally seat many more. The only other person in the room was Edna's husband Ralph, a tall, solid and elegantly attired man with self-assured features and an authoritative and competent bearing.

There were some small items on the table to eat and a set of cutlery laid out each side of the place mats, such that Jess was momentarily alarmed at their profusion. They had a chat and then a podgy little man waddled in dressed all in white and wearing a weird chef's hat. He had long hair under the chapeau and a neatly trimmed beard.

'This is Hubair, our esteemed chef,' announced Edna with some pride. Hubert bowed slightly and pretentiously and said, 'Bonjour mon petit, an' 'ow are you?'

'Bonjour Monsieur Hubair, je suis bien,' responded Jess quietly.

'Ah, mon Dieu! Parle-vous Francais!' he exclaimed.

'Oui, monsieur,' she replied demurely, staring him directly in the face, trying to take in the strange little man before her.

With that, Hubert swished up to her and embraced her openly, muttering all the time in garrulous French half to himself and half to the room. Edna was staggered. She thought Jess was a young city girl with little experience of the world and totally out of her circle in the vast outback. Yet here she was conversing in fluent French with her adored chef who so rarely was able to indulge this passion for lack of exponents. Edna peered adoringly at her surprised husband and smiled a little inwardly with a self-satisfied contentment. *This was going to be a good visit after all.*

Jess had never seen such elaborate food and so elegantly presented. Hubert fawned all over her and attended embarrassingly to her every desire. Each time he entered the dining room they would converse extensively in French. Edna could not help noticing that Jess had no table manners at all, which she put down to the result of poor breeding and inner-city living. Compounding the issue for Edna was the extraordinary clumsiness displayed by Jess manipulating her cutlery left-handed, a feat Edna had actually never seen before, despite years of working with the public in catering. *Poor child,* she thought, *she has never been trained to break this habit and now it was probably too late.* The others noticed it too, but at least had the manners to remain silent while exchanging glances.

The next few days passed in a hectic schedule of household chores, chats with Edna and vast amounts of time with Hubert. Edna managed to include a talk about 'that' subject, the actual purpose of the visit.

Jess tried to familiarise herself with the layout of Ravymoota, which possessed a huge and well-equipped workshop and several accommodation blocks where they could lodge paying visitors who wanted an outback experience. Jessie would eventually grow to be fond of the Coniston family over time, even the children, most of whom had moved away from the business to pursue interests in the city.

Over the course of what had stretched into a two-week visit, Edna gave Jess several pieces of more suitable clothing and footwear from her daughters' wardrobes.

Jess was beginning to like her stay at Ravymoota, but she could no longer burden the Conistons, and Stuart arranged for her to return to Milbark Station. The Coniston's pilot took her back in the station's helicopter and she was back again before lunch on the appointed day. She was unaccustomedly conscious of the difference in the circumstances of her previous two weeks and her condition here with the men of Milbark. However, she at least had George to continue on with his teachings and he seemed genuinely pleased to see her return.

Jess by now was beginning to despair of Donald. They had heard absolutely nothing at all from him since she bade farewell to him at Mascot Airport. In her mind, she began to imagine all sorts of evil that must have happened to him or that he had simply abandoned her, as her own parents had done. She wrote poignant and heart-felt paragraphs in her diary about him and their time together, and the sadness she felt at his apparent disappearance from her life.

She was growing rather fond of George, even Norm was bearable, and Stuart was always very kind to her, but none of these men were a substitute for the loving devotion she received from Don and his offsiders, Werner and Antione, back in her old life in Newtown. She immersed herself in the day-to-day needs of station life in an attempt to assuage her feelings of loss and disappointment.

As the outside work was becoming impossible with the advancing Wet, the men began to spend more time nearer the homestead. Usually, some of them would depart for weeks about this time of year to recover from the torrid life and constant work that occurred in the Dry, avoiding the oppressive heat and humidity that accompanied the Wet, especially the early stages. They would remain away until their money ran out in either Broome or Perth. George was well past this sort of activity and he spent the duration of the Wet safely tucked away with his machinery and station motors, which would all be totally overhauled during the downtime.

Because they were all so confined, it was inevitable that interaction was unavoidable. To this end, Norman Woods tried to discover more about the young woman who had been so unexpectedly thrust upon them all. At first, he found it difficult to break into the life of the withdrawn and diffident child who was wary of them and seemed very self-sufficient. Gradually, Norm increased his time with Jess, but this aroused a faint stirring in his memory of the enormous loss that had originally sent him to this corner of the world many years ago. Jess had very fine features, almost sculptured, with alabaster white skin and the finest of fine blonde hair that moved across her face with the slightest zephyr. Her small concave nose was perfectly proportioned to her gentle, longish face, and she possessed the whitest teeth he had ever seen, with two tombstone front teeth that often sparkled when she spoke. He had only ever seen such perfection in one other woman; the girl he wanted to marry.

Norm had a reputation of being brusque and short with people, but was acknowledged as having a well-educated and trained mind that led to him being called 'The Squire' by the crew. He began to detect in Jess that, with her elegant features and proud carriage, she might be susceptible to refinement and it would be conducive to pass on to her some of the etiquette he had so long abandoned. This idea arose after Jessie's visit to Ravymoota when she commented that she got lost at the table with all the cutlery.

He gradually began to impart some of the finer points of etiquette to Jess as they increasingly spent more time together over their meals during the confinement of the Wet. He found her a willing student, especially when she learned that such a field of learning existed, so unrefined had her upbringing been. She had no idea such things were important.

Norm introduced her to the few books he had with him as he could not resist the impulse to impart his learning, especially if the recipient was also willing. He hated wasted potential in others, but rarely had the opportunity to indulge in such pursuits in the outback. The only texts he brought with him were several poetry books, a small Bible, and a couple of the classic texts from his university days back in England. These he willingly passed on to Jess to peruse at her leisure and then get back to him so they could discuss it all.

Jess still maintained her diary, and every evening she wrote up the events and her impressions of the day. She was beginning to write a considerable number of words as all the new facets of her life tumbled upon her at an enormous rate.

The Wet season descended in all its fury accompanied by spectacular displays almost daily of night-piercing lightning, endless rumbling of thunder, and buckets of torrential rain so heavy it washed everything away that was not secured. The rain would fall in isolated cloudbursts in one spot and the sun would be shining brightly in another. Jess had never seen anything like it, especially the ferocious rain. During the intermittent breaks in the rain, the men worked in the sheds or in the house. Norm decided that if Jess was going to stay any longer, she must learn to ride, and the Wet was an ideal time to do it.

He gathered in a few of the quieter horses and ponies and began her instructions in the art of horse riding. At first Jess was scared and fearful of the animals. Norm could see that this was so and it was reflected in the reactions of the animals. He counselled her in methods of overcoming her fears, but more importantly, in convincing the horses that she held no fear of them. This he did by advising her on handling techniques that included always facing the horse and especially looking it directly in the eyes.

Jess possessed a rather disarming and beguiling stare, one that she utilised in a disconcerting way to the recipient, as it was an unflinching and penetrating sort of look that some found uncomfortable to encounter, especially in one so young. It was an effective tool when dealing with unfamiliar circumstances. Disconcerting for humans, it was a magnificent control method when it came to dealing with animals. Jess found that she could calm and steady a fractious horse by merely concentrating her eyes on its eyes. This was how she emphasised this trait even more so, by perfecting it while dealing with horses. It would surface to haunt her in her later life to the confusion of those around her.

Jess gradually settled in and approached each day's lessons and exercises with more enthusiasm. Norm was a patient teacher and encouraged her to attempt as much as she felt able to do. He determined that she would probably be a competent horsewoman but she seemed to lack that certain natural something that could have transformed her into a show standard rider. He warned her to keep close to the homestead and not to attempt risky ventures until she was more proficient. As her confidence increased, she began to explore further afield into the watery, riotous growth that was the vegetation on the station at this seasonal time of year.

It was on one of these solo jaunts that she had her first accident when the pony slipped in the sodden grasslands and threw her off sideways onto the muddy ground. She lay there for a few minutes before attempting to rise, but knew something was wrong with her right shoulder as every time she attempted to get up it hurt. She finally dragged herself up and looked down at her mud-stained clothes. She clasped her aching right shoulder and looked about for the pony.

He was contentedly munching on some of the plentiful lush greenery a few metres away. She walked gingerly over to him and secured the reins in her left hand. She patted him on the nose. He seemed all right. She was about seven kilometres from the house so turned and began the long walk back. Her shoulder was aching badly but she was more concerned about how Norm would react to her over-enthusiasm. Her mind was racing now and she was feeling a bit queasy from the fall and the implications that were beginning to present themselves to her.

Firstly, there was the issue of disregarding Norm's warning and incurring his wrath, but secondly, it was almost impossible to be evacuated from here at this time of year, another fact about which she was continually reminded. She could move her arm with difficulty, but painfully, so she hoped nothing was broken.

About two kilometres from the house, she decided she had better try to ride back into the grounds to allay any suspicions of injury. More rain was imminent, foretold by the crashing and rumbling of close-by thunder and the darkening sky. She managed to drag herself onto the pony and commenced to ride in as bravely as possible.

Jess cleaned herself up after attending to the pony and sat in her room shaking with fright and pain. She tried to disguise her problem and somehow managed to keep it to herself. Over the next few weeks, the pain subsided and she slowly regained her confidence, but this incident taught Jess a valuable lesson. She realised how isolated she was out here and that injury could have been fatal. It taught her to always be very careful and mindful of her surroundings. Luckily, she recovered sufficiently to regain most of her agility, but it would be months before she could resume full movement in that arm, something that restricted her training and exercising in her martial arts that she had kept up since arriving.

Chapter Three

The Wet usually began to ebb by March or April and disappeared rapidly once the wind changed to the south. Jess had spent her first Wet rebuilding some small motors with George and riding nearly every day, especially up until the time of the accident. By the time the Dry was settling in she was becoming more proficient in mechanics and passably adequate at riding. She had learnt a lot from, and about, George and Norm, as well as Stuart.

Jess continued to fill her diary at a rapid rate and regularly wondered what had happened to Don. Her desire to be reunited with her old life was slowly diminishing as she gained proficiency in the tasks presented by her new existence, but even so, she still missed Donald.

CHAPTER FOUR

The Dry season signalled the beginning of the serious work for the station. It took a few weeks for the water to begin to flow back to the larger billabongs and permanent lagoons. The weather became cooler and the enervating humidity of the Wet disappeared. George was keen to reconnoitre the road system to ascertain the damage from four months of incessant heavy rains. As soon as he was able to drive along the tracks, he would begin work. The task of mustering the cattle would soon begin, once most of the surface water subsided.

It had now been nearly a year since Jess had last seen Don and not a word had any of them heard. Stuart was in a quandary about what to do with her. He still thought of her as a child, albeit now becoming a useful one, but she needed to be educated and looked after by better people than were available at the homestead.

Jess was finding her new life had a lot of attractions. She still missed some of her friends and the martial arts training every night, but this place had compensations that had eluded her at first. She pleaded with Stuart to allow her to remain with the men she had grown to like and from whom she was still able to learn a lot of useful information and skills. Besides, she reminded him, she was now approaching seventeen; time enough to be leaving school anyway. Stuart had no counter to that argument.

During the course of her first Wet season, Jess improved her skills in mechanics and riding. The other topic that occupied her attention during this time was that of the local Aboriginal clan who lived by the permanent lagoon during the drier parts of the year. Their old ways were fast disappearing but they still retained some of their cultural traditions. They normally dispersed back up into the ragged hills where they could find shelter from the rain and the flooding in innumerable caves and over-hangs that littered the craggy ranges. Then, as the Dry permeated the country, they returned in tribal and clan groups back down to the savannah plains where there were permanent water holes in many of the ancient river beds. Here they could spend the long Dry season in relative prosperity and comfort as all the wildlife was also forced to return for both the fodder and the water.

Jessie found a strange and irresistible attraction drawing her to the clan who regarded the permanent lagoon three miles from the homestead as their home turf. These people lived in a world populated with spirits, which influenced every aspect of their living. George believed there was no way any culture could withstand the onslaught of technology possessed by the white people. This Aboriginal culture, which could see spirits in everything, acknowledged that the gods of the white man were demonstrably superior to their own deities. They trampled on the spirits of the ancestors and the spirits of the land, disregarding traditional laws and customs.

The people from the genesis of man had a simple, straightforward understanding of existence and Jessie grew to understand how they could philosophically accept their own passing. The elders rejected the young men following on as unworthy and would usually decide not to pass on the laws to those they perceived as unworthy, or worse, just not interested enough.

The five men closest to Jess in this new life had vastly differing attitudes to the subject of the Aboriginal clan. George was mystically and deeply attuned to their ways and understood as few men did. He passed on to Jess an abiding love and respect for their life. It was strange that a man with no connection to this world had such understanding and empathy.

Norm, on the other hand, was characteristically bitter about life. It would be a while yet before Jess would understand his reasons, but this bitterness was reflected in a casual and dismissive approach to the clan just as it was to himself, and indeed all humanity; a bitterness born of loss and regret. 'Sufficient unto the day is the evil thereof' was one of his oft-quoted sayings, signifying his discontent with all life and its travails.

Stuart was also dismissive, but for a more measured reason. He admired some of the things about the traditional inhabitants of the land, but was also scathing in his attitude sometimes. He observed that they sat around in the dirt and ate lizards, and were tribal in nature, a trait that was proving a hindrance to the evolution of an advancing technical human life.

'Had not we all been there thousands of years ago?' he would argue. 'But now we have moved on, or was that up? We cannot keep people in a museum for our own gratification or perceived loss or hankering for a departed existence, no matter how romanticised.'

All these differing opinions and ideas gave Jess much food for thought. For instance, one of the topics that always aroused arguments was about fire. She marvelled at the creation of fire, and how adept the natives were at its creation. *How did humans create fire in the same way despite their disparate existences? If God could give but one gift to humans, what would it be? Would it be fire?*

Stuart really had it in for the politicians. According to Stuart, the worst day for the Aborigines was the advent of the Whitlam government, which had stripped them of their last dignity by removing the need for them to work. Now they sat in the dirt and drank the free money that was given to them by the cultural vandals and European haters. The Aboriginal men loved cattle work and were surprisingly good at it if supervised and guided. Left to their own devices, they wanted to go walkabout and lived for the day. Stuart constantly complained that adoration of all things primitive and belittling of our own culture was detrimental to both societies. Josh was not of a mind to comprehend such weighty matters.

Peter, the elderly stockman, had a more considered view. He had been an overlander in the last days of that method of travelling stock long distances. With the advent of road trains, the need to overland stock had all but disappeared, especially up in the vast distances of the north. Many of his companions in that trade were mostly full-blood Aborigines or strongly part-Aboriginal, and Peter had spent most of his life with them. He treated them as he found them and, just as with the whites, their characteristics varied between themselves. He admired their horsemanship and their toughness in the saddle; almost as if they were born for it. It would be from the few short years that Jess knew Peter that she would learn all the old ways of the travelling stockman, and especially the enormous contribution the Aboriginal stockmen made to the industry.

Jess developed a deep and abiding friendship and respect for the small tribe of people who lived by the billabong. She learnt all their ceremonies and language and understood the nuances of it. They had seven different words in their language to describe what the whites crudely called the Wet and the Dry. Culture and family structures were complex and their language was literal and descriptive with beautiful sounding words that were attractive to the European ear, especially if the sounds were represented in an anglicised way, as the whites were often unable to exactly pronounce the words. Jess was accepted into all their affairs, possibly because she was viewed as an outsider and therefore it did not matter that their secret ceremonies were revealed to her as she had no influence on the outcomes, but was genuinely sensitive.

The station legitimately employed a few of the younger Aboriginal men in mustering and yard work but was not in a position to pay full wages. In days gone by, all who wanted work or to learn would assist, but now few did, as free money in the form of handouts stopped that. The half-castes often had more work ethic and aspired to climb the ladder, but meaningful work was now limited. They were all good horsemen and their talents were sorely missed.

Jessie's first experience of a Wet season prepared her for life in the outback. She and Stuart had many discussions during the confinements of the wet months. In total, all he was able to garner from her was that Donald had been assisting the police in some criminal matters and had fallen foul of some nasty types who had threatened him and Jess. She knew she would be safer away from their grasp, at least until Don contacted him. Stuart was reluctant to allow her to remain but she more or less begged him in the end.

The tipping point as far as Stuart was concerned was that she amused herself almost entirely with either George and his mechanics or with The Squire and his horse training. As these two in particular had no objections to her staying, Stuart was less concerned about her presence.

Jess found a neglected four-tyred tractor covered in

behind a pile of timber that was to be used to repair the homestead floors and asked if she could attempt to repair it. It was a large ungainly device with a homemade blade welded to the front. Before the arrival of the grader, it was used to maintain the network of station roads. As it had passed its usefulness and operating ability, it was left where it had died. George agreed to her repairing it provided she did it all herself.

Jess also discovered a monster of a truck slowly being revealed as the pile of timber reluctantly found its way to the homestead. She thought to herself that this might be next Wet season's project. She spent many hours late into the night dismantling, moving and reassembling the giant tractor, and managed to finally get it to start, if a little roughly. George was impressed, and at least acknowledged that it could be used to pull the trailer and other equipment about the run.

By the end of the first Wet, Jess was proficient enough at riding to be let out alone on the easier parts of the station. Stuart, however, forbade her to assist with the mustering, as it was highly dangerous and difficult work, especially in the wilds of the Kimberley, even for the old hands. She would have to content herself with improving her riding skills and utilising her driving ability to be useful about the property.

One surprise that did occur in March was an invitation from Ravymoota Station for Jess to spend a week or two over there. She was puzzled why they would wish to see her, but not half as puzzled as Stuart. She accepted the invitation more out of curiosity than desire, and Norm reminded her it would give her a chance to test out her newly acquired etiquette skills. It turned out that the main source of the invitation was Hubert, who was enamoured with her charms and Francophile traits.

Edna wanted Jess to experience more of a normal home complete with a woman. Edna found Jess very amusing with her quaint traits, but she certainly noticed that Jess had improved her table manners. Edna wondered at the transformation and had no idea how it transpired; and apart from occasionally using the wrong hand, could not fault her display.

The easing of the rains gradually ushered in the changing of the seasons as the Dry began to dominate. At the first opportunity, George drove the grader out to inspect the road network to see how much rearranging of the terrain had occurred from the heavy rains. He could not travel far because of all the surface water lying about, and the rivers that were still full.

The first priority for him was to repair the road on the west of the run. Milbark was unusual for a Kimberley station. Firstly, it was unusually small, only about fifteen thousand square kilometres. Ravymoota was more typical in that it comprised over fifty thousand square kilometres. Secondly, Milbark had a very difficult access road that was impossible to improve. This was the track that Jess had first used to walk into the place. The problem with this track was the river; it was not particularly big or even deep, especially later in the Dry, but its bed was enormously wide and very gravelly, which made it impossible to grade and for heavy transports to negotiate, especially loaded.

Milbark overcame this problem by rerouting the cattle road trains via the neighbouring station Bingarini, utilising that station's entrance road once George had regraded the access from a huge set of yards near their boundary. These were the yards to which Jess had been taken on her arrival. As a neighbourly gesture, George also graded most of Bingarini's road, at least up to the cattle yard turn-off and then all the way back to the Gibb. These yards were some distance from the homestead but were necessary if Milbark was to remove its cattle to market.

While rather small, Milbark was also unusual in that it was comprised almost entirely of savannah: open, lightly treed country with abundant grass and plenty of permanent water holes. It was nestled between much larger properties which had plenty of good country but also had more hilly outcrops and even ranges.

The Kimberley was geologically very ancient, with coral reefs and iron stone outcrops that were so old and hard that they were riddled with caves and overhangs, and possessed very sparse soil; it all having been thoroughly washed away in the heavy Wet season storms that had been transforming them for millennia. The lessees of Bingarini had cast covetous eyes on the Milbark plains, and Stuart knew that he would have no trouble disposing of his lease if and when that necessity arose.

Stuart assigned Jess the tasks of driving the station vehicles about the property delivering tucker to the yards when the men were working at those, and running errands for George to save his time. She became proficient in time with the nuances of grader blading, a difficult skill that required much practise to perfect.

The Gibb River Road was the only all-weather means of travel through the Kimberley. It was always rapidly repaired by the council road teams in order for the inhabitants, at least those without airstrips, to replenish their supplies for the long working months of the Dry. As it gradually became easier to venture into Derby, Stuart decided that Jess could accompany him on the first trip into town in order to buy her some suitable items of clothing and footwear. Jess insisted that she could afford to pay for her own things with the money Don had given her.

When Stuart saw the wad of notes Jess had, he suggested she open a bank account where he had his, and bank the money. It would be simple for her to open an account as his niece living with him at Milbark. She agreed. Stuart stayed in Derby two nights and was able to show Jess around the town. He attended to the station banking and sorted out the bills that accumulated during the off-season. Then he loaded up the Land Cruiser with supplies and headed back out to the run. The time alone gave both Stuart and Jess the opportunity to get to know each other a little better.

The next few years drifted by, punctuated by the rhythmic changing of the seasons and the steady growth of Jessie into a young woman. This was a critical time in the development of Jessie's life and there were several significant occurrences that strongly influenced her. The men that fate had thrown together with her each in their own way played just as a significant part as the location.

Peter Taylor was getting quite elderly now. He had known men who had overlanded with Kidman and Tyson among others, and who had travelled the Canning and other stock routes before the advent of road transport. Jess found him a wealth of historical information and always listened intently whenever he spoke about his life at the late-night campfires that finished each day's work in the yards or out mustering. He was finding the hard riding more of a challenge now and Stuart knew that it was only a matter of time before he would be forced to call it a day.

Peter had worked on many of the remote cattle stations in his early days in western Queensland. He hitched his future to a large mob of cattle being droved from the Gulf country to the then newly opened Kimberley. In those days, it was still possible for enterprising young men to select holdings and then lease them from the late 1890s onwards. At first it was nearly impossible to survive because of the climate, the isolation, and not least, the wild and mostly untamed natives. Many men and cattle were lost to the vagaries of the seasons, to tropical diseases that were then unfamiliar to the drovers and to the fierce and troublesome blacks who were much more robust than some of the arid tribal people. He recounted tales of incidents that were now lost to the present generation of cattlemen. Peter supplied the inspiration for much of Jess's later glory, consequent on developments in the future.

Chapter Four

It took Jessie years of painstaking attentive listening and judicious questioning, especially when Norman had a few drinks, to learn his story; at least what he was prepared to tell. Norman Woods was not his real name. It was Norman Melville Redveres du Bois. His mother was Catherine Bromwillis, born in 1881, and his father was Robert Charles du Bois, born in 1876, the fourteenth Earl of Bromley. Norman was their only child and heir to the earldom. He was born in 1912 and his parents, particularly his mother, had mapped out his entire future, including the well-connected woman he was to marry in order to ensure the line continued.

Trouble was that Norman fell for a ravishing beauty of a lesser light and, according to his mother, a totally unsuitable match. Her name was Charlotte Louise Brevis, the third daughter of Baronet Brevis, a member of a socially unacceptable lower order. The du Bois family was connected to the English royal family in several ways but chiefly through an illegitimate son of King Edward VII. This made the stakes even higher and it was essential that the correct marriage be entered into. His mother was a severe and domineering woman and she insisted that Norman discontinue his relationship with Charlotte Brevis, which he did. However, clandestinely he still continued to see her. His mother discovered this ruse and demanded its termination. When he was reticent to do this, she arranged for her butler, one Roderick Palmer, to sabotage Charlotte's saddle girth leather strap, which resulted in a fatal fall at the next hunt.

Norman had been riding close behind her and watched

as she tumbled. He was among the first to her broken body. She was an excellent rider and he suspected foul play. On discovering the cut girth strap, he raced home and confronted both his parents and the butler. A towering argument ensued in which the butler was severely struck and injured, and Norman stormed out of the castle vowing never to return. He gathered up a few precious items and walked out of their lives insisting that he would be disappearing to Canada. He arrived at the wharf but the next passenger ship departing was not for Canada but Australia. He had never considered Australia at all but on reflection decided that that would be even better than Canada. Besides, they would never think of looking there for him.

The whole thing caused an enormous scandal, not least because he was the only legitimate heir and that in itself caused considerable problems. There followed a controversial and grubby scramble concerning the claims for the vacant title. This was from various pretenders, as the earldom was a plum title with considerable lands and much wealth. Because it was associated with the royal family, that also caused much gossip.

Norman arrived in Perth on the ship from Southampton and disembarked. The only skills he possessed were riding and reading the classics. The latter was of little use in the colonies but horsemanship was still prized, especially in the outback. He found that there were vacancies aplenty in the north and headed that way. It was in the hotel in Derby that he had met Stuart. The items he brought with him were a few books, mostly gifts from his beloved Charlotte, a ring or two with the family coat of arms and a mourning brooch into which he had managed to secrete a small locket of her dark hair. One of the rings was attached to his finger and in his haste to depart, he was unable to remove it until he was well out at sea. Somehow, he could never bring himself to throw it overboard. Norm would be a major influence on the sponge-like Jessie and she listened intently to any conversation that turned to his former existence.

The next item Jess wanted to repair after the big tractor that she had worked on during the Wet was the enormous truck which was still partly hidden behind the flooring timber in the workshop shed. George did not know very much about it as it was already there when he arrived. It was working in those days but had sat idle for many years since the engine had died. Stuart knew a bit of its history and upon enquiry, Jess learned as much as he knew. It was a GMC six-wheeler that had originally been used in the Second World War.

After Pearl Harbour and the entry of the US into the war, the US army established bases in Australia, notably in the north. There were regiments sent to Brisbane, and when their trucks arrived in Australia, they were sent to Townsville in 1942 and then to Mt Isa. At that time, the railway line terminated at Mt Isa and there were no sealed roads in most of northern Australia so the GMCs were sent to forward supplies from the end of the railway at Mt Isa onto Darwin. Townsville was bombed by the Japanese in 1942 as well as much of the north from Broome to Darwin right around to Townsville.

Once the Japanese began to falter in New Guinea, the Americans applied increasing pressure on them and more troops were sent over. As the advance moved further north into Asia much of the US inventory was left behind, including many vehicles. After the war, many of the large isolated cattle stations in the north acquired the surplus US equipment for use on the properties and a few of these vehicles made their way into the Kimberley. This was one of them. They were not perfect. For a start, they had a petrol engine and this often proved a problem, especially as most modern vehicles in the bush were diesel.

Jess, for some reason, really desired to be able to retrieve this vehicle from out of its timber slumber and have the challenge of restoring it to running order. Stuart agreed, providing she moved all the timber and other rubbish herself and it did not interfere with any of the running of the property. It took her over twelve months of painstaking delays, interruptions and late-night manoeuvrings to finally get the old GMC, which she imaginatively christened 'Jimmy' because that was what Stuart called it, uncovered from its woody, trash-encased grave.

It was jammed hard up against the shed wall so, in order to work on it she would need to move it out a little. This entailed firstly inflating all the long-flat tyres, and worse, removing the locked-on nuts from each wheel and inflating those tyres that would stand up to the treatment after so long sitting idle on the hard clay floor of the shed.

The upshot was that eventually she managed to find

enough good tyres to move the vehicle out sufficiently to begin working on the motor. This particular truck still had its original motor, a six-cylinder 270 cubic inch overhead valve water-cooled engine that had seen better days. What Jess planned to do was remove the engine altogether and replace it with a more powerful four-cylinder diesel because petrol was almost unavailable on Milbark. There were several old diesel motors lying around in the workshop and George agreed that she could have the one that was the most suitable. It was an ex-generator motor and still serviceable, but would necessitate some judicious modifications to the motor bay and welding of the joints. By the time Jess finally got the truck to fire up, she had learnt just about all there was to know about rebuilding and maintaining a diesel motor.

The other significant episode during these formative years on the cattle station was the finishing of her diary. This Jess had meticulously maintained since the first day she began it over six years ago in Newtown. Donald would indeed be impressed with her usage in the intervening years. She had recorded in minute detail all the events of her life from age ten to sixteen. It was the last thing she did every night, often very late into the early hours.

As she aged, she found that she needed even less sleep. This peculiarity was compounded by the fact that she still occasionally suffered from reoccurring nightmares and vivid recollections of the murderous events that sent her to the outback. Sometimes she almost dreaded having to sleep. Completing the diary came as a sad finality to a pleasant habit when the last entry on the last line of the last page was entered by her late one night just after she turned sixteen.

Jess began to look for other outlets for her craving to write about her days. She spent much time thinking about this and began to jot down ideas from the stories she heard from the men around the campfires at night. Then a significant event occurred on one of the few trips when she accompanied one of the men, usually George, into town during the Dry.

She was in the newsagency thumbing through their meagre assortment of paperbacks when something struck her. She was glancing at the cheap, thin romance novels that were in a small carousel near the rear of the store when the thought suddenly hit her that these were very simple and uncomplicated books and she thought to herself that she could do this. She immediately bought three of them for a few dollars each and stuck them in her bag.

Jess waited until it was quite late in the evening and surreptitiously retrieved the three small volumes from her bag in her room and began to read. Jess read the three books in three nights but by the time she had finished she reckoned that she understood their makeup. The three all had a common theme and seemed to her to almost be written to a formula. She counted the words per line, the number of lines per page and the number of pages.

She noticed that the heroine was always similar, so too the hero in each of the stories. One was set in Victorian England, another in medieval England, and the third in modern Australia. The heroine appeared within the first

Chapter Four

pages, so too the hero. They embraced by page so and so; kissed by this page, loved by that page. The action seemed to follow a pattern and the endings were predictable. 'A piece of cake', as Stuart would say.

Jess began to formulate some ideas about a story, but her fertile imagination was running riot and she had the germ of at least five or six by the time she had given it a bit of effort. She was very taken by the English settings and could see endless possibilities for short romances based on the situations and stories that Norm had told her over the years.

She calculated how many words were required for each story and set up a little formula in order to comply with what she perceived to be the requirements of this form of writing. She became so excited at this new adventure that she failed to think it through enough as to how she would be able to carry it off. This reality did not really sink in until she had mapped out several stories and suddenly thought about how she could send off stories but avoid using her real name, which was still probably in danger from her unceremonious departure from Newtown. Then the thought struck her that she would use the name Don had used to buy her airline ticket all those years ago: Jane Ransom!

Jess grabbed one of the books and thoroughly read the inside cover and the first and last pages to find out where the publisher was located as well as instructions on how to submit manuscript copies. She decided that she would need to write to them first by way of introduction and ascertain whether they were in any way interested. That raised another problem;

what would her mailing address be? She then thought she would do what some of the people at Ravymoota did and get a post office box address in Derby.

Now she would have to wait until she could go back into town to arrange that. She could at least begin to write some of her stories while she waited. The next big hurdle for her was to obtain a typewriter. There was an old, barely working Imperial in Stuart's office but she was so inept at its use that she would not be able to utilise it. *No, I'll need to buy an electric typewriter similar to the ones that they use at Ravymoota. How to go about it?*

Jess spent some time contemplating this dilemma. Finally, she came up with a plan of action. She would order one next time she was in Derby and get it delivered to Milbark by the weekly mail run, ensuring that she was the one collecting the mail. As this was usually the case now, that probably would not present any problems. The next thing to do was to organise one of the small diesel generators and set it up in the workshop in a secluded corner where she could use the electric typewriter and run a small globe late into the night.

This endeavour took her most of the next three months to arrange and set up satisfactorily, but finally she was ready to go. She began typing some of her ideas onto paper and sorted out which one she would choose to forward onto the publisher if they accepted her offer to send something in.

Jess by now had become proficient enough on horseback to join in the mustering of the cattle. She was useful in that role as well as being both willing and able to do any of the driving that was required from the different cattle yards back to the homestead for supplies, thus freeing up the stockmen from that task. She often accompanied George on his road maintenance trips about the station and could passably manage the grader. Her hobbies consisted entirely of mechanics and perfecting her greatest love, 'Jimmy', which by now was fully operational and of considerable power. She impatiently awaited the next opportunity to get to Derby in order to acquire a post box.

When that arose, she found little difficulty in gaining one, even in the name of Jane Ransom, the only hiccup being her residential address. This she gave as being temporarily at Ravymoota, stating that she was an itinerant worker there and would be moving about different stations in the area, a common occurrence to the people at the post office apparently. She did ask if she could pay for two years in advance as she claimed that she might have difficulty in getting into town sometimes. She posted off a neatly typed-up letter to the publishers in Melbourne and crossed her fingers to await their reply.

Jess felt rather pleased with her own post box. For some reason, it gave her a sense of importance that she had never previously had. She could not wait for the publishers to reply and found it difficult to hide her excitement from the others at Milbark. She did, however, begin in earnest to implore Norm for more stories about his secretive past. This he obligingly complied with but only when off guard while under the influence of a few drinks.

Jess left her next visit to Derby for a couple of months as

she was not sure how she would react to no reply, or worse – a rejection. She had placed a lot of her hopes in this exciting new venture. In the meantime, she perfected her stories and prepared one as her choice to send off if that eventuality arose. She eventually had to accept the chance to go into town as the Dry would soon be drawing to a close and the onset of the Wet would render trips to town impossible.

This time she accompanied Stuart who was doing the final requirements for the year before the onset of the Wet. Jess could hardly disguise her anxiousness and desire to check her post office box on arrival in Derby. She nervously inserted the key and turned it. There was a muffled click and the door was free, but she hesitated for a moment, preparing herself for the worst. The box was rather high for her and she had to stand slightly on her toes to see in, but finally she could delay no longer and, standing on her toes opened the metal door.

She could see nothing in the box and her heart sank in gross disappointment. In desperation, she inserted her left hand and to her glee, a letter slid out from the floor of the box, it having been just the right size to fit snugly in the confines of the box. She closed the box, checking to ensure it was securely shut. She glanced at the letter for many minutes. It was a business letter with the name of the publisher on the envelope. Now she was afraid to open it. She walked calmly away from the public area with the rows of boxes and, fidgeting with the unopened letter, walked to a vicinity where she could open it in private.

She sat for quite a while flicking the letter up and down

Chapter Four

on her right wrist. Suddenly she decided to act. She retrieved the pocketknife Norm had bought for her years ago from the leather pouch that George had made her. She thumbed open the blade and slid it along the letter top. There was a double-paged letter within and she began to read every word from the beginning. It was formally addressed to Ms Jane Ransom of Derby, post box address, as she had indicated to the publisher. It began with salutations and indicating their pleasure in hearing from her, and yes indeed, they would be pleased to receive a manuscript from her, preferably typed. It went on to cover a multitude of topics relating to their requirements and conditions but offering much encouragement to the novice author.

Jess read and reread the letter several times. She resolved to try to submit just one manuscript at first, one that she had already written along with some explanations about her situation and that she had many more stories already prepared for them if this one proved satisfactory. She had brought with her this first draft and a note to accompany it and decided to post it off while she was there. She concocted a long and complicated story about her circumstances, lying to them that because of her handicap she was unable to travel, and suggesting to them that her actual address was various as she moved about a little but with difficulty. Meantime, she pointed out to the publisher that she had many more stories already prepared for them if that suited. She popped the letter and manuscript in the post box and headed back to find Stuart. She carefully hid the letter in her bag. The only cloud on the horizon so far was the disturbing request from the publisher for some life history accompanied by a photograph.

Jess concocted some more false information about her imaginary self and then rummaged through her meagre stash of belongings looking for a photograph. It was not of herself but rather of a girl Jess had briefly met while this girl was working as a kitchen-hand some years ago at the accommodation billet at Ravymoota. She was rather a sad figure and Jess had befriended her more out of total pity than genuine friendship. Her name was Helena and she was backpacking around Australia – the world really, as she was originally from Greece and had travelled all through Asia to Australia to see relatives and hoped to return to Greece in a few years via America. She was exceedingly plain – very short and plump with a large round face framed by untidy black hair that hung to her shoulders. She possessed small black eyes, large rubbery lips and a big crocked nose splayed out on sallow, pockmarked skin that always appeared dirty. However, she had a pleasant personality and was very self-effacing, almost apologetic, knowing full-well that she was a very unattractive person. She obviously made and kept few friends and Jess found that rather poignant so she attempted to socialise with her as much as she could bear to for the short time their paths crossed.

In return, Helena gave to Jess, as a token of her unrestrained thankfulness at such kindness, a photograph of herself that was more flattering than reality, but could not hide the plainness of her physical makeup. Jess never quite knew why she really had kept this reminder of a most unfortunate person, but could never bring herself to destroy it. This was the perfect photograph to send off to the publishers. This she did, along with the notes, at the next opportunity to do so.

Her first story was received by the publishers, Romantis Publications, with mild enthusiasm, but they did request follow-up stories if they were available. Jess found this enterprise quite unchallenging and was able to run off a complete story in a few days, especially during the Wet when no other work apart from mechanics was possible. When the first cheque arrived at the post box she asked to see the bank teller she had grown to know quite well through her dealings with Stuart's accounts and explained that she was writing small articles for a magazine in Melbourne under a pseudonym and had received a cheque for her first success and would probably be receiving more so she would need to operate a separate account using that name in order to keep the finances apart. The teller agreed and opened an account in the name of Jane Ransom into which Jess was able to deposit her cheques.

Over the next few years, Jess was able to churn out a variety of romances for Romantis featuring stories centred both in Regency and Victorian England and in rural Australia. Jessie assumed that her short novels were published solely in Australia but, because of her prodigious output and sparkling adventurous stories, she, unbeknown to herself, was now having them released worldwide through the international arm of the publishing company. The cheques began to roll in regularly, small amounts at first, but as time went by, larger amounts began to arrive.

Jess still spent much time with George on his grading trips about the isolated and undeveloped cattle run. From him she learnt many aspects about the northern Australia bush and began to understand its moods more fully. She would wander silently through the tinder-dry grassy plains and explore the innumerable hilly protrusions and ragged remnants of eons-old crumbling outcrops, walk through long-abandoned cave systems and rocky overhangs where once the Aboriginal people would have taken shelter and engaged in their rituals and unique paintings and scratchings.

She tried to learn about the strange and diverse animals and plants that abounded in this untouched wilderness, and at that enterprise, she found George an admirable teacher. It was on one of these trips with George to the outer boundary of the property that she obtained a true companion that she adored immensely and that accompanied her everywhere until its untimely death at the hands of the local constabulary six years later.

She was exploring a rocky outcrop some distance from the track that they were re-grading when she heard the muffled sound of animals emanating from a small cave-like structure containing numerous old hollow logs. In it she found three small dingo pups about six months old hiding in the burrow awaiting their mother's return. She managed to secure George's attention and he came over from the machine to see what it was. On discovering it was a dingo lair he announced to her that because they had been disturbed, the mother would probably kill them or abandon them. Jess asked if she could take a pup and George nodded, as they probably would die now anyway. She chose a plump little male pup and cuddled him lovingly while he licked her face and excitedly wagged his short tail. His fur was very soft and downy, not at all like a normal dog's hair, but furry and lustrous golden yellow. He had big dark eyes and a broad intelligent face with alert ears that darted about at the slightest sound. She adored him at once.

George sternly warned her in a serious manner that she needed to understand a few things about dingos. Firstly, he advised her that he would always remain a wild animal and could revert to type at any time and would probably want to wander incessantly. Secondly, he would need constant supervision and control, especially around the homestead. He advised her to ensure that she always remained in complete command of his actions. In days past, these pups would have been destroyed by the landholder on sight if ever found, as they were a constant threat to their livestock. The Aboriginal people used to break the pup's front leg to ensure it did not roam and to keep it about their camps. Jess was horrified at that suggestion and cuddled him even closer. She carried him back with her to the camp and began her long bonding process with her new companion.

CHAPTER FIVE

Once Jess had launched herself in her new direction of authorship, she found it advantageous to keep sounding out Norm for background settings and atmosphere for her novels. She now received considerable mail addressed to her post box in Derby. The one thing that did cause her some difficulty was the sending to her of a small packet of her books as each was published. Every time she had a novel published, Romantis sent her a few copies to keep for her records.

Romantis published these thin romance novels in great quantities, but left them on the bookshop shelves for only a short time – about three months. This necessitated the recalling of unsold copies from the bookshops for their destruction. Jess was writing so many now that she was accumulating quite a store of each one published. These she semi-hid in a large trunk in a corner of the workshop.

Chapter Five

The other decision she needed to make involved her now completed childhood diaries. She was of two minds what to do with them. One thought was to bury them forever in the bush somewhere and forget about them. She found that idea distasteful because these two volumes held the details of her now long-removed and totally different past, including her first real father-figure in the form of Donald.

In the end, she decided to thoroughly wrap them in plastic and secure them in an ammunition box, which she in turn covered in heavy canvas. This packet she painstakingly hid in the rafters of the machinery shed. It was near the hidden diaries that she secreted the trunk that now began to fill up with a few copies of every romance novel she published.

Jess was making more frequent trips into Derby at every opportunity now and it began to be noticed that she was doing so. Norm was getting more irritable as his advancing years were filled increasingly with regrets, and pain from his many niggling ailments. It was this combination that led him to request Jess for some much-needed assistance with his few requirements in his fading years.

Norm, as were all the men, was paid irregularly by cheque by a cash-strapped Stuart. These needed to be deposited in the bank, usually in Derby. Mostly the men did their own banking; sometimes Stuart did it, but not often. On one of the last trips that Norm made into Derby, he specifically asked Jess to accompany him and requested of her that she could do him a big service by becoming a counter-signatory to his bank account in order that she might be able to withdraw money for him. It was becoming so distasteful and difficult for him to travel the long distances now that he wished to avoid it if possible. She agreed instantly and was rather touched that he so honoured her. As she was already known there, it was no trouble to arrange. In future, she would be able to deposit into, and withdraw from his account, and then purchase his few requirements, mostly alcohol and tobacco.

Jessie was now approaching eighteen years of age and she had actually driven 'Jimmy' into Derby a few times. This was a gamble as the truck was not registered, but even worse was the fact that Jess had no licence. She had lied to Stuart about that issue but was terrified for her life that there should ever be any records of her whereabouts. She normally accompanied one of the others into Derby and occasionally Broome, but rarely had had to take 'Jimmy'. Stuart insisted that she never travel alone on the Gibb, not only for her own safety but also in case of breakdowns.

She had modified the old GMC to cope with the long return trip to Derby. She had added a large five-hundred-gallon fuel tank mounted behind the cabin and rigged it to connect to the original fuel tank, which held only forty gallons that would normally take her only four hundred miles, totally insufficient for Kimberley distances. When she first discovered it, the truck had a huge bull bar welded onto it that protruded well out in front beyond the bumper bar. There was a long cable attached to the original winch mounted on the front bumper which she always made sure was in working order. She also added two large spotlights for the frequent night driving that she needed to do in order to cover the distances from Milbark to town.

The truck also was still a left-hand drive, possibly also illegal in Western Australia but she was never game to ask. She had to fix the passenger side seat so that someone could accompany her on the longer trips. Stuart would not allow any of his workers to waste time going with her to town but instead arranged for one of his most trusted and reliable Aboriginal elders to go. His tribal name was Mookargey and he had been, in his younger days, a proficient stockman. With the introduction of full pay for all Aboriginal workers on the cattle stations, most had to be released from work. This was a devastating blow to both parties as the Aboriginal workers all lost meaningful and useful work and the station owners lost most of their, albeit until then, almost cost-free workers. In place of this, the native stockmen began to either drift to the towns or try to subsist about in their own country in the more traditional way. Mookargey fitted the second pattern and had remained in his country and become over time a respected elder of this tribal clan. He loved going to town in the truck as it afforded him the opportunity to meet relatives and renew acquaintances with his extensive and complex native family and clan structure.

Jess was almost becoming embarrassed with her financial position but was unsure how to handle this issue without raising suspicions about her activities. It all started rather simply as a silly girlish pastime. She thought that her venture into romance novels would peter out and die a natural death after only a few attempts. However, she secretly enjoyed the clandestine writing and therefore continued to produce acceptable products for Romantis, and they kept on paying her.

She had now accumulated a considerable amount of money that she had difficulty utilising. She had managed to arrange a tax-file number in the name of Jane Ransom so at least that kept the tax office away from her affairs. The only thing she felt capable of doing with her money was to pay some of the station accounts for Stuart without his knowledge. As she was now a major user of the fuel on the property, she was able to pay most of the station's fuel accounts whenever she was in town. She also paid many of the other accounts that were set up in other businesses in town, but could not pay those that were sent to Stuart at Milbark, which he paid out of the station cheque account. She did manage to deposit some money into that account but not in large quantities as it would have been noticed.

Jessie's little pup grew rapidly under her devoted care. He was playful and loyal but she had taken George's advice and maintained a very tight rein on his activities. She was occasionally harsh with him but he returned her devotion with total loyalty in return. He also always accompanied her in the truck, usually riding on the tray, flitting from side to side between the rails and behind the fuel tank she had installed, his nose permanently sniffing the passing air as the truck slowly travelled the long dusty roads.

Jess could see that Norm was deteriorating and that his life was nearing its end. She spent a lot of time with him when she could, especially as his days of serious horse activity dwindled to nil. She continued to ask him questions about his past and he opened up a little more each time. She continued also to do most of his financial work for him. Norm had stipulated clearly that all his meagre worldly possessions were to go to Jess on his death. This he had reiterated several times in the earshot of Stuart so there was to be no confusion. His only requests were that he be buried in the small plot set aside as the station graveyard and that the mourning brooch be buried with him. This contained the twirled lock of dark hair that he had removed from the dead body of his only love following her fall from horseback caused by the instructions of his mother. Jess had always acknowledged that she would comply with that request and Stuart to the other. In his last days, Norm had also removed a sprig of his own sandy, wispy hair and inserted it on the reverse side of the brooch.

'There,' he said to Jess, 'now both of us will be together in eternity as God intended.' Jess felt a bitter tear swell in her eyes at the sad melodrama of lost love. It haunted her often to think of the tragedy of Norman's loss and his wasting away. It certainly gave her much material for her novels.

Towards the very end of his life, he actually told Jess more details of his childhood and position. He obviously realised that he would soon be gone and no one was ever going to learn his secrets now, especially not from this sweet young woman living in this isolated dead-end. It was gratifying for him to be able to tell someone his tale, especially someone so understanding. He had already confided to Jess that his real name was Norman Melville Redveres du Bois. Jess sat up knowingly.

'Forest. Woods,' she said with a slight smile.

'Yes,' he replied. 'Don't you think that's cunning?'

'Yes. What a brilliant idea.'

'And as no one out here is ever likely to speak French, the possibility of it being found is almost nil,' he said with a wry smile. Jess smiled at him in return, shaking her head slightly.

He went on to explain more fully his family connections and the association with the royal family through King Edward VII. All this gave her wonderful background for her novels. She tried to observe in detail all his little quirks for authenticity. Norm still often rolled his own cigarettes from the tobacco Jess bought for him in town. Jess found the smoke from all the cigarettes that most of the men smoked irritating, but understood that it was taken for granted that they would all do it. Norm was different in that he often held the smokes in either hand but between the ring and middle fingers, not the usual middle and first as most people did. She noticed that this gave him more dexterity to manipulate his fingers in doing other chores with them.

One conversation left a life-long effect on her and influenced the way Jess would direct her life. Late one afternoon, as the fading sun sent a melancholy drabness over the quietening air and the few resident birds twittered in the adjacent bushes, Norm was in a particularly restive and reflective mood. He had been especially open with her regarding his romantic attachment and became quite glum.

Chapter Five

He sat by the veranda pillar and turned to her, 'The dreams of men are slain on the altar of pride and hope, Jess.' There was a long difficult pause as he gazed into eternity across the plain. He turned back to her and said earnestly, almost pleading, 'Don't waste your potential in dreaming and in imprisoned isolation out here Jess. Cast your vision away from here. Spread your angelic wings beyond the lost world of this desolate dreaming Jess, spread your wings beyond the Dreamtime. You are capable of, and hopefully destined for, much more than a life discarded to this dross.'

Jess stared at him in confusion, not certain exactly what he meant, but knew that there was something prophetic in this secluded moment between them. In the future, she would often cast her mind back to those words shared by a loving old man in his last weeks on earth. She clearly recalled the comment, and identified with its meaning.

Late in the Dry of 1986, it was evident that Norm would not see out another Wet. Jess began to remain with him almost incessantly, picking his brains and caring for his needs, which were few, mostly a few drinks and a roll-your-own from his tobacco pouch. Norman finally died in peaceful silence in the early hours of a still November morning. Jess shed a few tears, not only for Norm, but also because no one else was there to do that for him; a melancholy thought which saddened her immensely. It gave a different perspective to Jess about life in general and her own life in particular, and the strange cards that were dealt at the beginning. Norman's haunting words came back to her:

'Spread your angelic wings beyond the Dreamtime'.

Stuart arranged for Norm to be buried and all the station personnel attended a solemn affair that was accompanied by much wailing from the clan. He was buried in the fenced-off plot that contained a few other old graves, including Stuart and Donald's father, grandfather and mother. Jess was quite upset, but also very guilty. For some reason, she could not bring herself to throw in the mourning brooch as she had promised Norm. She grasped it tightly in her hand, feeling the smooth, golden frame and the clear, glassy covering. She had an emotional and mystic sensation that it was not to be lost, but remain above ground. She disobeyed Norm's dying wish, but cold shivery sensations prevented her from dropping it into the grave. Jess would put it with the ring that Norm had kept with the family crest, the one he was initially unable to remove from his finger once on board the ship.

Jess left Norm's things untouched for several days and joined the men in the late Dry clean-up of the remaining stock. She worked long hard hours to try to ease the pain of Norm's passing. The traumatic sadness of his passing had a strange and unexpected side-effect on Jess.

The sudden onslaught of grief instilled in her a different approach to her writing. She was rather amazed at its effects, but deep down she wished to utilise this feeling to its fullest for as long as it lasted. She found deep solace in producing copious quantities of writings inspired by the new sensations welling within her. She created madly while she could. It was almost a week before she was able to venture back to

Chapter Five

the quarters where he had made his home for the last few decades.

Norm had had an eventful, but unfulfilled and incomplete life. She had assured Stuart that she would attend to his affairs and close off his bank accounts. Among his few possessions were the books with which she had become thoroughly familiar and which he had pledged to her on his departure. There was also the ring that she had seen many times, a couple of other small pieces of jewellery that she would investigate later, and some papers that she did not know existed. She would read those later too.

For some reason, Jess felt in no hurry to close off Norm's bank account. She knew not why, but something told her not to hurry. She had assured Stuart that it was dealt with. She began to feel uneasy about herself. She was accumulating a disturbing array of dishonest attributes that was a worrying sign and she hoped not indicative of a warped personality.

She had lied to Stuart from the start. He genuinely believed that she was his niece. He would be hugely offended to discover the truth. He thought she had a driving licence and that the truck was registered. She just put old plates from the shed on it to disguise the fact. He was totally unaware of her foray into literature; well, literature might be slightly grandiose a term when describing a romance novel, but nevertheless she had hidden that fact from them all. Stuart also knew nothing of her finances, now growing to be substantial. She disobeyed a dying man's last request to send the mourning brooch with him on his journey, and she now contemplated keeping Norm's accounts operational for herself. All this and she was not even twenty.

Norm's death set Jess to thinking about her environment. Apart from Edna Coniston and the Aboriginal women, her list of acquaintances consisted entirely of men, mostly aged at that. These had all been the source of her knowledge and insights into the world and from each she had learnt something different. Peter had relatives in New South Wales and Jess thought he would probably end up with them when he was totally infirm. Jess could see that he was steadily deteriorating with age and that his time with her might be short. She began to engage him in earnest conversations in order to glean the last drop of his knowledge.

Alas, Jess miscalculated with that source as well, for rather unexpectedly, Peter died in 1988, just two years after Norm, leaving a big hole in both Jess's life and in Stuart's, as he was steadily losing his reliable workforce. Stuart contacted Peter's relatives in country New South Wales but they were content for the 'old codger' to be buried in the station graveyard. They did not even bother to come up for the funeral or show much interest in his few belongings.

These two deaths were a turning point for Jess. She was tiring of the drudgery of the Jane Ransom novels. They were not particularly onerous, just not much of a challenge for her anymore. She now cast covetous eyes on another prize. Norm had inspired her to spread her gaze further afield. The germ of an idea for an adventure novel had been forming for some time in her mind and she was keen to try it out. However, she would need to ditch the shallow meaningless work involved with the romance novels.

She typed up a long letter to Romantis Publications advising them that she was finding it difficult to continue with her novels owing to the increasing impositions of her handicap. She told them she had made the acquaintance of a budding fellow writer who lived much further out on one of the cattle stations along the Gibb River Road. She asked Romantis if they were in any way interested in a new author who wrote a different genre.

In due course, Jess received a reply indicating the publisher's disappointment at her impending departure as one of their authors. Their publishing house only published romance novels, however, as they were part of a bigger publishing enterprise, they might be able to refer him to them. They were willing to forward on a manuscript, especially if Ms Jane Ransom would agree to still producing a few romance novels per year. Jess thought this might be acceptable, at least in the early stages, so agreed to the offer.

She had acquired a computer capable of operating on her variable power. This made life for her much easier although she still pecked at the keyboard as she had always done. She had compiled a massive manuscript consisting of over four hundred and fifty pages based on the life histories of Stuart and Peter. It was a novel of epic proportions, giving a detailed account, with poetic licence, of the early pioneering days based mostly on the stories and experiences that both Stuart and particularly Peter had recounted.

The novel spanned the time period from about the 1880s up to the present but concentrated on the early times. It also touched on the natural history of the region and covered in a cursory manner the life, conditions, and plight of the original inhabitants, and the impact on them of the arrival of the white man and his cattle. She called her first novel 'Unkind in Every Season', an appellation indicative of the social norms of the earliest settlers emanating from an oft-quoted line by Norm of a Wordsworth poem.

Jess wanted to progress her abilities to this level of output but still wished to remain anonymous. To this end, she gave grave thought to achieve both her aims. She finally decided to use another pseudonym, one that reflected her desire for anonymity but also paid homage to the sources of her inspiration. She wanted to acknowledge the contribution that George had made to her life as well as the enormous influence Norman had made. Norm was now dead, as was Peter, but George was still alive.

Jess chose a male name to further dilute the chances of her discovery. The name on which she finally settled was George Norman Thaler. The thaler was a large silver coin, and George had two. They numbered among his meagre possessions that he was able to bring with him on his hasty departure from Austria. The thaler had an ancient lineage going back to the glory days of the Austro-Hungarian Empire and had been one of the few artefacts that had a connection to George's family, having been passed on from his father. More importantly though was the cunning fact that Jess could honour her other main inspiration, Peter Taylor, by disguising his name from Taylor to thaler, as the correct German pronunciation of thaler was tarler, thus disguising Taylor but still with the connection to George.

Jess bundled up the manuscript and posted it off to Romantis, who would pass it on to their associated publisher who handled these sorts of publications. Jess also acquired a second post office box solely for the use of George Norman Thaler. She waited with mixed feelings for the reply that she expected to take some time. Firstly, she was unsure how this more serious work would be received, and secondly, she had misgivings of her whereabouts being revealed by increasing any publicity involving herself.

In due course, Jess received a lengthy reply from her new publisher, addressed to her second post box. It was a mixed bag for her. The publisher, Advent, was the Australian arm of a massive international organisation dealing with many famous and popular Australian authors, a fact that escaped Jess. It accepted her manuscript with what she found to be rather overly demonstrable enthusiasm, praising the author for an exceptional piece of literature.

Jess was slightly embarrassed by the effusive manner of their praise and the pointed way in which they stressed that they would accept any other manuscripts he could produce. There were two more disturbing aspects in the letter that she had not anticipated. One was the request for a profile of the author accompanied by a suitable photograph to place on the fly or cover of the books, and the second was a request for bank account details into which any payments could be directly deposited from Advent Publications.

On the long drive back with Mookargey, she had plenty of time to decide what to do. The further she removed herself from Derby and the nearer she got to Milbark, the clearer her line of attack seemed to come to her. Jess recalled that she had never closed the account belonging to Norman to which she was a co-signatory. She could nominate that as her preferred account, so that would solve that problem. The issue of the photograph also resolved itself in a similar fashion. Norman had a couple of photographs of himself taken at Ravymoota a few Christmases ago when they had all travelled over there for a huge and fun-filled social event at which many pictures were taken by anyone having a camera. Norman was given a few in which he was included and she would be able to utilise one of these. She concocted a lengthy personal profile that basically reflected someone resembling Norman Woods and doctored a picture of him to accompany her notes. As a final touch, she acknowledged that George Norman Thaler was a *nom de plume* and requested that his true identity remain hidden in order that he may continue with his secret life of novel writing unencumbered. She deviously also hinted that his domicile was a large cattle station named Ravymoota, but secrecy was paramount.

Jess was rather pleased with her deception and posted off the lie on the next trip to town. It did disturb her slightly the ease with which she managed to concoct untruths and the sensations of achievement accompanying such deceptions. It

Chapter Five

was yet one more misdemeanour to add to her growing list of dishonesties. In the meantime, she commenced work on a second novel.

Jess settled into a steady routine over the next year or so. The Dry was filled with endless cattle work and she became very proficient at horse riding. She was now capable of joining in the toughest of cattle work and was particularly useful with the early bang-tail musters that occurred at the beginning of every Dry. She accompanied George occasionally and was able to effectively control the grader. She became so proficient at motor mechanics that she was now able to repair and maintain any machinery on the station. She indulged her interest in traditional Aboriginal ceremonies at any of the camps located variously about the run.

During the Wet seasons she amused herself with engines, writing a few romance novels as Jane Ransom, but concentrating on her books written by George Norman Thaler. Her life held few surprises now and she grew less fearful of ever being discovered. She rarely gave a thought about where her life was heading as she was exceedingly content. The heart-felt plea of Norman about spreading her wings was slowly fading from her horizon.

When Jess was twenty-three, her settled life received a sudden jolt one day from a totally unexpected quarter. She had taken occasionally, though not often, to driving her trusty 'Jimmy' to Derby if she needed something that was bulky. She always took Mookargey with her as well as Wornor, her faithful dingo companion. This day, she fatefully decided to take the truck in to pick up a new engine that she had arranged to be delivered to the depot in Derby.

The Gibb River Road turns off the main coast road some miles out of town and at the turnoff was a tavern and small accommodation facility where she often stopped to pick up final supplies, mostly alcohol for any of the men if requested. This particular day, early in the morning, she pulled up and Mookargey got out of the cab to socialise with some of his people and Jess purchased a few items. While she was in the shop a police car arrived and two officers alighted and strolled over to the bottle shop. Jess was nervous at seeing them and prepared to depart.

The two men, one very young and the other much older and quite a tall, solid man, glanced at the truck located away from the shop but continued to proceed to the hotel. They bumped into Mookargey as he was leaving and the older officer, a sergeant, passed a rather offensive comment casting aspersions on both Mookargey's heritage and his parentage. They were engaged in earnest conversation when Jess approached and indicated that Mookargey should follow her to the truck. The sergeant eyed her off in a somewhat lecherous manner, which Jess resented. She had an uneasy feeling and just wished to be gone.

About an hour later as she drove slowly up the Gibb she was startled to see the four-wheel drive belonging to the two police officers close behind her and attempting to pass. Her fears suddenly rose to huge heights.

Chapter Five

At an appropriate spot in the road, they sped past and drew to a sudden halt in front of her truck. 'Jimmy' was a lumbering hulk and not used to sudden enforced stops so ground to a squeaky halt almost on top of the police car. The two men got out of the car and the sergeant, donning his hat, strode over to Mookargey's side of the vehicle, thinking that he was the driver. The other man went to the left expecting the passenger.

The sergeant demanded in another offensive manner that Mookargey get out of the truck. He was about to comply when the younger man indicated that the driver was actually on his side. Sergeant Moore then told Mookargey to remain where he was and marched around to the other side.

'Get out, you,' he demanded of Jess, who was by now very jittery.

'Turn that motor off.' Jess obliged and turned off the engine.

Wornor was also beginning to grunt. Jess jumped out of the cab onto the dirt surface. Sergeant Moore then grabbed her left arm above the elbow with his huge rough right hand and pushed her towards his wagon. He was muttering the whole time in quite a disrespectful manner that Jess found irritating. He also smelt slightly of alcohol. He shoved her against the wagon and then kicked her on the ankles to force apart her legs.

He slowly began to frisk her from the knees up. Jess protested by attempting to move but he firmly restrained her by grabbing her right arm and bending it back behind her and pushing her again against the vehicle. This time he began again at the top and ripped her shirt open and fumbled with her before progressing to her moleskin trousers. He began to undo her belt.

Jessie's mind was racing. The critical line from her old martial arts instructor was ringing in her mind: 'If you are going to strike, strike first and strike hard.' Just as he was fumbling with her belt, Wornor leapt from the tray of the truck and bounded over to the scene. Sergeant Moore immediately drew his service pistol and shot him dead with two quick shots that landed the dog almost at his feet. Jess was dumbstruck. She attempted to move again but Moore pushed her in the back and put his face next to hers and began again.

Jess decided it was now or never before she was totally incapacitated and unable to react because of lowered trousers and belt. She whizzed about in a lightning manoeuvre that was accompanied by two lightning-fast, fierce jabs of her left arm that landed destructively on the right side of the sergeant's face. She heard the bones cracking and felt them give under her jab. In the same move, she connected with his knees, shattering them completely and finished with a high leg kick that completely destroyed his right elbow. He was out cold before he hit the ground.

Jess was shaking violently but her mind was as clear as crystal. She did up her belt and clasped her open shirt with her right hand. She looked at the body of her dead and faithful dog and then, with a fearful and penetrating stare turned her gaze to the young officer standing close by with a stunned and confused look on his face. She peered steadfastly and mesmerisingly at his eyes and he returned her gaze in an almost hypnotic state.

She strode purposefully the few steps separating them and, continuing to stare menacingly into his eyes, and with almost invisible movement, landed a shattering left kick on his unsuspecting right knee. The note book into which he had been jotting down any unlawful infringements Sergeant Moore bothered to mention during his attempted undressing of Jess went flying to the side. He grimaced in shock and pain and crumpled to the ground.

'That's for just standing there and watching,' she said in a soft and low voice so full of menace that he feared for his life. Mookargey was still in the cab staring unbelievingly at the events that had just unfolded in front of him. When Jess went back to pat her dead companion, she was almost distraught with rage and momentarily contemplated finishing off both of them. She tried to pick him up but he was too heavy for her. She looked back at the truck as much as to say come and help to Mookargey. He hesitated than leapt out of the cab and ran over to her and together they lifted the body of Wornor onto the tray of the truck. She reverentially covered him and ensured he was securely on the truck and then cast another glance at the scene. The sergeant was still out cold. The younger man was whimpering slightly and returned a fearful shocked look in return. She momentarily again contemplated another swift kick but decided against it. Both these men would never forget this day and would always have painful reminders of their encounter.

Jess climbed back up into the cab and sat for a moment. Then she started the engine again and let it idle for a few minutes. The police car was still in the way. She looked out the split-glass windshield and engaged first gear. The massive bull bar connected with the defenceless police wagon and it yielded to her superior strength by sliding unceremoniously into the grassy roadside ditch. She drove off in a mild daze of fear and shock, and unbridled hatred for the world, people and especially the police.

Jess drove on in dazed silence for many hours. Her racing thoughts were only disturbed by the reassuring and responsive sound of the massive GMC's engine purring away in front of her. Finally, she brought the truck to a gentle halt by the side of the road, miles from anywhere. Mookargey sat in confused silence. She turned to him and said in a calm and soft voice, only talking loudly enough to be heard above the idling engine,

'Mookargey, you must promise never ever to tell anybody about this. Is that clear? No one. Never.'

'Yes Miss,' he stammered. 'But won't you tell the boss?'

'No, definitely not. And you must promise never to tell him either. Promise?'

'Sure, Miss. If you say so.'

'I do.' Jess was now thinking about the possibility of her whereabouts being revealed after all this time. She feared that her happy existence might all come apart if anyone discovered who did this.

'We'll go back just as if nothing has happened and I'll bury Wornor before we get home.'

'Yes Miss,' was all he could say. But then he managed, 'Are you okay Miss Jess?'

'I'll be fine when we get home. Just don't mention it to anyone.'

Jess engaged first gear with an echoing clunk and drove off. They buried Wornor in an isolated spot not far from where she and George had found him in his lair as a pup six years ago. She was terribly sad and a burning anger rose in her.

Mookargey was true to his word in his understanding of the agreement. He told no one about the incident; that is no one who was white. He did, however, tell and retell the story to his relatives and at each telling the details grew more heroic and the actions more stupendous. The news of the event travelled far into his country and was rapidly expressed at all the local stations including Ravymoota. Evidence of this was clear to Jess on her next visit there. On her arrival she was greeted as a long-sought-after spirit person worthy of all their adoration. Her celebrity for what they regarded as defending Mookargey's honour was astounding and widely celebrated in song and dance.

CHAPTER SIX

The unfortunate interaction with the local police was a turning point in Jessie's life. She henceforth resolved never to take 'Jimmy' back to either Derby or Broome. This had a detrimental effect on her outlook. Firstly, it was a reminder of the ever-present fact that she was still probably being hunted for being a witness to the deaths of the two policemen in Newtown. Secondly, it reawakened long-dormant emotions connected with her despising all officialdom and authority, and reinforced her attitude that they all seemed to be corrupt and evil. It also reawakened how fragile was her happiness and her circumstances. She now had to find a more secure and reliable way to get into town, probably only by using one of the men's registered vehicles if they would permit her.

The incident involving the police on the Gibb reverberated

throughout the district. The police were convinced that a car load of drunken local Aborigines had perpetrated this deed and wasted much time in hunting the imaginary offenders. Jess wondered why that story did the rounds but certainly was relieved that all suspicion seemed to be directed away from her.

She was now so insecure that she was unable to venture into Derby for several months and this was interfering with her projects. She continued to write a few romance novels but put much more effort into George Norman Thaler. She wrote and submitted a second novel under his name, this time dealing with more modern issues and other foreign influences, especially the Chinese. It also covered a lengthy deliberation on the *bêche-de-mer*, or trepang trade, also known by some as the sea cucumber, that had operated for centuries between the Macassar men and the northern coastal tribes of the Arafura Sea and how far inland their influence and trade items penetrated. In this second novel she also based a lot of the characterisation of one of the main people on George and his experiences. This she titled 'The Measure of My Days', referring to the life-spans of individuals in the context of endless time. It was a biblical Psalter reference often espoused by Norm, usually sarcastically.

Unbeknown to Jess, and totally unanticipated by her, was the enormous success of her two novels. She was unaware of their critical acclaim within Australia, let alone the huge popularity overseas, especially in Europe, notably Britain and North America. The reason for this acclaim was the unique

Australian bush settings and the lyrical, knowledgeable and sympathetic manner with which the subject matter was dealt.

All this was of little consequence to Jess, as she was so isolated from the world in general, and the literary world in particular, but her success was reflected in the payments that she was now regularly receiving into the account in the name of Norman Woods. She received favourable and encouraging letters from Advent Publications and continued to develop her ideas for further novels.

Jess published a third novel in 1992 called 'Serpents Bite Without Enchantment', a convoluted reference from Ecclesiastes that embodied the role of the Rainbow Serpent in the mythology of the Aborigines. This account concentrated almost entirely on the Aboriginal and natural history of her realm. She was careful not to expose the sources of her inspiration, but on the native aspects she was entirely dependent on the mystic customs of those she dealt with on an almost daily basis.

This novel allowed her to discuss one of the aspects of her life in the Kimberley that offered her the most solace. She gave free rein to her ability to describe the geology and scenery of her region and, with the aid of some research, was able to enlighten her readers about the ancient primordial province that had remained largely untouched by colonial intrusions.

Jess included all the flora and fauna with which she was familiar, and described the seasons and the events that occurred which were regulated by them. Her ability to accentuate the nuances in eloquent and striking language captivated readers. It was clear to all that the author was thoroughly conversant with his subject.

A year later, her much anticipated fourth novel was released. Jess was now almost twenty-seven. This novel deviated from her previous ones in that it was based on the life of Norman and as such was set for the greater part on his earlier life in England. She called this one 'Forth Goes the Woodman'. She thought this was a clever play on the name of the main character, which came from a Cowper poem that Norm was rather fond of quoting around the campfire.

The staggering aspect of this novel was not so much its setting, but the apparent authenticity and knowledge of the author about that subject. Readers were quite stunned and amazed at the historical and social accuracy of the details of a life of privilege displayed by someone who was supposed to be an untrained bush author domiciled in the isolated back blocks of the Australian wilderness. It only served to enhance his reputation in the European sector and resulted in a healthy increase in the sales figures.

The book also aroused much interest in England, as Jess had unwittingly alluded to several things about Norm's life that she did not realise were still a mystery there. She had indirectly set investigators into a frenzy on several fronts, but the one that started them off was the reference to an earl of the family du Pont. This in itself was innocent enough, but she had hinted at circumstances that were eerily similar to those of the du Bois. In the novel, Mr du Pont had called himself Mr Bridges. This began a trail of questions by various people in England: Was it possible that Mr du Bois was now known as Mr Woods, and not living in Canada as always supposed but in Australia?

Some of the detail in the book was so esoteric that it sent some historians scurrying for their history books just to ascertain whether this author was accurate or merely using poetic licence. As a case in point, Jess had described in detail the design and use of the Norman curved horse bit as used by the Norman knights and described to her by Norm. It had been one of the many ancient artefacts dating back to the Norman invasion in 1066 that were still lying about the ancestral home of his forbears and that he had discovered while playing about the castle.

Jess had always had a fascination with technology so to her this had been a natural inclusion and she assumed that its knowledge was universal. She was totally unaware that its use was long lost. The fact she was also able to accurately describe the small size and manner of the ponies used by the knights was to her normal, not unusual. She had included other facts about medieval life and martial activity that aroused suspicions and interest.

Jessie MacIntyre possessed a powerful intellect that needed constant exercise. Her mind had several facets, so over stimulation in one component could often satisfy her need to work in another that was being underutilised. Thus, her foray into literature went a long way towards meeting that need but she required increasing doses of that elixir in order to assuage her growing dependence on this form of outlet for her need to create.

Jess inhabited a wildly exotic fantasy world peopled by the characters she had created or was reinventing or remoulding. The dilemma was for her that she was constantly bombarded with an incessant stream of new ideas and situations from the people surrounding her. From these, her fertile imagination could not resist casting into ideas, testing out theories and following up leads. She lived in a make-believe world of characters and situations, which she either admired or fashioned into her ideals. She could alternate between the hum-drum of daily toil and the excitement of her imagination.

Ironically, this position was compounded by a sensation that was probably peculiar to her alone. For some reason, Jess never entirely felt at one with her Kimberley surroundings. She loved the life and the country but she always had a sensation of not belonging. She regarded the Aboriginal people as at one with their environment. She could never quite regard herself as either part of the country or fully in it, as they did. As always, the stirring words of Norm returned to her constantly: *spread your wings beyond this dream world; do not be trapped here under its spell.*

As Jess immersed herself deeper into her only stabilising influence, her creative writing, she found that she was accumulating self-rejected output. In the beginning, she merely discarded it by deleting, but occasionally she realised that some of this output had literary merit, if not the subject matter. Sometimes it was too deep and esoteric for the novels of Jane Ransom, and sometimes it was too racy for the novels of George Norman Thaler. Sometimes it was just not appropriate for either genre. Jess collected these rejected passages and accumulated them into a discard file.

In her meanderings about the property, Jess spent many engrossed hours inhabiting her other worlds and developing stories for her novels. She began to get the germ of an idea for the creation of a third channel for her insatiable need to create. She slowly began to entertain the thought of creating a new pen-name for herself. This alone would create several nearly insurmountable difficulties, but part of the attraction for her was to overcome these impediments and triumph by the final output. Once achieved, much of the gloss dissipated, despite any success. The challenge was in the achieving, not the continuation.

She had actually collated great swathes of rejected text into passable story lines in what she thought of as airport novels, better than the slim romance novels of Jane Ransom, but nothing like the calibre or quality of George Norman Thaler's novels. She wished to have them released but under another name.

Jess came up with a name quickly enough: Kimberley West, a suitably frivolous and flighty sort of name to reflect both her domicile and the nature of this form of output. However, the main problem was going to be publishing them and arranging for payments without revealing herself. She feared her chances of yet another false bank account under another assumed name would be too difficult to arrange and another reclusive author located in the same region as her two previous ones would certainly arouse suspicion.

She contacted a literary agent in Sydney by telephone while in Derby on one visit and asked if she would be interested in receiving a manuscript for perusal. Jess was informed of the procedure and duly complied. She gave the small grocery store in Australia Street, Newtown, as her address, the one next-door to Don's workshop where Paddy had his store, as she still well remembered that address clearly, where Antoine and his girlfriend, Micheline, had been so kind to her.

Several months later, Jess rang the agency in Sydney to ascertain the results of her submissions. They had read the preliminary material and were prepared to accept a full version in order to ascertain its merits. This Jess did, slightly more encouraged than at the beginning of this enterprise. It took several more months before the agency was prepared to further her pursuits, but finally she had a contract to sign if she agreed to their terms.

Jess concocted a story that she was travelling around and the documents could be sent to the post office in Broome. She thought she could utilise the Milbark Station accounts as she was a well known signatory to them. Furthermore, she reasoned, the pen-name of Kimberley West could also stand for a property name or a location of part of a station, muddying the tracks even more. *Can I hide all this from Stuart?*

When next in Derby, Jess approached the teller in the

bank and asked if it were possible to create a new cheque account attached to the existing station accounts that could be used for a new development they were contemplating on the west of the property. As it turned out, it was a simple matter to create a new account number for the station that had her as a signatory and that she could operate solely. That account number she forwarded to the new publishers in Sydney still indicating that the address was in Australia Street. It all went without a hitch.

A few months later, Jess rang the agency in Sydney to be informed that they had been successful in finding her a publisher prepared to publish her first novel as Kimberley West. Jess contacted the publisher herself and expressed her gratitude. During the conversation, she intimated that, despite her first novel being rather lengthy, she had several more in the pipeline of a similar ilk. They requested that she wait to see how this one was received and they would then decide. It was up to the book-buying public as to how this new enterprise went.

Meantime, Jess began collating more of the great swathes of text she had accumulated but rejected for her other two enterprises. She could now experiment with a more ribald and coarser style of writing. The only clouds that Jess could see on the horizon so far were those involving hiding this subterfuge from an innocent and trusting Stuart. He hated bookwork and rarely checked the details of the station's books, especially where the finances were involved. As far as he was concerned, they were always unfavourable.

Chapter Six

In due course, Jess established a system of communicating with the Sydney publishers by initiating the contacts herself, usually from in Derby. She managed to get any paperwork that was sent to her, sent to Broome and then sent on by the post office. *That should cloud the track*, she reasoned.

Her first attempt as Kimberley West was a lengthy tome of over seven hundred pages. It was filled with action, complications and many devious turns. It was set mostly in North Queensland. Jess followed that one with an equally lengthy, more torrid and fast-paced extravagant work that she devoted scant time to sorting out detail. She was far more interested in output with this task, not quality. Besides, it allowed her to remove enormous swathes of collected text from her records and gain some minor return for her effort. It certainly was easy for her to turn out these manuscripts and at the same time assuage her growing desire to create and produce.

It took some time, but finally Jess was slowly forced to take stock of her life. She was now approaching twenty-nine. The episode on the Gibb River Road with Sergeant Moore had forced her to focus on her own mortality. She could see that, no matter how rewarding were her writing efforts, in the end this life was surely about more than personal amusement. She realised that when she died there would be no one to mourn or notice. The death of Norm had removed one cornerstone of her life and that was followed by the death two years later of Peter. George was making noises about moving on to Darwin while he still had the ability, and every time she looked at Stuart, she realised he was getting older too.

There was no way for Jess to take over the lease that Stuart held on Milbark. Apart from a single bank account in her own name in Derby, she had no legal existence. She possessed no Medicare card, was not enrolled to vote, had no driving licence or vehicle registered in her name, and certainly had no credit cards, let alone a passport or visa. She did not even submit a tax return in her own name: she did not exist.

It was becoming impossible to employ suitable stockmen and Milbark had to rely on the less dependable local native stockmen whose loyalties often lay elsewhere, especially during the Dry season when their labour was most needed. Along with all the increasing government interference and pressures to accommodate conflicting requirements regarding land tenure, native title, ecological issues and tourist pressure, managing a large and demanding cattle station was becoming more difficult. Jess was unsure whether she was able or willing to cope with those demands.

Jess had no real spiritual beliefs either to comfort her. George almost never mentioned the subject and, in any case, he was a lapsed Catholic who had forsaken their rituals long ago following his wartime experiences. Jess observantly noted that George now worshipped the creation, not the Creator. Peter had seemed to hold no particular attitude to the subject except to indicate that he was animistic and could identify with the Aborigines. Stuart was essentially an atheist; or if not, gave the subject no attention. Norm had been brought up emersed in the faith of his class but had forsaken it following the death of his love. He was antagonistic towards God and held Him responsible for his present plight.

Jess had never had the opportunity to formulate her own considered opinion about spiritual matters as her only experience with religion was a bitter one where she had been unmercifully beaten by its practitioners in her earliest childhood. She had no reason to backtrack. Norm was the only one who had a meaningful experience of the subject. He quoted extensively from the Bible, as he did also from other classics and English poets, and had obviously once been very familiar with its contents. Jess was always fascinated by the eloquent and powerful manner of the Bible's message, so succinctly expressed. Given her own enthusiastic endearment to the wonders and intricacies of the English language, it was no surprise that she found its manner of expression so attractive.

She had never had access to the source of this mine of inspiration until, on the death of Norman, she inherited his ancient Bible. It was a small leather-bound volume with tiny, closely spaced type that discouraged exploration. She had opened it a few times but found its contents too difficult to navigate and had no idea where to begin to make sense of it. She found it very difficult to devote her valuable reading time to something that was not advancing her own research and writing.

She was always dissuaded from the Bible's message by the sadness instilled in her every time she picked it up only to read the neatly written ink inscription penned by the long-dead hand of Norman's unfortunate lover, Charlotte Louise.

Herein lay another telltale sign that further weakened Jessie's anonymity. Norm had occasionally referred to Charlotte Louise as Weesey, the secret name by which she was known by only a very few souls. Unfortunately for Jess, she inadvertently used that appellation as a designation for one of the characters associated with her hero set in the fourth novel about England, thinking that it was a name known only to Norm and herself. However, it was recorded in the saga of the missing fourteenth earl of Bromley.

The Aboriginal people with whom she had become so familiar had no real concept of a god as such, especially a single god. Their world was controlled entirely by spirits, mostly malevolent, and every effect, every outcome was held to be caused by one spirit or another. They spent their lives in an attempt to avoid upsetting the spirit world and they could perceive spirits in everything such as the endless little willy-willies (dust devils) that danced about in the dusty grass of the hot Dry season days.

Even Death, the great leveller, was attributed to the work of spirits through the agency of some person. Every death of an Aboriginal was accompanied by the search for the culprit. In the region where Jess lived, this was manifested by the act of placing a circle of stones around the bones of the dead in one of the countless caves in the hills. Each stone represented a person, and the first stone to receive a drip of water from the cave roof was the perpetrator. Alas, some poor innocent would then have the bone pointed and would die. Jess was always trying to understand how philosophical they could be. She was not too keen on hurrying up the process, even though she sometimes did wonder why she was here and what her existence had contributed to the world.

Jess had only known old men. She had never had the experience of young men in her life since leaving Sydney as a thirteen-year-old. For the first time she began to think about children and all that she had missed. Jess was not a mirror-gazer but she had of late taken to observing herself in the only mirror that the station possessed, located in the wash room of the house. Jess did not regard herself as particularly attractive. After all, it had been drummed into her by the nuns as a child. When she looked into the fuzzy mirror on the wall, she saw a rather characterless face with pale skin, thin light eyebrows, a rather prominent forehead and a small concave nose above a generous mouth full of very white teeth and thin lips. Her eyes were very blue, and set within almost overlarge orbs of milky white. She was so different from all the others that she almost detested her appearance.

Her blonde hair was so fine that it lay flat on her head and hung in a short rough cut over her long head. She was short, only five-foot-two with a rather thinnish frame, due mainly to deprivation as a child. She had thickened up in her early youth through hard exercise and training at the gym and from a life of constant physical work, but nothing was going to increase her height. She wondered what a young man might see in her and what, if any, traits would attract his gaze.

There was one other aspect to Jessie's life that she was prepared to acknowledge. She had always been taciturn, almost aloof, but had grown to be sullenly silent. She realised that this was a part of her character makeup that evoked coolness in people towards her. After her horse fall at the beginning of her stay at Milbark, her approach to things slowed to a deliberation and she became much less impulsive. She was never able to determine if this was a product of her experiences or from her unknown genetics.

One consequence of all this introspection was that Jess began to spend more time over at Ravymoota. She was always made most welcome, especially by Hubert who somehow the Coniston's had managed to keep. He was a superb practitioner of the culinary arts and was the head chef for the paying guests that were arriving in increasing numbers during the southern winters. Edna was a sympathetic and kindly woman who treated her as a deserving soul needing constant reassurance. Jess found the experience of a more normal family life inspirational and rewarding, if only for brief periods.

Jess's immersion in her imaginative world of make-believe and adventure was so cathartic that it became like a drug to her. She was glad that she had retained access to the short stories of Jane Ransom, as she was able to relay anonymously her desires for the ideal romance that she felt were slipping further away from her as each year passed. These unchallenging works fulfilled that need, but not the need to produce quality writing of which she knew she was capable.

This was fulfilled in the serious novels as George Norman Thaler. Her fertile imagination and unquenchable thirst for the authentic resulted in long, detailed novels that enthralled the reading public because of their authenticity. She completed a fifth novel early in 1994 and had the draft almost ready to send off to Melbourne. This novel was lengthy and more modern than the first four. She called it 'For All His Days Are Sorrow', a quote again from Ecclesiastes that Norman often espoused when melancholia set in about the camp fire during the long Dry season nights.

She still had the same main hero, but the futility of his struggle was becoming evident as he approached his end days. This extensive work covered crime, hunting, mining, and especially the romance of the Kimberley diamond exploration and the subsequent discovery of the unique coloured stones from the kimberlite pipes of the rugged ranges.

In this novel, Jess also covered the extensive history of settlement in the main towns of western Kimberley, of Broome and Derby, and the development of the Gibb River Road. She was able to learn a lot of the information from some of the local stockmen as well as a few of the elderly residents of the main towns. The Western Australian government tourist and lands departments also freely distributed information that she was able to utilise.

In the meantime, she also continued to pour out a copious harvest from her wildly energetic and fertile imagination as the racy new author of paperback romantic thrillers under the guise of Kimberley West, supposedly domiciled in what she still thought of as the seedier working-class district of Newtown. So far, she had managed to remain undetected by a totally unsuspecting Stuart.

Actions however, had been set in train by the success of the publication of the first four novels of George Norman Thaler. Unbeknown to Jess, investigations were under way in an attempt to locate the mysterious and immensely successful reclusive writer. The investigative reporter for Channel Four, Anna Delaney, was an avid fan of the works of George Thaler. She also acted as an occasional reporter for life-style and travel programmes for Channel Four.

It was in her capacity as a travel reporter that Anna convinced her network boss that, if she could use the guise of writing a travel report on the family-run farm-stay of Ravymoota, she might be able to ascertain the whereabouts of the allusive Mr Thaler. Preliminary investigation had revealed that he apparently was domiciled either at that address or close by. Advent, his publisher, was reticent to reveal anything, but had indicated that he was located in the Kimberley around Derby and connected to a station that resembled Ravymoota.

Anna arranged a four-day stay at the cattle station's home-stay billets for herself, a cameraman and a sound assistant. She had four days to discover Thaler's whereabouts and that was all. They arrived on a Thursday, planning to remain until the Monday morning. The first two days were completely occupied in filming and describing the facilities, the scenery and the activities that were available on the property.

In the evenings, Anna would casually endeavour to discover surreptitiously if anyone had any knowledge of the novels of George Norman Thaler. She was surprised to discover that very few of the inhabitants of the run had even heard of him. The hosts, Edna and Ralph Coniston, had heard of him, mostly through the incessant tramp of visitors journeying to the property in search of the ethos generated in the novels. On the strength of these occurrences, Edna decided she had better acquaint herself with the books and had thus become familiar with the contents. She was rather staggered to learn that George Norman Thaler was considered a local as she certainly had never met him, at least not knowingly.

In tandem with Anna's visit to Ravymoota, fate had decreed another peculiar event to coincide. This involved Jessie. She had taken to driving the GMC regularly about the local area, but not into town anymore. She used it to travel the thirty or so kilometres to the mail box in order to keep it running. On this occasion, however, 'Jimmy' broke down a few kilometres inside the river side of the Milbark property. He needed constant attention in the form of maintenance and occasionally, though rarely, actually stopped dead in his tracks. This was one of those occasions.

Unfortunately, 'Jimmy' had slipped a cog in the gear box train and Jess, after preliminary searching, decided it would need to be disconnected from the engine enough for her to be able to get at the offending parts. This required her to construct a tripod of stout tree timber in order to support the disengaged engine while she slipped out the cogs and attended to them.

It took Jess over a day to arrange the supports to her

satisfaction and to dismantle the components. She was slightly closer to Milbark, but Ravymoota had a much better workshop, equipped with machine tools capable of manufacturing a cog. She decided to walk the slightly longer distance to Ravymoota overland, in a direct line from where the truck had stopped. She gathered a few items, the damaged cog and the heavy-gauge rifle that hung behind her in the cabin, and set off in the direction of Ravymoota at first light on the Friday morning. She walked quickly and arrived near dark on the same day.

Jessie made straight for the homestead and found Edna in the throws of preparing the evening meals for the paying guests. Jess wasted no time in conversation, but asked if she could attend to the broken piece in the workshop. She rummaged about in the metal heaps around the building to find a suitable piece in order to manufacture a new cog wheel then began to machine it to size. This would take some time.

Anna and her team returned just on dark to discover from the hubbub occurring about the property that a strange woman had wandered in from the wild bush and was constructing some part or other for her truck. Edna emphatically announced to Anna that there was the real story of the Kimberley: a young girl thrust into a rugged life of toil and struggle and making a huge success of it. Anna would do well to feature her. Anna was intrigued. She had made no progress at all in her efforts to reveal the presence of George Norman Thaler, but had made some successful segments for the travel episodes. Maybe this might give her a spicier story.

Chapter Six

After a sumptuous evening dinner provided by Hubert, Anna proceeded over to the distant and well-lit workshop where she could hear the busy sounds of industry as two people were working at benches and on various vehicles. Over in the far centre of a long assemblage of press drills and machine tools was Jess.

Anna walked over, 'Hi there, hello.' Jess gave a slight jump of surprise and turned to face Anna. Anna was immediately struck by the fine-featured young woman facing her. In Jess's hands were some instruments, and a cutting machine was grinding slowly on the bench behind her. Jess peered slightly upwards and gave the barest glimmer of a smile. She replied in a barely audible soft voice, 'G'day.'

'I hear you've just walked in from the bush?'

Jess frowned a little and looked puzzled.

'I mean, you've come in to repair something I'm told.'

'Yes.'

Anna could see that this woman was quite reserved and reticent so she excused herself and departed. She went back to the house, intrigued. Edna told her all she knew, which was not all that much, but indicated that Jess would be there for a day or so to repair the part.

Jess worked all night and most of the next day preparing the new cogs. She announced to Edna that she would be leaving next morning early in order to get back to the truck in daylight. Edna would have none of it. She insisted Jess have a proper dinner and breakfast then the Ravymoota chopper would ferry her back to her truck. Jess was embarrassed with all the fuss. She outwitted poor Edna by leaving well before daybreak and made good time on her way back.

Edna was sorry that Jess had snubbed her invitation but admired her pluck. Anna, rising quite late, discovered that her prize story had departed. With a little goading from Edna, it was arranged that Anna and her crew alter their filming schedule to track Jess and investigate the truck.

About mid-morning, they took off in the Ravymoota chopper, headed for the river crossing on the Milbark road. En route, they spied Jess walking over the grassy plain between two spurs of craggy hills, the rifle slung over her left shoulder and a small backpack on her back. They could not safely land there so headed off in the direction of the river. Skimming the top of a small rise, they saw on the road ahead the dismembered blob that was the damaged truck. There were parts strewn all over the road on tarpaulins and a huge gantry of trees supporting the dismantled engine over the engine bay.

The chopper pilot realised he had better land at some distance as he did not want to throw up too much dust onto the uncovered parts. Jess was estimated to be a couple of hours away yet so Anna arranged for the photographer to take plenty of pictures of the site and surroundings while they waited.

Jess arrived just after midday, surprised to see Anna and her crew. Jess ignored them and began to uncover the compartment and re-strain the chains supporting the engine. She crawled under the raised body of the truck to fit the remade wheel. She announced to Anna that it would take her the best part of the night to reassemble the truck and advised that maybe the visitors should depart.

The next morning was Sunday. Anna had postponed her departure by a day to learn more about this strange, capable and talented person who had just spent the night alone in the vastness of the bush. As early as possible, they again flew back to the truck. Jess had reassembled most of it and had removed the three trees that had acted as a tripodal support for the engine block. She was still under the truck attending to final adjustments when the familiar whirr of the Ravymoota chopper softly infiltrated the still and cool air of the Dry season morning.

Not them again, she thought.

The chopper landed nearby and Anna enthusiastically ran over, joyously carrying a large wicker basket of items supplied by Edna. By lunch, Jess was ready to tentatively turn over the engine and attempt to move the cumbersome truck. The motor started immediately. Jess moved the truck slowly back and forth and then along the track, changing gears and getting out to inspect underneath for signs of failure. *So far so good.*

Anna heaped praise on the efforts of Jessie's handiwork. She did not fully appreciate the significance of what Jess had achieved but nevertheless did understand that it was a remarkable effort under the circumstances.

Anna was about to say goodbye when Jess announced that she could not go home, not yet anyway, as she needed to return to Ravymoota to finalise the cleaning and tooling of the gear wheel interfaces to ensure they were all within acceptable tolerances. Anna was both surprised and excited at this development as she sensed an opportunity to achieve an outcome of significance if she could accompany Jess on the relatively short drive back to Ravymoota, rather than going in the helicopter.

The others departed in the chopper about four in the afternoon while Jess turned the big truck around and pointed it in the direction of the river. When Jess was finally ready to attempt the drive, she and Anna climbed into the smallish cabin and Jess gingerly drove to the river where she got out again and inspected underneath the truck, noisily poking at it with metal prods and wiping the seals to check for leaks.

Jess said with a wry smile, 'Hang on Anna, here we go. If we stop in the middle don't get out whatever you do.'

'Why not?' asked Anna.

'Crocs,' said Jess in a matter-of-fact tone.

Anna went silent and hung on tightly as the big truck slipped into low range with a heavy metallic clunk. The engine revving loudly as the truck crawled and bumped at a reasonable pace along the gravelly tracks and into the wide but shallow river bed. The GMC bumped and jigged more violently as it hit submerged boulders and other objects in the river bed but Jess kept the pace up and the water began to bow-wave in a large mass in front of the vehicle.

On emerging onto the other side out of the riverbed, Jess gunned the old truck and in a crescendo of revving engine and displaced water, emerged onto the long expanse of the other side, slipping and sliding about in the soft gravel that was the road at this point. It was not until they were well clear of the gravel bed that Jess stopped the truck and let it idle for a few minutes while she got out to inspect it again.

There was not much to see with water cascading down the chassis and engine compartment. Jess re-engaged the gears in high range and eased the truck up the track, venturing a faster speed out onto the Gibb. It was about an hour to Ravymoota.

About thirty minutes into the drive, Jess came to a wide gravelly space that was obviously used by travellers to stop and enjoy the view. Jess pulled over onto the area, stopped the truck at the edge of the clearing, and pointed the nose out over the extensive valley view. Anna looked at the view and was spellbound at the vista. She turned towards Jess to speak, but noticed that Jess seemed to be in a daze. Her right hand was on the gently vibrating gear stick with her palm down and fingers extended. Jess was delicately and minutely manoeuvring the stick about in the gate with a dreamy far-away look on her face. It was some time before Anna realised what she was doing. Jess was actually listening to and 'feeling' the engine and the gear box through the gear stick. Anna could see Jess's concentration as she deftly and slowly moved the stick about, oblivious to her presence in the cabin.

This went on for about two minutes before Jess realised someone was with her. She turned the engine off and a sudden eerie silence fell upon the two women. Then they chatted for over twenty minutes, after Jess had thoroughly inspected under the truck again. They talked about the scenery and the pioneers and the Indigenous people, Anna marvelling at the knowledge and stories this strange person was telling her.

It was this fateful moment, more than any other, that twigged Anna to the astonishing possibility that Jessie MacIntyre and George Norman Thaler might be the same person. The reasons for this deduction were manifold, but central to her conclusion was the peculiar turn of phrase that Jess utilised, and her choice of colloquialisms that Anna clearly recalled occurring many times in the books of George Norman Thaler.

Then her suspicions increased as she began to realise that Jessie MacIntyre was an expert mechanic, a topic that was raised several times in the novels. To top it off, this woman expounded knowledgeable details about the geology, the Aborigines and the climate of the area in such a way as to indicate an affinity to the settings of George Norman Thaler's novels.

Anna began to observe Jessie much more closely now, looking for a telltale sign to conclusively confirm her suspicions. The remainder of the trip back to Ravymoota was concluded in silence because Jess had difficulty speaking over the noisy motor and Anna was deep in her own thoughts.

Jess dropped Anna off at the homestead and continued on over to the workshop where she hoped to complete the reaming of the casings holding the new gears in one night. Anna began making discreet enquiries about the strange woman from the bush. She also managed to contact one or two of the Aboriginal people who seemed to be everywhere about the station. It was from them that she learned how much they respected her and how much she knew about their customs and life.

Anna Delaney and her team packed up the next morning and departed from Ravymoota with their travel segments fulfilled, and possibly, Anna hoped, some beginnings about the identity of George Norman Thaler.

Jess spent two days completing the machining of the metal components before she was able to reassemble them and rely on their serviceability. She gave no more thought to the young woman with whom she had spent some of the last few days.

On Anna's arrival back home, she immediately began to research any information she could obtain about George Norman Thaler. The travel excerpts were not due to be aired for a few weeks but she was very pleased with her trip.

Channel Four was located in Melbourne but the programmes went nationwide. The team had surreptitiously taken many photographs and film footage of Jess, and on the rare occasion that she had actually seen them doing it, had insisted, rather gruffly, that no pictures of her were to be shown. She had even extracted a promise from Anna, to which Anna was only too pleased to agree. However, her producers and others involved with the programme had no such scruples and, on seeing how photogenic she was, and realising how astonishing Jess's story would be to their travel show, some shots of her were included along with the fateful insertion of her name.

Inspector Mick Stolt, now Deputy Commissioner of Police in New South Wales, did not see the programme when it was aired but several others of his ilk certainly did. Stolt was alerted and there was suddenly a flurry of enquiries emanating from Sydney into the mysterious woman portrayed in this travelogue. Anna was startled to learn from her boss that the police had seized all the film and photos of Jess, plus other material.

Anna gave it little thought, though the idea of alerting Jess had occurred to her. Anna simply did not understand the seriousness of the position into which she was about to place her new friend from the remote outback of the north.

Deputy Commissioner Stolt had all the seized material sent to his office. He realised that he had never actually seen Donald MacIntyre's daughter, but on further investigation, it was discovered that the property where Jessie lived was leased to a Stuart MacIntyre; a very good portent. Stolt had carried with him for years the latent fear that one day he would be exposed by the only other witness he had been unable to eliminate. In an attempt to assuage some of his guilt, he had befriended one of the rather attractive widows of the slain men, rashly promising her that he would eventually track down the perpetrator of the deed. Their friendship had developed into rather more than platonic, and his vow had taken on more of an urgency. He was constantly on the lookout for a scapegoat. Jess was the person he had always hoped would best fulfil that role.

He studied the footage at great length and familiarised himself with its contents. He spent many hours preparing the arrest. He seriously contemplated trying to eliminate her before that could be achieved as that would reduce the risk of exposure. But in the end, he decided that to parade the perpetrator would be more beneficial, eliciting much greater public adoration for his life-long devotion to redressing this monumental wrong.

The problem was that she was domiciled in another jurisdiction. He would need to emphasise to them the dangerous nature of this person and indicate how desperate she would be to avoid capture and extradition back to New South Wales. He was unable to emphasise how much he wished her dead though.

CHAPTER SEVEN

The programme about the Kimberley was aired in early September, and even though travellers could not take advantage of the remainder of the Dry season to travel north, they could plan for next year. It also gave the New South Wales police time to organise their counterparts in the west to arrest Jessie MacIntyre and arrange her extradition on murder charges, among others, before the onset of the Wet.

The Western Australian police had never heard of Jessie MacIntyre and there were no records of her existence in that state. They were puzzled when the request came through indicating that they were dealing with a vicious and dangerous criminal wanted for the murder of two policemen in Sydney and other criminal activities. The Western Australian police believed that their New South Wales counterparts were exaggerating the position but heeded their advice to the extent of appointing four Special Branch operatives to arrest her, partly because of the difficult terrain in which they would have to operate and the extra preparedness of this group for such challenges.

In charge of the operation was Sergeant James Musgrave, a highly trained and skilled policeman who would be accompanied by three also well-trained men. They were to fly to Derby then sneak in as close as possible by helicopter and support vehicles, then make the arrest. Prior to their arrival, several flyovers were performed by the local police in unmarked aeroplanes to ascertain the layout of the property and the whereabouts of the homestead. The plan was to get into the homestead and make the arrest there. It went without saying that they would be heavily armed.

Jess was with all the station hands over at the big set of yards that bordered the neighbours at Bingarini, about thirty minute's drive from the house. As was becoming her custom nowadays, Jess usually drove back to the house to retrieve any stores that were wanted for the camp while the men worked until dark. As normal, she had planned to drive one of the station utes back to the homestead just before dark to retrieve some items and return to set up the campfire. The police were unaware of the system but assumed they would all return to the homestead, not realising that they all camped at the various yards about the vast and spreading property.

Jess set off about an hour before dark in order to be back in the light. She was, as usual, covered in dust and dirt from horseback and yard work; her face and hair were grimy from the day's toil. She normally remained this way until well after dark in keeping with her habit of going to bed very late and rising before dawn. At about midnight, Jess would have a short warm shower from the twenty-gallon drum she set up on the fire as an 'elephant', transferring the water to a hanging bucket some distance from the camp.

As usual, she pulled up at the front door and the four policemen inside readied themselves to arrest her or to apprehend whoever arrived first. The kitchen area of the homestead was fairly large but cramped as there was a large wooden table occupying most of the centre of the floor. This was surrounded by several disparate wooden chairs scattered under and about the table. The room was cool and dimly lit by sunlight to keep out the heat. Jess hopped up the stairs and bounced into the kitchen, heading for the pantry cupboard. Suddenly there was a loud command,

'Don't move, you're surrounded!'

Jess was startled by the unexpected voices and she jumped to one side and turned to face three large men with guns dressed in dark-blue overalls. She had no idea who they were, but she was not about to ask.

Remembering the advice of her instructor, *if you are going to strike, strike first and strike hard*, she tried to sum up the position in a split second. She instantly concluded that this was not good. They were not here for her benefit and she feared the worst. She concluded that she was about to die, so nothing would be held back.

In a flurry of lightning-fast manoeuvres and evasive

movements designed to confuse, disorientate, and stun her attackers, Jess lashed out with her left leg into the right knee of the nearest officer, combining that attack with a chop to the falling man's head, rendering him disabled. She scattered and chucked the wooden chairs about the room in a profusion of mess and noise as she ran back towards the door near where another man was standing with a drawn gun.

Jess kicked a chair in his direction, and while he was trying to dodge that missile, she was able to smash her clenched and joined hands with an almighty swing into his elbow and chest, which, combined with the attack by the chair, sent him backwards onto the floor. The resulting jolt and tumble ensured that his hand gun discharged, sending the bullet skyward through the timber roof and raining debris and dust down onto the tumbling policeman.

The third man in the room, also dodging randomly, scattering and tumbling wooden furniture, charged towards the now fast-disappearing woman as she darted through the doorway. Amid much confusion and shouting from the officers, he fired a shot that hit the door frame. Jess was unaware that the fourth man was hidden outside on the veranda. She ran out of the house, intending to leap wildly over the stairs, but the fourth man tried to impede her movement with a foolhardy stand near the doorway.

Jess saw him just in time to leap swiftly up onto his chest sending him tumbling backwards onto the wooden veranda floor. The last man from within was by now on the edge of the veranda, and while trying to dodge falling bodies, was able to discharge two more shots at the rapidly departing figure. One shot grazed Jess on her upper right arm just as she was darting and changing direction. The shot thrust her awkwardly sideways into a small clump of bushes and stacked tree limbs. She bumped her head in the mix of branches and tree trunks, which stunned her and she tangled her legs in the scattering sticks and branches. The pain from the bullet was severe and she was unaware how serious the damage was. She tumbled into the pile of debris, fleetingly losing track of her circumstances.

This momentary interruption of her retreat was all the last man standing on the veranda needed in order to get to her and prevent any further escape. He ran over to where she laid facedown in the dirt, blood oozing from the wound on her upper right arm. The fall into the branches had temporarily stunned her and those sticks that were now entangling her legs slowed her regaining movement. This allowed the man to pounce on her prone body, shouting at her and roughly shoving her arms back behind her.

He pushed her violently in the back with his large left hand, cuffing her roughly as she struggled and then leaning down to her right ear, leant heavily with all his weight on his right elbow and arm squashing her into submission and straining Jess's old horse-fall injury to her right shoulder. She yelped as the burning pain of the bullet wound joined the new muscular pain of the now-returned shoulder injury.

Jess was panting wildly from fear and pain, as well as the exertion of the escape, sending up little puffs of dust from her face that was still pressed firmly against the dirt. Sergeant Musgrave pressed his considerable weight onto the slowly subsiding woman and then said to her in a shaking voice exuding furious rage, 'Stop it! Stop it now.'

Jess gave a stifled grunt and attempted to struggle some more. Sergeant Musgrave shoved her harder into the dirt, hurting her shoulder more. Jess moaned. He could see the patch of blood spreading about her torn shirt sleeve. He rolled her over and gave her a swift backhand across the face, hurting her jaw, stunning her more, and sending her into a mild daze. By this time, the man from the veranda had arrived. Sergeant Musgrave was very tempted to thump her again but the other man said, 'Boss! Steady mate. You sure this is her?'

'Yeah. This is her all right. Just as they said, mad and bad. And I didn't believe them.'

'Are you all right?' he asked Musgrave.

'Yes. I'm okay. Listen,' he puffed out at him, 'You wait here with this wild animal while I check on the others. Contact Ray and get that chopper here immediately.'

Sergeant Musgrave shoved her face-up onto the ground and cuffed her ankles while she was still dazed. Then he turned her back onto her front and walked over to attend to his injured men.

'Watch her,' he said. 'If she moves shoot her.'

The first man lay on the kitchen floor still dazed from the crack on the head with his right leg probably broken. The second man had a painful dislocation of his elbow.

Sergeant Musgrave attended to his wounded men. He

was angry. The New South Wales police had warned him Jess was a vicious and dangerous criminal and he had dismissed that advice as an exaggeration; an attempt to diffuse their failures to apprehend her themselves. He calculated that if she could be cornered by surprise alone in the house and unarmed, the four of them, armed and much bigger than Jess, would be able to arrest her quietly and without violence. In the distance he could hear the sound of the chopper rotors as they approached from the river end.

The chopper landed in a cloud of rising dust and grass with spotlights lighting up the make-shift landing pad. It was a big chopper, but it would be a squeeze getting the four of them, two wounded, and the prisoner into the machine. They loaded up the two injured officers and then Musgrave and the uninjured man went back to collect Jess. Musgrave turned her over and looked into her face. It was covered in dirt, and blood had trickled from a wound over her left eye caused from contact with the logs as she fell from the shot. There was also blood from the corner of her mouth from the thump Musgrave had inflicted on her.

He grabbed her shirt by the collar and gripped it very tightly around her neck. She had difficulty breathing and tried to turn her head to the side, but his grip was too strong. All the time, she peered unflinchingly at him, only grimacing slightly when the pain hit her. He shoved her back onto the ground with a solid heave, crawled to his feet, and roughly removed her boots. He had seen what devastation she could wreak with those. Then the pair pulled her off the ground and dragged her to the chopper and shoved her, still partially dazed, onto the vibrating floor of the swishing machine. It took off and headed for Broome.

The helicopter and its cargo did not arrive in Broome until well after midnight. They had radioed ahead to alert the hospital that there were two injured officers on the flight and a vicious criminal that was also injured. On arrival at Broome, the two injured officers were transferred to an ambulance and ferried off to the hospital. Jess was left laying on the floor in some discomfort. Musgrave come over to the chopper and dragged her onto the tarmac.

Again, he grabbed her by the collar and half lifted her off the ground. Jess was by now in a mild daze of pain and fear. She assumed that she had been arrested for the assault on the two policemen on the Gibb River Road.

Musgrave pressed her tightly against the body of the helicopter. 'You little bastard. If I could kill you I would. If there is one thing I really hate it's cop killers and drug runners. You're lucky there were others about tonight. I hope you rot in hell.' With that he sent her flying to the ground by chucking her sideways. Jess fell heavily onto her left side, still trying to protect the very painful right shoulder that Musgrave had already re-injured for her.

Jess was taken to the police station and charged with multiple offences, but it was now that she had positive confirmation that she was hunted not for the assault on the Gibb River Road but for the much more serious offences that happened years ago in Sydney. In fact, she was to be extradited back to Sydney to face charges of murder, among other things. She had wondered all these years what was the outcome of that night, as she had never heard a word about it in her isolation of the outback.

She had never expected to be charged with those murders, but she had expected to be hunted down as a witness to something so dastardly. She wondered how it had all been turned around and she was the one accused of the crime. Added to those unexpected murder charges were now going to be a string of offences incurred during last night's arrest. There was a police photographer who took shots of her in the state in which she first arrived. She was questioned and shoved in a cell until morning so the injured officers could first be patched up.

Several times during the night, Jess was visited by various officers, not to attend to her but to gape at the wild woman from the outback who had managed to cause so much damage. Jess was filthy and smelled badly of cattle yards and dirt. Her clothes were stained and grimy, and she had blood on several parts of her body. The worst was on her right arm where the stinging bullet had ripped through the outer part of her muscle. It was not too serious but had bled considerably. The police were not prepared to get her any hospital attention until the morning when more staff would be around. They did remove the handcuffs from her back but only to secure her arms in front of her. The cuffs on her ankles remained in place.

In the morning, Jess was taken to the hospital under heavy guard and attended to by nurses. Jess was stoic and resigned to her fate. She did not complain and expected no sympathy from hospital staff. After several hours and a cleanup, she was then returned to the Broome lockup and proceedings were put in train to extradite her to Sydney.

Stuart wondered what had detained Jess for so long at the homestead. When she did not return by eight o'clock that night, he decided to drive in to check. He found the kitchen in turmoil and no sign of Jess. There were signs of a struggle, and dust and grit from the roof bullet littered the floor. Stuart was worried. He did not know what to do. He rang Edna but she had not seen Jess. He contemplated ringing the police but they were hundreds of kilometres away.

Next morning, not long after day break, a police Land Cruiser trundled into their busy cattle camp and two officers rounded up all the men to ask questions. They wanted all their names and ages, and were unceremoniously officious about it. They also wanted to know who knew anything about Jess MacIntyre and the allegations against her of murder committed back in Sydney.

They were all warned that they were suspected of collusion and involvement in crimes; or at least being accessories. There must be some kind of mistake they kept on saying.

Stuart was asking as many questions as were the police. They were not forthcoming, though they did intimate that she was bound for Sydney. He realised that if she was sent to Sydney, he might have to go to ensure she was looked after. Stuart began to plan how he could manage that in the middle of mustering and shipping stock. He would now be two hands down.

Jess was charged with multiple offences in Broome and then a hearing was set for her extradition to New South Wales. That was accomplished rapidly, as the New South Wales police were very keen to gain access to her and begin proceedings relating to the crimes with which she was charged. She was flown quickly to Sydney and remanded without bail pending charges, and a trial that was expected to assemble in a few months.

Stuart arranged for George to oversee the cattle work and flew to Sydney within a few days. He had trouble finding out exactly what Jess was being charged with, or any of the details. He had to learn how to get her a defence lawyer and trudged about finding all sorts of other support. Stuart was staggered at the expense of reputable defence attorneys or barristers and also found many were less than enthusiastic to defend her, given the seriousness and controversy of the case. This he slowly learned as he trudged about the city alone, trying to gain her some assistance.

About three weeks after her arrival in Sydney, with Stuart still unable to secure a reputable defence lawyer, Jess received a mysterious visitor. She was told by the supervisor of the prison that she had an unknown caller and that she would be escorted to an interview room and guarded. Jess sat in the room alone except for visible guards about the hallway and outside the door, which was securely locked.

After about twenty minutes, there was a heavy metallic clunk and the glassed panel of the door revealed a stranger on the other side about to be let in.

A man wobbled in, dressed in an ill-fitting suit. He was short and rather corpulent, with a shabby coat covered in cigarette ash. His face was rotund and fleshy with large bushy eyebrows over smallish, piercing dark eyes. He wore heavy black-rimmed glasses over which he had the habit of peering. He also had flapping jowls and a big rumpled nose, slightly crooked on his pasty-skinned face, and pouting lips, spotted here and there with small discolorations that probably bordered on cancerous. He waltzed up in a smooth action as he headed for the chair. Jess found him quite repulsive.

'Caxton Tennex,' he said in a gruff and gravelly low voice that exuded authority, which seemed to her incongruent with his appearance.

She peered at him incredulously and wide-eyed. *Who is this peculiar and uninspiring morsel of humanity?* Jess just stared at him in wonderment and then knitted her brows slightly, trying to understand the purpose of this intrusion.

Caxton Tennex casually placed a black, battered briefcase on the table with a thud, all the time not taking his eyes from Jessie's. She felt a shudder of discomfort at his penetrating stare, which seemed to be drilling through her in an attempt to reveal her inner secrets. She hoped this was not the best that Stuart could arrange as her lawyer.

He stood motionless by the chair with his right hand still unmoving on the briefcase while he stared at the seated woman. He then began to sit by pulling the chair out from the table with his free hand, all the time maintaining direct and piercing eye contact with an unnerved Jess. She stared back at him unflinchingly.

Caxton puffed nasally as if just having exercised and then said to her, 'How are you standing up to the rigours of Her Majesty's pleasure?'

Jess knitted her brow even more and just stared right back at him, not muttering a word. He seemed to accept that his question was rhetorical. He placed two large rough hands onto the table with a sudden move. Jess jumped a little nervously. She looked instinctively at the source of the fright and noticed his plump short little digits, one encased in a huge signet ring with some sort of motif that almost covered the whole finger. Otherwise, his hands sat motionless on the table.

Looking at her steadfastly, he said in a brusque and serious tone, 'Miss MacIntyre, have you yet retained a suitable defence team to represent you at the trial?'

There was a short delay before she replied, saying simply, 'No.'

Caxton began to chat in a strange and peculiar vocabulary about matters that appeared to Jess to have almost nothing to do with her predicament, but were aimed at extracting opinions and feelings. She was very uncomfortable and spent most of the interview merely staring silently at him and remaining confused. He did manage to extract from her that Stuart was assisting her and that he was in fact actually out right now trying to obtain help. Caxton finally asked if he could contact Stuart and discuss the matter, to which she shrugged her shoulders and nodded agreement.

Caxton coolly summed up what he thought he encountered in the young woman seated before him. She presented herself as a rather elegant woman with attractive features that beguiled his gruff old heart. She possessed the biggest pair of pale blue eyes he had ever seen – that was when she was not peering at him through a furrowed brow. She presented a certain innocence and sophistication that his instincts told him were genuine.

A few days after this meeting, Caxton finally managed to arrange to meet Stuart in Caxton's small offices in the city up from the railway station. Jess had passed on the request from Caxton to Stuart, but intimated that she found him rather abhorrent. Stuart was not concerned about that aspect because he was having trouble locating suitable representatives willing to take on her case.

Stuart found the chambers of Caxton Tennex in a small building that consisted of a diminutive waiting room and two larger separate offices. He was ushered into a grubby office in which was seated the strange man just as Jess had described him. Caxton introduced himself and got straight to the point by asking Stuart to describe his understanding of the situation.

Stuart explained that he was mystified as to the events described as being Jessie's crimes and was very worried and upset at how things were going and the prognosis. Stuart kept insisting that Jess was a child when all these events were supposed to have occurred. That was the one point upon which Caxton seemed to pounce repeatedly, and hinted to Stuart to keep that fact quiet at present.

Caxton closed the session with a remark that he would like to think about things and asked Stuart to contact his office in three days. Stuart left the office feeling a little comforted that someone was finally at least listening to him.

Caxton sat back in his chair and lit a cigarette. He sat thinking so long that the ash began to fall onto his shirt. He brushed it off and sat up suddenly. He leaned over to his telephone and picked it up to dial. The telephone rang for some time before a woman answered and Caxton said to her, 'Good morning, Mrs Knuckey, it's Caxton Tennex here, from Sydney. Could I possibly speak to Mr Knuckey, if he is there?'

There was a long delay before Ian Knuckey picked up the telephone.

'Ah, Mr Knuckey, it's Caxton Tennex here. How are you going? Good, good. Listen Ian, have you ever heard of a Miss Jessica MacIntyre?'

Ian Knuckey explained to Caxton that Jessica MacIntyre was the daughter of Donald MacIntyre, the man who was assisting him in his attempt to implicate Stolt, among others, in corrupt activities using their positions in the police force as a cover.

The murder of the two policemen was the scandal that destroyed Knuckey's career all those years ago. He had never actually seen Jess, but understood that at the time she was about twenty-three and Donald protected her lovingly as best he could. Knuckey was unaware of her involvement in any of his clandestine affairs that also included Donald, who was at the time assisting him in catching other corrupt police. Knuckey again reiterated his long-held belief that Jessie did not commit the crimes of which she was now accused; in fact, he knew for certain she had not committed them, but someone else, whom they suspected but could not prove.

He suspected accomplices of Stolt's, if not the man himself, of committing the murders, but was never able to prove it. Caxton confirmed that Knuckey understood Jess to be twenty-three or more and that he had never actually seen her. Knuckey also mentioned that Donald had a girlfriend about that time by the name of Dawn Hobbs. He knew about her from Don as they had split up and Dawn was working at his old pub as a barmaid. After some more pleasantries, Caxton hung up the receiver.

Caxton sat back again in his ancient, creaking chair. He thought deeply about the one case in his life that he most regretted losing, not only for the loss *per se*, which was always regrettable, but for the manner of the loss and the nature of the person who had inflicted that loss on him and, worse than that, on his honourable and respectable client, Mr Knuckey.

He recalled clearly that Ian Knuckey came across as a very honest cop who had been severely wronged and set up by his colleagues, notably, he suspected, Stolt, as the fall guy for the most heinous and despicable crimes it was possible for a policeman to commit. Caxton particularly disliked his opposing barrister of that day, Mr Ivan Sebeski QC, a notorious and flamboyant character who had the reputation of sailing as close to the wind as was possible and had a clientele that included some of the most disreputable souls in Sydney. It still rankled with Caxton the glee with which both Stolt and Sebeski gloated over, what was to Caxton, a miscarriage of justice.

Caxton drifted into his thoughts about the Knuckey case of years ago. Almost directly opposite Don's workshop was the large and ornate late-Victorian Newtown police station and courthouse. A perfect location for what transpired. When Ian saw criminals and Stolt conversing, and cars being driven away from the workshop, he got suspicious. According to Ian, the only people he knew who lived at the Australia Street address were Donald and Jessica MacIntyre. Donald disappeared from the scene and was never heard from again. They tried hard to locate him, but he vanished. Ian suggested that he was probably at the bottom of the Hawkesbury. Jessie simply disappeared. The two policemen assisting Knuckey were killed that night. Stolt's offsider, Constable Josef Hindler, was killed in a motor accident two weeks after the event. There was no investigation into the possibility of any connection with the deaths that night at Don's, and now no one could corroborate Ian Knuckey's suspicions.

Caxton was at a loss to understand, after all these years, why Stolt would risk pursuing or reopening that case when there was always doubt, at least in the mind of Caxton, that justice was served in the original case. *Stolt must be driven by other motives to be taking such a risk.*

Caxton sensed a weakness, a chink in that former, foregone argument. He could not put his finger on it just yet, but somehow, he sensed it all centred on that reticent and reserved young woman.

Caxton got up out of his chair and walked briskly out of the office into the neighbouring one, which was occupied by his son Seton, who had taken over the small chambers with his wife that Caxton had held for many years. Caxton had basically semi-retired, passing the practice onto his son and his wife, who was also a qualified lawyer.

'Got a minute?' he asked them both as they looked up. They nodded.

'What do you think of this MacIntyre case then, eh?'

'Nasty business that one,' answered Seton. 'Don't like their chances there at all.'

'Funny you should say that,' said Caxton slipping his fingers into his belt at the side of his trousers.

'Why?' asked Philippa.

'Now don't leap on your high horses both of you, but I want you to think about us taking that case on.'

There was a stunned and noticeable silence. Both Seton and Philippa held Caxton in the highest regard, his knowledge and experience were of the highest order, but he had a reputation for taking on the unconventional. They were horrified at the mere thought.

Caxton continued, 'Listen, I've been to see her at digs and

I've formed a feeling about this case that could be the makings of you both and also right a major wrong that I was unable to fix the first time.'

'Not that old one again Dad,' said Seton. 'You never give up on that case. You should just drop it as a bad loss.'

'No, there's something fishy about this and why it's suddenly cropped up again after all this time. I want you two to meet with her and myself in the next few days. What d'you say, eh?'

The other two looked at each other in a resigned and slightly mortified manner.

Stuart returned to Caxton's office in three days as requested and was introduced to Seton and Philippa. They agreed a time for them all to meet with Jess at the prison the next day. It was proving difficult to arrange meetings between Jess and anybody else, as she was regarded as a dangerous prisoner, but finally the prison authorities agreed to a meeting.

Jess was ushered into the meeting room in handcuffs and waited for twenty minutes. Stuart entered first, followed by Caxton with his ungainly coat and old case, followed by Philippa and Seton.

Stuart was showing signs of the strain and Jess despised herself for placing him in this position. Caxton waddled up to the centre of the row of seats and flopped down with a gasp. The other two, however, were new to her and she wondered what they could want.

Jess observed that the younger man was astonishingly like

Caxton, and she deduced that he was his son, only a slimmer, slightly more elegantly dressed version. Seton wore a dark suit that hung uncomfortably off his narrow shoulders, and Jess decided he had the kind of physique that no amount of tailoring would flatter.

The young woman, on the other hand, was very smartly dressed in a dark-grey dress suit and minimal jewellery. Jess was rather impressed with Philippa, but wary of her.

Stuart asked how she was going and intimated that she already knew Caxton. Then he introduced Seton and Philippa as possibly interested in taking on the case; no guarantees yet, just preliminary enquiries. Jess nodded her understanding, all the time peering intently at each of the new arrivals.

'Miss MacIntyre,' began Caxton, 'my son and daughter-in-law need more information before agreeing to take on this case. Can you explain exactly what happened on the night in question?'

Jess knitted her eyebrows again and sighed a mildly audible sigh. She stared with a penetrating intelligence and disarming glare at the three of them in turn, concentrating in the end on Seton. Her short blonde hair sat neatly brushed over her head and her big eyes gave no hint of fear or dread, just stoic and determined resignation; almost as if she were accepting of the pointless attempt to remove herself from this predicament.

Jess described that evening in lucid and minute detail, recalling every nuance of feeling and actions that she endured and witnessed. Caxton noticed that every time she was interrupted, she stopped immediately without annoyance, stared intently at the interrupter or the cause of that interruption. She always paused before answering. At first, Caxton thought that she was displaying displeasure and rather arrogantly showed it by emphasising her delay in responding, but he slowly realised that this was her manner and she really was deliberately thinking through her response.

This was the first time Stuart had heard all the details of the now infamous night, and he was totally horrified at the trauma to which she had been subjected.

There was a long and meaningful silence when Jess had completed recounting the story. No one really knew what to say.

'And what happened after that?' asked Caxton.

'When I was sure they were gone, I ran inside and told Donald.'

'And what did he do?'

'Donald told me to collect a few things and meet him in the yard in the old van. He took me immediately to the airport.'

'But I thought it was not even midnight?' asked Philippa.

'That's right,' said Jess softly, turning to her and replying after the usual short pause.

'We waited at Botany Bay until morning and he got me onto a flight to Perth that morning.'

'And how old were you, Miss MacIntyre?' asked Caxton, leaning on the table with his big elbows.

Jess turned to stare at him with her familiar penetrating

gaze, knitted her brows again and stated, with a slightly puzzled tone, 'I was thirteen. Why do you ask?' she replied, turning a guilty gaze towards Stuart. That was the first lie that she had told him all those years ago. *How many more would emerge*, she wondered.

'Oh, no reason at this stage,' he replied. 'But keep that fact quiet, please.'

Stuart finally piped up, 'Look, there must be some horrible mistake here. You can see she was just a child at the time, besides, she's five-foot nothin' now, you should have seen her when she first arrived, she was only this high.' He waved his arm just above the ground.

'That's no guarantee, Mr MacIntyre. Children can kill,' said Caxton.

They spent another twenty minutes in the room with Jess after the story was told. Finally, Caxton asked Jess to sign a small piece of paper indicating her agreement to them taking on the case if they so decided. Jess looked at Stuart and he nodded.

'We are very lucky to get such reputable people,' Stuart assured her. Jess took the piece of paper and read it thoroughly. The others sat in silence, each trying to sum up their impressions of this enigmatic woman. Often clients just signed and never read anything, but not Jess. She asked a couple of questions and extended her left arm to accept the pen being proffered by Philippa. Jess stole a long and questioning look deep into the eyes of Philippa as she took the pen and turned the paper slightly to the right to sign. She hesitated for a moment then placed a neat, smallish signature onto the dotted line, returned the pen with another long look at Philippa and slid the paper over to Caxton. He in turn passed it to Seton.

Seton drove Stuart back to his motel and then returned to their office. Caxton sat contentedly in the back seat inwardly smiling at the possibilities. Back at his office, he lumbered into the rooms and flopped into his chair, thudding his case on the desk and smiled.

'What?' asked Philippa.

'Well, what did you think of all that?' asked Caxton in return.

Seton considered his response and said, 'Well, what an amazing story. But it's her word against his. And he's the deputy commissioner. I can't believe he would do such a thing. And so blatant.'

'I can,' insisted Caxton. 'What about you, Phily?'

Philippa took some time to answer. 'She's a remarkable woman. Not just very pretty but seems sincere and gentle. I find it hard to believe she has done any of those things she's said to have done. We'd better get Stuart back in here.'

'Yes,' agreed Caxton. 'Did you notice anything else important?'

There was a strained silence.

'Did you not notice she is left-handed?' asked Caxton.

'Now you mention it – yes, you're right,' said Philippa. 'Is that important? It's not that uncommon you know.'

'No. But very well could be. Keep that bit of information quiet too.'

Chapter Seven

The next day, Stuart was called into their office again for some more questioning. They asked repeatedly if she had ever shown any signs of aggression. All he could reply was that she seemed to have interminable patience and understanding when dealing with the animals, the men, and the Aborigines.

'I've never known her to hit a soul, or raise her voice, let alone severely injure three burly policemen!'

'What about being left-handed. Was that definite?'

Stuart looked at them quizzically for a moment.

'You know, I've never given it much thought. It's not that unusual. I've had a couple of cacky-handers before, but it never interfered with her work. Now that you mention it though, she is definitely a lefty, almost never uses her right hand much for anything.' That information was stored safely in Caxton's brain.

CHAPTER EIGHT

They were getting nowhere. Caxton asked Seton and Philippa to attempt to find Dawn Hobbs to confirm some of Knuckey's story, while Caxton went to Melbourne for two weeks on another matter. Dawn was not difficult to locate as she still lived in the older part of Newtown. Together they went around to her terrace house that she rented not far from the hotel that Ian Knuckey had named. They knocked on the door and after a small delay, a wizened and frail-looking woman opened the door and peered at them quizzically.

'Yes?' she asked in a rough, raucous voice.

'Would you be Mrs Dawn Hobbs?' asked Philippa.

'Yes.'

'My name is Philippa and this is my husband Seton. Could we talk to you about Jessica MacIntyre?'

'Oh, her. I'm not surprised someone's come about her,' she said with a slight sneer. 'Yes, come in.'

They entered a dark hallway that led into a small adjoining lounge. It was roughly furnished in tired-looking chairs that had faded with time. Dawn sat in a single chair that was obviously her television chair and the others sat in the small two-seater.

'I see they've reopened that cop's case over them two that was killed years ago,' said Dawn in a croaky, high-pitched voice.

'Yes,' said Philippa. 'We are here about Jessica, however.'

'Her name's not Jessica.'

'Oh. What is it then?' asked Philippa looking at her husband quizzically.

'Her name's just Jessie.'

'Just Jessie?'

'Yes. That's what Don called her when he picked her up.'

'What do you mean?'

Dawn went on to explain about the episode at the markets, the nuns, the orphanage and the picking up of Jess by Donald. She explained how the nuns had called her Jezebel, but Don refused to call her that and instead called her Jessie.

They detected that Dawn was not enamoured in any way with Jess. When they realised that Jess was not Don's daughter, they were flabbergasted. Dawn was obviously jealous of the child and intimated that her coming had contributed to the break-up of her relationship with Don.

'What sort of a child was she?' asked Philippa.

'Strong-willed little blighter,' said Dawn. 'She had all the men twisted around her little finger, what with her blonde hair and big blue eyes,' she continued bitterly. 'Don taught her mechanics and the other fellers also, plus she was always muttering away in all them different lingos. They tried to teach her to use her right hand on all the tools, she refused but. She was a stubborn little bitch, about that anyway.'

They chattered on a little longer then departed in a high state of confusion. Dawn had acknowledged that, as far as she had been aware, Don was not into criminal activities himself. He was no angel but drew the line at crime. He was involved with a few cops, as far as she knew, to help catch crooks. They sat outside in the car for awhile digesting this barrage of conflicting and distressing information.

Philippa and Seton returned to their office and compared notes. They decided to try to contact the Catholic Church, which had run the now-defunct orphanage. It was not easy to find their way through the maze of bureaucracy.

After several days, they were unable to locate any records of a baby born around that time who went missing. They were, however, able to locate one retired nun who had worked and lived there for many years. Her name was Sister Mary and she was located in a western Sydney retirement village for nuns. They arranged to pay her a visit.

Sister Mary Travail was an elderly, slightly plump and short woman with a gentle face and a quiet, deferential voice. She sat in an old armchair in the sunny room set aside for contemplation and visitors. She was dressed in drab attire.

Although she was very plain, Sister Mary exuded an inner beauty with her welcoming smile.

'Good morning, Sister Mary,' greeted Philippa. 'How are you?'

Sister Mary nodded and answered softy, 'Hello. I'm fine, thank you.'

'This is my partner, Mr Tennex. We have come to ask you a few questions, if that's at all possible.'

'Certainly. I'll do what I can.'

'Sister Mary, I believe you worked at the Quin Street Orphanage for many years.'

'That's right.'

'Do you by any chance recall a child there by the name of Jezebel or maybe Jessie?'

Sister Mary's face turned noticeably harder and her gentle smile and calmness seemed to dissipate. She sat rigidly, staring at them and replied in a less friendly voice, 'No, I have no recollection of any child by that name.' She continued to eye them directly and said nothing else.

'I see,' said Philippa diplomatically. 'She would have been a very young child at the time. She had blonde hair and very blue eyes. It would have been about twenty-five, thirty years ago now.'

'No. I don't remember anyone like that at all.'

Her coolness was becoming palpable. This change only served to convince both Seton and Philippa that Sister Mary did know something. How to extract that was the difficulty.

Philippa leaned a little closer to Sister Mary. 'I know it

was a long time ago now, but this child is now in serious trouble and we just wish to learn a bit about her in order to help her. Any small thing that you can recall might help her.'

Sister Mary sat silently for some time, nervously moving in the chair.

'I'm sorry to hear that. I don't see how I can possibly know anything that could be useful.'

'Well, she has been accused of serious crimes and we are convinced that she is innocent, but we can't find out about her childhood. Things that might be useful in proving her innocence.'

Sister Mary turned and gazed momentarily out the large window into the vista of green trees. She clasped her hands in her lap and wrung them together nervously. She was obviously struggling with her conscience.

Philippa sensed her turmoil and said, 'Look, we are not hunting anyone. There certainly is no trouble for anyone. We just need to know about her arrival there. You know, things like when, how old, when she left, that sort of thing. There don't seem to be any records at the church about her at all.'

Sister Mary turned to face them.

'Very well, I'll tell you what I know, but only because all those responsible are now dead. It was one of the saddest episodes in my time there you know,' she said with some sadness. 'There was a child like you described deposited on the steps in August 1967. I clearly remember it for several reasons, but mostly it was the day of my mother's birthday so I clearly remember the date. She was very new, still had the cord, couldn't have been more than a few hours old, maybe a day or so.

'She had the blondest hair. A lot of kids have blonde hair but most grow out of it in a year or so, but not this one. As she grew, it got blonder and her eyes were the bluest I ever saw. But she was a terror.' Mary saw the puzzled look on Philippa's face. She continued, 'Yes, she was headstrong and used her left hand all the time despite us punishing her.' Again, the puzzled look from Philippa. 'Yes. It is, well was in those days, considered sinful and from the Devil himself to be left-handed.'

'But you must have had other left-handed children there?' asked Philippa, horrified.

'Oh yes, a few. Not many. But we always managed to correct them straight away. But not this one. No matter what we did we could not get her to change. Mother Superior was beside herself with rage on many occasions. We beat her, tied her arm up, starved her; nothing worked. No matter what we did she never cried nor changed. Never. Mother Superior called her a Jezebel. She defied us all the time. Just stared at us with big blue eyes and all that blonde hair. She was such a pretty child. We all thought she was the Devil's child.'

'What happened to her in the end?'

'She ran away once. Someone rang up from the markets and we retrieved her. She didn't half get what for for that episode. Still, she would not change. We cut her hair very short to keep her from tempting others, but she was a real Jezebel.'

'Then what happened?'

'It was pitiful what some of the sisters did to her. But eventually she ran away again. She was about five at the time. We never saw her again.'

'Did you not enquire after her welfare, or at least her whereabouts?'

'No,' said Sister Mary, looking ashamed and embarrassed. 'We were rather glad to be rid of her. She was hated for her looks, her stubbornness and her disruption.'

'I thought you would have kept some records of her being there?'

'We did at first, but after she ran off the last time and didn't return, Mother destroyed the records. I had a bad feeling about that one all along.'

Philippa was very grateful to the distraught old nun for unburdening herself about what was, for her, a painful recollection. They had also learned a lot more about Jess's amazing story and the puzzle was not coming together but only getting more complex. They thanked the old lady effusively and assured her that there would be no more visits and nothing further would be asked of her about the subject. Outside the building, they sat immersed in their thoughts for many minutes before either could speak.

Back in the office, Philippa commenced enquiries into records of any births that were registered in Sydney on the day Jess was left at the orphanage. There were several, but all the girls were accounted for. The puzzle deepened. *What would Caxton make of it? Worse, how would Stuart react?*

Chapter Eight

Caxton arrived back in the office on the Monday morning after his two-week sojourn to Melbourne. Philippa and Seton had been occupied with several other clients as well as court appearances during this time. They were anxious to inform Caxton of developments. This they did as soon as he arrived mid-morning. He was stunned by the enormity of this unexpected development and its implications. He wondered how much of this story Jess really knew or remembered and if she had ever told Stuart. He decided to visit Jess first.

Caxton arranged to visit Jess on Wednesday with some trepidation. On entering the visitors' room, he sat down with a hint of less bravado than normal, though this was undetected by Jess.

Caxton opened with a tricky question, 'Do you remember a Dawn Hobbs, Miss MacIntyre?'

Jess shot him a glance that resonated with a malevolence he had not witnessed before. It rather unsettled him.

'I forbid you to discuss me with her,' she said in a cold, but soft tone.

'Miss MacIntyre,' sighed Caxton, 'I don't think you fully understand the seriousness of your situation.'

She stared menacingly at him. For the first time, he comprehended that possibly she was capable of any action if provoked. He had never seen such power in a face and such menace in a stare as was emanating from this previously passive and gentle soul. It worried him enormously.

'You don't understand what's at stake here, Mr Tennex. You, with your grotesque comedic exterior wandering the world in covert derision of the undeserving outcasts, jocularly jousting with the lesser-lights in a mind game of intellectual chess where you win or you lose. Well, Mr Tennex, it's not about you, and you have no idea what and who you are up against here. Destroying my life is a small price to pay to protect the ones I love. I forbid you talking to that woman and you must promise me you will not do so.'

There was a long delay before Caxton replied. He leaned slightly towards her, his large lips revealing a wry smile, and said to her in a moderate and conciliatory voice, 'Look Miss MacIntyre, I've learnt over many years that truth will eventually come out. This may be difficult for you and, yes, I concede that there is an element of truth in your opinion of my motives, but many others will benefit from the revelations that you may be required to sustain.'

She glared at him in an unblinking glower, her intelligent blue orbs contracting like those of a hunting animal.

Caxton Tennex, for one of the few times in his career, was at a disadvantage. Jess was proving truculent and defiant, disguising her fury and meaning in menacing words that resonated with intent. He realised that he could lose her if he did not attend to her request with sympathy, subjugating his aspirations to accommodate her fiery soul. Suddenly the game had turned. It resonated again with him the effect the devastating loss that the Knuckey case had on him, and he could sense his chance at redemption might slip away because of his own pride.

'Jess, I have not yet mentioned any of this to Stuart. I

understand your feelings but I can only reiterate that there are bigger considerations here than your shame at your accident of birth. I do understand what we are facing. Together we can extract retribution on those who have caused you and Donald so much pain in the past. They have destroyed people that it may be possible for you to restore. At least consider Donald, if not yourself.'

Jess glowered at him and pulled back slightly in her chair.

'You won't get me by eliciting my sympathy for Donald, Mr Tennex.'

Caxton was using all his enormous talent of persuasion. He could only hope that some of it would rub off. He noticed a mild flinch in her otherwise steadfast gaze at the mention of Donald. *Maybe that was her Achilles heel.*

Jess eased her intensity and relaxed her rigid body perceptively, but not her intense gaze. How he admired those ice-cold, blue eyes that spoke so eloquently of all her feelings. He felt almost as a captive mouse with the cat slightly relenting its fatal grip.

Normally, insulting words dripped off him as water off a duck's back, but somehow her stinging appraisal of him cut him deeply. He could not find the words to answer her.

Jess continued. 'You don't honestly believe this will be allowed to get to court do you, Mr Tennex? You're sadly mistaken in that belief. There's too much at stake. I've already been threatened and no doubt I will be killed long before it gets to that stage. I don't understand why I was arrested and not just killed at the time. Stuart knows nothing of this and I don't want him involved in any manner that would jeopardise him. Do you understand? So, there is nothing to be gained in pursuing this to the point that he is hurt by unnecessary facts. Am I clear here?'

'Yes indeed, Miss MacIntyre,' he replied, then added firmly, 'but I beg to differ. I believe he is man enough to cope with any news and would be prepared to support you to the end. That is how he comes across to me.'

'I'm not prepared to risk it. So please don't discuss my affairs with Dawn Hobbs.'

'What about restitution for the crushed soul of our Mr Knuckey? Would not that be a fitting goal and some recompense for a few perceived or imaginary wrongs on your part?'

Jess flinched slightly at the mention of Ian Knuckey. Caxton saw the slightest glimmer of hope in her reaction. *Maybe that was also a possible chink in her hardened heart.*

Caxton left the jail with a heavy heart. He so wanted the chance to redeem himself for the Knuckey case and seek restitution for Knuckey himself, but he was unsure whether to follow his instincts and ignore Jessie's plea or risk everything on his intuition. Her stinging and derogatory words, honestly felt he feared, were still ringing in his ears. He was indeed downcast.

Caxton was totally unfamiliar with parental shame. In fact, he saw little shame in any of life's impediments and in some ways felt Jess was overreacting. He gave the subject serious thought, but in the end, he felt the stakes were just too high to be influenced by the niceties and scruples of a seriously endangered client. He called Stuart into his office to break the news to him about Jess's parentage.

Stuart was devastated and severely offended that something so important could be kept from him by someone he truly loved and sacrificed for. He was so traumatised that he refrained from contact with anybody for several days. He finally pushed aside his hurt and visited Jess. Caxton had already told her of what he had done and they parted with bad feelings.

Jess was contrite and upset at the turn of events and kept apologising to Stuart.

'Please don't hate me, Stuart,' she pleaded, with tears rolling down her puffy white cheeks and dripping onto her arms. 'Please don't hate me.'

Stuart had never seen her cry so much in all their fifteen years together. She had shown emotion at the burial of Norman and also for Peter, but nothing like this. He was touched and it went some way to easing his own pain, but not entirely. He was both hurt and disappointed that she was no longer 'family'. He still loved her as a daughter and could see her heart-felt despair at her concealment.

Stuart was slow to recover from this devastation. It would be many weeks before any form of recovery was evident on all sides.

This was hastened by startling information that surfaced. They received advice from the prosecution that Sergeant Moore of the Western Australia police had been prompted to come forward after publicity about the case had surfaced in Perth. He decided to seek some revenge on the person who had confined him to a wheelchair, and he was encouraged by the coverage to change his version of events that occurred out on the Gibb. The reporting had indicated that Jess was a violent criminal with a long history and he felt he might be able to add to her woes and ease his own suffering at the same time.

Stuart and the three defence lawyers were less ruffled at the unexpected news. Caxton asked Stuart if there were any other witnesses, to which he replied that he hoped Mookargey would come forward as he had accompanied Jess on that day.

Stuart rang George and asked him to find out if anybody had seen or heard about it and was astonished to discover that all the clans people knew the heroic story, and even some of the people living in the surrounding properties.

Jess refused to discuss it, but a full and detailed account was provided by Mookargey, and Jess acknowledged its accuracy through silence, if not its embroidery.

In the meantime, Caxton and his team were now quietly confident that they could counter the barrage of evidence aligned against Jess. Their chief defence was predicated on two main arguments that they considered watertight. All the character assassination could simply be deflected as lies by the incontrovertible fact that Jess was thirteen at the time. They would call at least three witnesses to prove that fact.

The other aspect for which they had high hopes was the also undeniable fact of Jessie's left-handedness, an issue that needed to be delicately and thoroughly exploited at the appropriate time. Caxton was sure that Seton would be able to turn the jury around over that assault on the arresting officers and on the latest hiccup with the officer on the Gibb River Road, given Mookargey's account of that incident. In fact, it began to emerge that that incident might actually benefit their arguments. All seemed to be falling into place.

Alas, not quite so. The prosecution advised them of Jessie's bank account in Derby with hundreds of thousands of dollars in it. They contended that this confirmed her continued involvement in drug and other activities.

Caxton was a little annoyed, and Seton was full of despair at the continued arrival of unexpected issues. They immediately confronted Jess with the news but she rather dismissively suggested in her usual cool and off-hand manner that it was an irrelevancy and of no interest to any of them. Caxton informed her they would have to investigate it, with or without her acquiescence. She peered at him disdainfully as much as to say, 'See if I care'.

Stuart was totally dumbfounded by this news. He had no explanation for that amount of money in her account. The station did not have that sort of money so he wondered where she would get such an amount. Caxton suggested that Stuart return to the station and go through all the station accounts for the last few years to try to determine if she had been fraudulently skimming it from there. This he agreed to do. It would take him several weeks to complete this task so he bade her farewell for the time being and departed. Jess was devastated at the prospect of yet another of her hidden secrets emerging, dealing another blow to her injured honour in her eyes to her most respected friends.

Only a few days after this, the information relating to a large sum of money being in her possession was printed in a national newspaper as a small by-line on an inner page. Shortly afterwards, Seton's office received a visit from a stranger requesting to see him in connection with the MacIntyre case. It was Anna Delaney, the popular and well-known television reporter from Channel Four. She asked for a confidential meeting with the lawyer defending Jessie MacIntyre.

Seton asked in what way it related to the case, he being suspicious that she was merely seeking publicity. When she insisted it was not, Seton then asked if his father could also sit in on the meeting as well as Philippa. The story that Anna unfolded kept them spellbound for about twenty minutes. She expounded her theory that Jessie MacIntyre was probably the famous and very successful Australian novelist George Norman Thaler. She explained in detail her reasons, and the evidence she had so far amassed. Anna had advanced as far as she could unassisted, as the publisher was not prepared to divulge any details about their prize author to anyone, let alone a television reporter. Besides, she insisted, the publishers did not seem to know all that much about 'him' either.

So far, Anna was able to learn that mail for George Norman Thaler was always sent to an address in Derby and that he was supposed to live on one of the outlying stations along the Gibb River Road, the main track that connected Broome and Derby with Kununurra and Wyndham. Anna

Chapter Eight

explained her epiphany regarding George Norman Thaler on the Gibb River Road while in the company of Jessie MacIntyre. Following this unexpected revelation, and because Seton was committed to court appearances, Caxton agreed to go to Melbourne in an attempt to learn more about George Norman Thaler from the publisher.

Before going off to Melbourne, Caxton paid a visit to Stuart, who revealed that he had never heard of George Norman Thaler and doubted very much anyone he knew would have been capable of writing anything let alone a novel, with the possible exception of Norman Woods.

When in Melbourne, Caxton arranged to see the publishers and interview the agent who dealt with George Norman Thaler. Caxton entered the building mid-morning and was conducted into a neat and sophisticated boardroom where he was confronted by a young man in a light-grey suit and two young women, one of whom was Anita Norton, the representative of Advent, the publishers of George Norman Thaler. The young man was their legal representative who looked after all the legal aspects of the complex mix of creative artists and finances.

Caxton began the meeting in a gruff and direct manner, 'Thank you for seeing me. I have come to determine if a client of mine who faces serious charges is in fact George Norman Thaler.'

'Well, as I'm sure you understand, Mr Tennex,' replied Anita, glancing at her notes and trying to pronounce his name without stumbling, 'we have very strict rules and laws governing the divulging of confidential information.'

'Look,' said Caxton, 'I only want a few answers and that may satisfy our inquiry. Then I will need go no further. I can of course obtain a subpoena to garnish all the files when all I need from you are some simple answers. I can assure you of the strictest confidentiality at this point.'

The last thing the publisher wanted was legal complications. They understood the law enough to realise that Caxton was not bluffing.

'What is it you want to know Mr Tennex?' asked Anita.

'What I need to know is the following,' he said, passing over a piece of paper with a list of questions.

Anita picked it up and read out aloud, 'What is the postal address of GNT? What is the number and location of his bank account to which you send any remuneration? Where does he live? Have you ever met him or seen him? What details do you possess about him? How long have you known him? How does he send in new work?'

Anita looked at the questions again and pondered. She picked up the heavy file and flipped through the papers. She looked up at Caxton with a stern face and then back down at the file. Then she said, 'We send all correspondence to a post office box in Derby in Western Australia. His bank details are also located in Derby in the Westpac branch but I'm reluctant to divulge that number. It is in the name of one Norman Woods and the address is given as Ravymoota Station. And no, Mr Tennex, no one has ever met him or seen him, in fact we have never even spoken to him. We do have a profile on him and we have known him since his first novel turned up in 1991. Nowadays, he sends in his work electronically, but originally it was on paper.'

'You mean it just turned up out of the blue? Is that normal?'

'No, not exactly. He was referred to us by one of our subsidiary publishers, Romantis.'

'Who are they?'

'They publish our Romantis range of romance novels, inexpensive fantasy stories aimed at the lower, less-demanding market. There was some sort of agreement between Romantis and one of their top writers at the time that she would continue to supply romance novels if we would look at her friend Mr Thaler.'

'That simple?'

'That simple, Mr Tennex.'

'So, who is this contact in Romantis then?' asked Caxton.

'Julie Devlin. I can get you a number for her if you wish.'

'Thank you, yes that might be helpful.' he said gruffly.

Caxton departed the building in a state of mild confusion. Rather than clearing up this matter, he had been given more work do. He had a brief lunch at one of the many cafes and then rang Julie Devlin at Romantis. He met her at three o'clock in a shabby little room that evoked a make-do atmosphere. Julie was pleasant. Caxton surmised that she had already been contacted by Advent because she offered few objections to revealing most of the information Caxton requested.

His first surprise was to discover the existence of a Jane Ransom. Not delving into this kind of literature, he was totally unaware of its intricacies. What he was most interested to learn was that Jane Ransom had a post office box also in Derby and that her bank details were at the same branch of the same bank as George Norman Thaler.

On the way back to his hotel room, Caxton purchased a copy of the latest book by Jane Ransom to add to the book by Mr Thaler that he had bought in Sydney in order to acquaint himself with that author while in Melbourne.

He set out all the details he had so far gleaned and sat back to think. His next job would be to learn about the bank details of the people involved. He made an appointment the next day to see a financial manager in the head office of the Westpac bank that held the details of the writers. Caxton obtained a court order enabling him to access the details, and thus armed, presented himself at the bank the next afternoon. He came away from that meeting with some alarming data that he felt he needed to digest carefully before advancing. He went back to his room to think.

Caxton had a brainwave. He obtained the telephone number of the post office in Derby and rang them. He enquired about the two post office boxes that he had been given from the two publishers. The post mistress recalled quite clearly who emptied them both; it was the same young woman, a short, blonde woman, quietly spoken, and she came in from the Kimberley outback about every month or so. No, she had not been in for some months now and her mail had mounted up considerably. Caxton felt a shiver run up his back.

Caxton rang Stuart and enquired whether he had heard of a Jane Ransom or a Norman Woods. Stuart had never heard of Jane but he told Caxton that Norman Woods was his head stockman for many years until his death in 1986. Now Caxton had most of the pieces, it just remained to make sense of them all. He lined up the information and wrote it down in a list.

Caxton returned to Sydney to an expectant troupe anxious to learn his results. He discussed it with them at length and they were, to say the least, stunned by these latest revelations. They determined to attempt to ascertain from Jess any information she was prepared to divulge, though going on her past performances, this, they anticipated, would prove difficult. They would, however, await Stuart's return from Milbark and his researches into the station's finances.

Stuart returned in a confused state of mind because he had inspected all the station's accounts and did indeed find discrepancies. These, however, were in the station's favour and he was at a loss to explain how this could have happened. He was in front to the tune of many hundreds of thousands of dollars. Caxton thought he might have the answer, and explained to Stuart all the details he had gleaned from his trip to Melbourne. They were only waiting for Stuart's return before confronting Jess with this evidence.

Jess was surprised to see them all visiting her at the same time, and it had been awhile since she had seen anybody.

Caxton commenced by asking her directly, 'Miss MacIntyre, have you by any chance ever heard of George Norman Thaler?'

Jess glared at him. Then she peered at the others. She

remained emotionless and set her face in a non-committal way and remained silent. Caxton knew instantly he had hit a nerve and that they were going to experience another unpleasant episode with this fractious client. *How could she be one and the same time so gentle and malleable a person and then be so truculent the next? And always over issues for which she should be proud or contented to have exposed.*

Caxton said again, 'Why make us struggle to arrive at an agreement, Miss MacIntyre? I'm almost convinced you are him.'

'I have nothing to say about that. It's a total irrelevancy.'

Caxton, and the others for that matter, knew immediately that she had confirmed their suspicions that she was indeed George Norman Thaler. Therefore, by deduction, she was probably Jane Ransom.

'Just confirm you are he and I'll ask no more for now,' continued Caxton.

'No,' said Jess defiantly.

'Very well, Miss MacIntyre, but there's no way we can conceal this from the court and you may as well prepare yourself for whatever affront, real or perceived, that you imagine will result. Are there any more shocks we can expect before this is over?' Caxton asked in an irritated tone.

Jess just looked at them and turned her face to one side in resignation.

The trial was set for some months ahead so Stuart returned to Milbark for a short visit before the onset of the Wet season.

Chapter Eight

He would return for the commencement of the trial. Jess received spasmodic visits from the long-suffering Tennex clan and prepared herself for the trial.

The only other distraction of note that occurred during Jessie's confinement was the tangential event of the Salvation Army visitor. The only reason this was significant was the markedly influential effect this particular woman had on the future life of Jess. Her name was Loraine and she was a frequent prison visitor to the most notorious felons there. What Jess liked about her was her complete and total non-judgemental interaction with her.

Loraine was a caring and gentle woman in her sixties. She was totally incongruous in the confines of the penal system where all those with whom she dealt were almost diametrically opposed to her philosophy. She nevertheless ministered to those who would sit with her and, surprisingly, that number was many. It seemed the further from goodness they drifted, the louder the call to seek redemption. Jess found it quite a solace to listen to Loraine's renditions and to be able to try and discuss some of the features that confounded her. Jessie's life experience was certainly novel for the members of the Salvation Army and often they seemed just as interested in her approach to the big questions as they were at trying to impart any message to her.

Jessie looked forward to the infrequent discussions with Loraine. She plied her with questions relating to the afterlife and tried to elicit compromise and comparison with what she knew of the Indigenous people's attitude to this ubiquitous question.

CHAPTER NINE

The long-awaited trial of Jessie MacIntyre was finally scheduled for Wednesday in the first week in April. The first two days were set aside for preparations, advising the jury and the securing of witnesses, so the trial proper did not commence until the Monday. Stuart was able to remain in Sydney once the trial dates had been set.

The prosecution had an extensive line-up of witnesses to process but Caxton Tennex in particular was not overly worried at this point. Not so his son, Seton, and his wife and partner, Philippa, both of whom still had misgivings about the possible outcomes and their impacts on them all and their careers.

There was a general introduction by the prosecutor Ivan Sebeski QC, outlining his case and some of the evidence that would be presented. The first witness was a well-known petty criminal and reprobate who gave evidence purporting to indicate that Jessie was involved in prostitution, drug dealing, money laundering and stand-over tactics. There were several other witnesses that promulgated the same line, casting vivid and lurid accusations at both Jessie and especially Donald. Caxton was convinced that these accusations could be dismissed once Seton began to present his evidence, so he found it rather amusing that the prosecution would indulge in such misrepresentations when it would become evident that it was all a fabrication. The more they slandered her, the deeper the hole they were digging.

There was a total of five witnesses on this theme. One thuggish and uninspiring character even claimed to have witnessed Jessie's involvement in a knifing incident in one of the back streets of Newtown in which a notorious young villain was slain over a drug deal. Seton, in cross-examining him, got him to describe in detail the actions he had claimed to witness, ensuring he emphasised that Jess used her right hand in wielding the knife. This witness described in every detail how she had used the knife, in her right hand, not two-handed or left, but definitely in her right, all without prompting.

The most devastating accusations were directed at her involvement in prostitution and drug dealing. Through all this, Jess sat shackled and clad in ill-fitting clothes, emotionless and coldly staring at her accusers. She was offended by the implications and the slurs on Donald that he was involved in so much criminal activity. She was inwardly seething that his good character was so sullied.

Once the preliminary froth was completed, more

substantial witnesses were presented, some with unexpectedly disturbing accounts of the matters to which the defence had been alerted. The next serious issue came in the form of the arresting officer's report and the account of her arrest over six months previously. Most of this evidence was suppressed, as the prosecution did not want to jeopardise the trial by releasing disparaging information about the defendant, thus rendering the possibility of a fair trial more difficult.

The defence was unaware just how violent the arrest had been. The arresting sergeant stunned the gallery and court with his graphic account of the violent arrest. He listed the outstanding charges that the Western Australia police still had pending against her and hinted that they wished to process these once her trial here was completed. The list read as follows: resisted arrest; failed to stop when directed; assault causing grievous bodily harm; attempted murder; firearms offences; unlicenced driving; driving an unregistered vehicle; driving an unroadworthy vehicle and driving in a manner likely to cause harm; left the scene of an accident; failed to render assistance; not reporting accident; manoeuvred a vehicle with intent to cause damage. There were further charges pending imminent information and evidence that was to be presented in court. There was a long silence after the officer had completed his list, followed by a low murmur and coughing in the courtroom.

The prosecuting counsel then asked the sergeant to describe the arrest in detail. This he did with dispassion and in a professional manner, detailing for the first time to the court and to Stuart and the defence team the violent struggle that had ensured in the homestead, the damage and injuries caused to the arresting officers, and for the first time, the fact that Jessie was severely beaten and actually shot in the upper right arm. More groans from the court. The defence was unprepared for such a graphic account and asked some clarifying questions of the sergeant.

Seton tried to elicit from Sergeant Musgrave exactly how they had sneakily assembled in the house and how a surprised and isolated individual might react if suddenly confronted with gun-wielding strangers.

Jess was driven to the courthouse each morning in a heavily guarded security van accompanied by several guards. This was not for her protection but for theirs. She was regarded as a particularly violent prisoner with a proven record of damaging attacks on police.

There were two incidents involving her on her trips into the courthouse. One concerned the prison van being rammed in an accident at a busy city intersection in which the van was severely damaged and two shots were fired into the back. The other concerned another van she was supposed to be in being again rammed and this time an explosive devise set off under it as it was stationery. The only reason she was not in it was that the prison governor had been alerted by a tip-off that something was afoot and had set up a subterfuge to get her to the trial.

These two incidents were of no concern to Jess, after all, she had warned Caxton that the case would not advance to trial but did severely worry her team. This was the first confirmation within the defence that there may indeed be more to this case, just as Jess had alluded.

Then came the revelation of the incident on the Gibb River Road that involved Sergeant Moore. Jessie originally thought that only she knew about this and never wanted to discuss it at all with anybody. With the gathering publicity Australia-wide about the case, Sergeant Moore had finally decided to come forward and report the truth about the incident with one minor change; he failed to mention his assault of either Mookargey or Jessie.

Sergeant Moore now assumed that he was the only credible witness to the event and, as he heard of the increasing litany of crimes attributed to Jess, he assumed he would be just one more and at least get some redress for the pain and suffering imposed on him by her actions that day beside the road. Councillor Ivan Sebeski then read out a submission from Sergeant Moore that read in part as follows: *On the morning of the eleventh, my partner and I were following a heavy vehicle from Derby along the Gibb River Road when we came upon this vehicle. It was apparently unlawfully on the road in that it breached several road rules and regulations. We passed and stopped and flagged the vehicle down.* He went on to describe the incident from his perspective, completely reversing the onus of blame and the intent of the combatants.

Sergeant Moore explained the change in his story as follows: his offsider at the time was a young constable from Perth. After the attack by Ms MacIntyre he, Sergeant Moore, was rendered unconscious for some days. The young constable, Mr Constantine Grabbo, was so shaken and shocked by the ferocity and violence of the attack that he was not prepared to acknowledge that all this damage had been inflicted by a single female person. He therefore erroneously alleged that it was perpetrated by a car load of drunken Aboriginal men in a crowded four-wheel drive utility from one of the adjacent stations. On regaining full consciousness, he, Sergeant Moore, was unable to fully speak due to the damage to his jaw and face and was not made aware of the untruth until well into the investigations. He regretted not correcting the story but by the time he had the chance he felt it was possibly too late.

Seton pounced on the fabrication about Aboriginal offenders, knowing that later on they hoped to present further incriminating evidence about his attitude to Aborigines from Mookargey. *Why, for instance had he originally attributed the assault to a group of Aboriginal men and not the single woman he now claimed.* He did not intimate that Mookargey was to testify but ensured that he confused the story sufficiently so that when Mookargey took the stand and, later on Jess, their stories would contradict Moore's sufficiently to destroy his testimony.

The next witness was a finance investigating officer from the Western Australia police force who indicated that he was requested to examine financial documents that came to light during the course of their scrutiny of her case. He reported that there was a bank account in the name of Jessie MacIntyre located at the Derby branch of Westpac that currently held many hundreds of thousands of dollars. To date they could not account for the source of these funds or their purpose. There was another muffled murmur buzzing around the room. Seton made little interrogation of the officer as he wished to remain silent about their discoveries until later.

The final witness was the central figure of the prosecution case. He was Deputy Commissioner Michael (Mick) Stolt, the man who had originally accused Jess of the crime and supposedly the only witness to her actions. He gave a polished and well-rehearsed version of events totally laying the executions at the feet of Jessie MacIntyre. This time, however, the defence was more prepared. They asked him to describe in minute detail the events of that evening especially the actual shootings.

Deputy Commissioner Stolt was asked twice to demonstrate the shooting, and he deliberately emphasised his use of the right hand. He stated emphatically that he had a clear view of the events and that he had lucid recollections of the night. The prosecution's entire case rested on this one witnessing of the event, corroborated by peripheral character assassination to prove the case.

Through all this so far Jess sat stony-faced and resolute, showing no emotion whatsoever, such that she was being dubbed the Kimberley wildcat and the ice-maiden. She was unaware of these appellations, but Stuart found them most disturbing and offensive. He was quite distraught at her treatment in the press.

The defence would begin with a two-pronged attack on the evidence; the first was to establish the true age of Jess and thus discredit the witnesses that had based all their evidence on a false premise regarding her age at the time of the offence. The second planned attack was to stress she was left-handed, a fact so far purposely not revealed to the court.

The first witness for the defence was to be Stuart.

'What was the age of Miss MacIntyre at the time of her arrival at your station?' asked Seton.

'She was about thirteen.' There was an audible gasp in the courtroom.

Seton went on, 'Thirteen? That seems very young for someone to be accused of these crimes. Can you substantiate that claim in any way?'

'Jessie was quite small at the time, which led me to believe that she was about that age. But a give-away to me was the Aboriginal women giving her a jacdat.'

'And what is that?' asked Seton slightly puzzled.

'It's a necklace of special beads and shells woven by the tribal women and given to the young girls when they first begin their cycle. It was given to Jess about six months after she arrived. I was so concerned about it that I rang Edna at Ravymoota Station to help me.'

'And, for the court, who is Edna?'

'She is the station boss's wife, our neighbour at Ravymoota Station.'

'And what did she do?'

'She agreed to take Jess for a visit to explain to her these woman things.'

'And did she?'

'Yes.'

'Just wait there Mr MacIntyre, please,' said Seton in finishing.

Stuart was cross-examined by the prosecution, but maintained his story as originally recalled.

The second witness was Edna Coniston. She was able to add that during the visit of Jessie to Ravymoota Station for that fortnight she had actually confessed to her that she was indeed only thirteen and had just commenced her cycles as a young woman.

Dawn was an unknown factor in all this. Caxton was unsure whether she would be beneficial or detrimental to Jessie's case. He did, however, concede that she should be able to further the sympathy vote from the jury if it were handled properly. They were all unsure what the reaction would be to her startling revelations. She began, in response to a question from Seton, to explain the genesis of Donald MacIntyre's relationship with Jessie. Dawn answered this question, indeed as she did all questions, with an arrogant self-assurance that manifested itself in brusque, and often offhand, responses that did little to endear her to the court.

'Don just found her at the markets and bought her home one day,' she said.

'And why did he do that?' asked Seton.

'I don't know! He just found her there wandering about.'

'But surely he gave a reason?'

'She had run away from the big house, the convent place, because she was being beaten by the nuns.'

'And why would she have been mistreated by the nuns?'

Chapter Nine

asked Seton.

'She was left-handed, you see.'

'She was left-handed!' pounced Seton in a slow and emphatic manner, stressing deliberately that fact in clear and slow resonance, pausing dramatically and turning to face the jury.

Caxton took a good hard look at Stolt to judge his reaction to that information. He detected that it was not favourable at all. He appeared quite uneasy.

Dawn was surprised by the interruption, but then continued, 'Yes. They didn't like that at all. She was also very cheeky. I can vouch for that.'

'So, you are saying that this small child was picked up in the markets after running away from the nuns who were beating her?'

'Yes.'

'And you say they were mistreating her because she was left-handed?'

'Mostly, yes,' answered Dawn.

'Members of the jury,' said Seton, 'here is a child that showed a strong propensity to utilise her favoured left hand at an early age such that she was actually being punished for it. I can vouch for the fact that the accused is still solely left-handed and strongly so. It seems to me that it would be impossible for a person who is left-handed in every aspect of life to suddenly change that preference for something so demanding as knifing an opponent or shooting another person.'

There was a murmur about the courtroom. Seton paused

for the information to sink in before continuing on with the other startling revelation that Dawn had divulged.

'Another thing, Mrs Hobbs, you are also saying that Jessie MacIntyre is not the daughter of Donald MacIntyre?'

There was tension in the room as Dawn said loudly, 'No! Never was. Just a kid off the street.'

A large hubbub circulated audibly about the courtroom.

'And how did you react to that, Mrs Hobbs?'

'I was furious. I told him so. You can't just go around kidnapping kids. We had arguments about it all the time. I threatened to go to the police. That's when he threw me out.'

'What, straight away?'

'No. About five years later. We argued all the time about her.'

'Why?'

'He doted on her. What with her blonde looks an' blue eyes and pretty little face. She had him wrapped 'round her little finger. She had 'em all falling over 'emselves.'

Caxton began to feel the contented happiness of a small-time gambler who had a little flutter and a minor win. Just as he had hoped, Dawn was revealing her not so latent dislike for Jess because of her appearance, not her substance, and as she fell further into the abyss of aversion, he sensed a rumbling of sympathy arising in the court, especially among the men. He hoped Dawn's display of a lack of maternal caring would also help assuage any aversion the female members might harbour towards Jessie because of any antipathy they might feel for her because of her attractiveness.

Chapter Nine

Before he let the prosecution loose on Mrs Hobbs, Seton made another short oration. He began,

'Members of the jury, since the first mention of this case arising, two of Miss MacIntyre's school friends have come forward from her days in Australia Street Primary School corroborating Mrs Hobbs's story about her age and dates. What's more, the owner and instructor from the Fang My and Associated Martial Arts and Self-defence School has also come forward. He further corroborates those details. Additionally, he shed some light on the abilities of Miss MacIntyre in that endeavour. He advises that Miss MacIntyre was a particularly proficient exponent, even at a very young age, at his particular brand of self-defence. He also advises that, unlike most other branches of this industry, his school is not philosophically based in any way. It is strictly a method of defending oneself from attack under any circumstances, based on an ability to hit hard and hit first. He confirms that Miss MacIntyre was indeed only ten when she first commenced with him in 1977.'

The next witness called was Mookargey, the Aboriginal elder. Luckily for the defence, he had accompanied Jess on this fateful occasion and he was the only other witness available to the event. He was a quietly-spoken, self-effacing and respected man in his own right and highly regarded by the white folks who knew him. To the surprise of all in the courtroom, the event was not only well known to the Aboriginal people of Milbark, but also to his relations on Ravymoota. He made it known that the incident had at the time caused such a stir in the camps that Jess was forever afterwards regarded as quite a heroine because of the way she defended him after he was racially abused and the fact that Sergeant Moore was well known as a bigot by his people.

Mookargey was asked to give his version of the event outlined in the written submission presented to the court by the prosecution. He began, speaking slowly, deliberately and very softly in his characteristic Aboriginal accent, 'We bin drivin' along for long time. Then the police car raced past and stopped in middle of the road. Two men got out and walk back to the truck. I was about to get out when udder fella said to his boss, 'Boss, I think is this side you want.' Boss tells me to stay put and then he went round udder side. He spoke some time to Miss Jess then he told her to get out. He drag her by the arm over to their car and make her lean on hood.' Mookargey demonstrated how she was held and led to the police vehicle. He continued, 'Now Wornor get very cross and jump off truck.'

'Who is Wornor?' asked Seton.

'Wornor is magic dog belong Miss Jess. He big strong dingo she had since pup. Wornor jump over to men an' Boss jist shoot 'im dead. Miss Jess verrie cross. He yell out bad name to me to stay in truck.'

'Who yelled at you?'

'Boss policeman.'

'You mean Sergeant Moore?'

'Yes.'

'Go on Mr Mookargey, please.'

'Next thing, Boss man grabbin' all about Miss Jess, all over her clothes.'

'How do you mean, Mr Mookargey?'

Mookargey again demonstrated with his hands and arms the actions he had witnessed.

'You mean he was undressing her?'

'Yep. He undo her shirt and get to trouser when she thump 'im bigtime.'

'What do you mean? Can you explain more?'

'It all happen very quick time. She turn and hit a few times an' he go down. She continue to kick. Then she do up belt and shirt and walk over to udder man and thump 'im too.'

'Then what happened?'

'Miss Jess very shaky. I jump out and we pick up Wornor together and place 'im on truck. Then we start up engine an' she push off police car into side of road an' we drives off.'

There followed a stunned silence in the court. Most eyes had turned to peer at the small, lonely woman who sat motionless throughout the whole tale. Jessie stared directly ahead, displaying no emotion whatsoever.

The prosecution rose to cross-examine the dignified black man still seated in the witness box. The cross-examination was torrid but Mookargey never varied his story except to grow more animated as the questions kept coming. He was warming to his exposure and the opportunity to sing the praises of his revered friend.

This retelling of the events on the Gibb River Road involving Sergeant Moore confirmed in the minds of the story-hungry press that the solemn woman in the dock was entitled to the description of Kimberley wildcat. It explained why she always appeared in court in such a restrained manner.

The first witness to appear for the defence the next morning was called without the prosecution's knowledge. It was known within the legal circles that the television reporter was instrumental in the case coming to light, but it was not generally known to the public, or how she could add to the evidence substantially. After all, she had only indirectly exposed Jessie's existence through her travel programme.

'Please state your name and occupation for the court.'

'Anna Lucile Delaney. I'm a reporter and presenter for Channel Four, mostly travel programmes.'

'Please state for the court your involvement in this case.'

'Well,' she began, 'it all started back in about 1993. There was a book published by an author called George Norman Thaler. It was about the fourth book by him and I wanted to do a programme on him, but after some research I discovered that he was impossible to find.'

'And what does he have to do with this case and the crimes alleged against Miss MacIntyre?' asked Seton. There was a general murmuring from the prosecution benches and also from some in the gallery.

'Well, our legal people were able to discover from the publisher that all mail addressed to George Norman Thaler was sent to a post office box number in Derby. All we were able to discover was that the box number was registered to him and gave his address as Ravymoota Station. I convinced

Chapter Nine

my producer that if I could do a segment on farm stays in the Kimberleys on that pretext I might be able to find out a bit more about him. It would be a real scoop for us. Anyway, he finally agreed so we went up with our travel crew to stay at Ravymoota which, as you may know, runs a big tourist accommodation business. It was a perfect ruse because it gave us the travel segment plus we hoped it might result in a real scoop for our arts division.'

'What has this to do with the case, Your Honour?' asked Ivan.

'Yes Mr Tennex, is this leading anywhere?'

'Oh yes indeed, Your Honour. If you will permit?'

The judge nodded condescendingly at Seton.

'Please proceed, Ms Delaney,' said Seton.

'Jessie was a strange woman. She talked in a funny way, you know, using funny words and expressions that I'd never heard. It began to dawn on me that she would make a beaut story alright but she was very shy. Anyway, we drove very slowly back to the house and on the way, it hit me.'

'What hit you, Ms Delaney?'

'Wouldn't it be amazing if George was Georgina, eh?'

'And why would you have come to that decision?'

'Because of something she said. Something special I mean, apart from all the other stuff she said.'

'And what was that?'

'Have you ever heard the expression "wallaby teds"?'

'No Ms Delaney. Can't say I have.'

'Exactly! That's my point. You see no one I spoke to

has ever heard that expression. But you see, it occurs about seven times in a whole lot of different ways in all the books of Thaler.'

'And is that important?'

'Yes sirrey. We stopped on a ridge that had this enormous view right across the plain. I asked her something or other and she replied, "It was Wallaby Ted's". When I asked her what that meant she went into a longwinded explanation that finally led me to believe she was him, or at least could be him.'

'How come?'

'It's complicated. Do you want me to explain it?'

Seton peered over to the bench. The judge peered back, momentarily dumbstruck then nodded a reticent agreement, 'If we must,' he said to Seton. The judge, as indeed was everybody else, was beginning to become intrigued with this insight into the life of the defendant.

'Proceed, please Ms Delaney.'

'She said to me that Wallaby Ted is Kangaroo Edward's little brother.'

'And?'

'Well, Kangaroo Edward? Kangaroo Ted? Roo Ted? You know Roo Ted. Oh please? Do I have to spell it out?'

Suddenly there was a mix of giggling and gasping from within the court as an anonymous voice from the public galley blurted out, 'Rooted, mate'. The judge banged his gavel and demanded silence as the disturbance subsided. It had gone over his head as well. Not dwelling on this complex phraseology, Seton continued, 'That led you to believe Jessie MacIntyre was George Norman Thaler?'

'Not immediately. But when I got back to Melbourne, I reread all the novels and sure enough there it was in all its guises, several times in different ways. Shortly after the travel segment went to air, I learnt that there had been a lot of high-level enquiries about the programme but didn't realise that it was about her, not the travel – not until I heard about this court case. Then I remembered that she had made me promise not to show any pictures of her.'

'And did you? Promise I mean.'

'Yes, I did and I meant it. But my producer wouldn't hear of it. He said that these were priceless pictures, you know stuff like 'chic in the bush', 'chic meets country', all that. I was a little annoyed, as I had promised, but it was good copy.'

'And is that why you came forward Ms Delaney?'

'Yes. I felt responsible for exposing her, so when I heard she was on trial I offered to help account for why she had so much money.'

There was a long and profound silence in the court as Anna finished her story. All eyes were on the defiant figure seated in the defendant's chair exhibiting no emotion whatsoever. Anna was cross-examined at length by Ivan Sebeski but it only enhanced the story of the potential discovery of one of Australia's most intriguing publishing mysteries.

When proceedings recommenced after lunch, the defence wished to add to the information alluded to by Anna Delaney and to relay the results of Caxton's endeavours into the investigations about George Thaler. Seton asked to be permitted to read a report of the results of the research that Caxton had finalised on this issue. The judge agreed, and Seton commenced to read the report to the courtroom.

'So let me get this straight, Mr Tennex,' interjected the judge. 'You are saying that this Jane Ransom, who writes these trashy romance novels has all the proceeds sent to an account in Derby to a man who has been dead for years?'

'No, Your Honour. Jane Ransom has her remittances forwarded to an account in her own name in the bank in Derby. But George Norman Thaler has his money directly deposited into an account in the same branch of the same bank but in the name of one Norman Woods. As far as we know a Mr Norman Woods did live at Milbark Station until his death there in 1986. That bank account has a joint signatory authority in the name of Jessie MacIntyre.'

'And you think that person is this same Jessie MacIntyre?' asked the judge.

'Yes. I'm certain of it,' replied Seton.

'Have you any proof?' asked the judge, mystified.

'No. Not yet. But the evidence points directly to Miss MacIntyre.'

'Well, why don't we just ask her Mr Tennex?' asked the judge, exasperated.

'We are getting to that, Your Honour.'

The time was approaching 3.30pm and the judge looked at his watch and announced that as it was now so late, he might adjourn proceedings until the following day. This was because Jessie MacIntyre was due to be called and her evidence would require considerable time; much more than was available now, even for preliminaries to commence. He enquired if there were any more witnesses to be called before Jess. To this request he received a last submission from the prosecution seeking permission to investigate the latest revelations about the two authors, and if possible, to refute those suggestions if evidence surfaced. In effect, they requested to be able to call one last expert witness to comment on the revelation that Jessie MacIntyre might also be Jane Ransom and/or George Norman Thaler. To this the judge acquiesced.

The next morning began with Ivan Sebeski calling an expert witness to comment on the suggestions raised on the previous day regarding the identity of the two authors. Sarah Cronin was a middle-aged woman dressed immaculately in a dark suit and matching shoes and with her dark hair neatly groomed over the back of her head. She wore dark-rimmed spectacles and red lipstick. She was one of the leading literary critics with a syndicated book reviewing column in most of the leading Australian newspapers, particularly the Sunday editions.

Sarah was also involved with a company that acted as an agency responsible for managing authors and their contracts and for the intellectual and quality integrity of the company's products. She was highly respected. She focused primarily on Advent but also was involved on the periphery of Romantis, among other publishing houses.

Ivan began by asking her in her expert opinion whether

she considered it possible that Jane Ransom and George Norman Thaler were one and the same person.

'In my opinion it is just not possible.'

'And why would you consider that, Ms Cronin?'

'Because George Thaler is a wonderful exponent of his craft. His writing is well balanced, grammatically and technically superb with divine story lines and believable characterisation. The settings are, for the most part, uniquely Australian, which are popular in North America and Europe, particularly Britain. He writes with authority and deep knowledge of his subject and is obviously a well-educated man with wide experience and a unique turn of phrase.

'The writing of Jane Ransom is, on the other hand, rather naïve and simplistic, featuring single story lines with minimal character development, often displaying an immature and unsophisticated language and technique and method of structure totally opposed in every way to that displayed in the writings of George Thaler. She lives in a fantasy world of impossible romance, vigour, wealth and health, fuelled no doubt by her own lack of all these attributes. She writes distant and unfamiliar period pieces often riddled with social, time and locational inaccuracies, though for this particular genre her output is more than adequate. No writer of the calibre of George Norman Thaler would also produce such pieces. It would be like asking Shakespeare to write Phantom comics.'

'Have you any other evidence to support your opinion?' asked Ivan.

'Yes. Both these publishing companies have notes on all

their authors filed away in their archives and I managed to retrieve the author's notes on both of these two from their files. It is from these notes, usually provided by the writers themselves, that the sleeve profiles are composed, often accompanied by a picture.'

She opened a folder, retrieved a sheet of paper, and began to read, 'Jane Ransom: I am a single young woman with a disability living in the town of Derby. Because of my disability I have difficulty in travelling. I write novels as an interest and a way of filling in my time.'

Sarah Cronin continued, 'These brief notes are accompanied by a rather poor-quality photograph, which clearly shows a plump, plain young woman who is possibly part-Aboriginal. It is from this information that we composed the sleeve data.'

She replaced the piece of paper and retrieved a second piece. 'Here are the notes sent to them by George Norman Thaler, and I quote: I am an itinerant rural worker currently employed as a stockman at various Kimberley stations. George Norman Thaler is a pen name that I utilise in order to maintain anonymity. My real name is Norman Woods but I request that this information remain confidential. The inspiration for my novels comes from many of my colleagues and this source of stimulation would be jeopardised if my true identity was revealed.'

Sarah looked up. 'Again, it is accompanied by a photograph, but following his request it has never been published. It shows an elderly, dapper man dressed in cowboy clothes.'

'May we all see these please, Ms Cronin?' asked the judge. 'You say these photos have never been issued?'

'No. The one of Ms Ransom is rather unflattering, not a suitable look for this class of novel. The one of George Norman Thaler is very suitable but Advent respected his request to remain anonymous. I do ask that at this stage their confidentialities be respected, however.'

'So, to reiterate,' asked Ivan, 'you maintain that it is impossible for Jane Ransom and George Norman Thaler to be the same person?'

'Yes, both stylistically and from their own self-provided data that I have managed to acquire from the publishers – as an enormous favour, I might add.'

The judge looked at the defence desk as much as to say, 'Any questions?'

Seton rose from his seat with a hint of a smile and asked simply, 'Are you sure these two authors could not possibly be the same person?'

'Yes, I'm positive.'

'How so, Ms Cronin?'

'I have already described why I believe that to be so. The novels of Mr Thaler display the emotions and knowledge of an elderly and very experienced man, albeit of a sensitive and caring nature, who nonetheless exudes a deep knowledge of his subject. He writes almost exclusively about his known subject. On the other hand, Jane Ransom displays the output of a rather immature and uneducated, but very imaginative and creative, personality with a lot of time on her hands

Chapter Nine

to produce the output she has managed. I don't think the defendant fits any of those descriptions.'

'We have no more questions at this stage, Your Honour.'

There were rumblings around the courtroom but it soon subsided when the judge announced that the defence could call its next witness. This was the moment that the gallery had been eagerly awaiting. The room was filled to capacity and there was an atmosphere of hushed excitement.

CHAPTER TEN

The highly anticipated moment in the long, drawn-out trial had finally arrived. Questions were being asked: Who was this woman really? Was she as vile as had been made out? Had she committed the contemptible crime of which she was accused? Indeed, had she committed any crimes? Had she been provoked and molested into committing the other crime of which she was also accused? If she did not commit the heinous assassinations, then who did? Was she an unwitting witness to the crime? Was she really the author of the seedy little publications by Jane Ransom and the now-famous George Norman Thaler?

The courtroom was packed with more people than any previous day, not only members of the public, but many press representatives. The other major question on everybody's lips was: If she did not commit the crime for which she was on trial, who was the person Deputy Commissioner Stolt had seen doing it?

The security procedures for the trial were more stringent than most trials. This resulted from the two known attempts to disrupt Jessie's arrival and possible attempts on her life during her transport from the prison. As usual, Jessie was escorted into the courtroom heavily manacled, both feet and hands, and wearing drab prison clothes.

After the judge had seated himself and the court quietened down, Seton turned to the bench and to the jury box and said to them collectively, 'Your Honour, before we commence the testimony of the defendant, I would like to submit to the court some information for clarification. This concerns the matter of the moneys that appear in the various accounts as mentioned previously. On subsequent investigation, it has come to light that Romantis Publications is paying money into an account in the name of Jane Ransom as indicated. Her address is given as Ravymoota Station. Advent Publications is indeed paying into an account in the name of Norman Woods, whose address is given as Milbark Station. But this account is operated by Jessie MacIntyre, and Jessie MacIntyre has her own account in her own name into which she is depositing money withdrawn from the other two accounts.

'However, it might interest the Court to know that she has also been personally paying bills for Milbark Station, which came to light when the books there were checked. The only discrepancies in the station accounts are ones in their favour; that is, in the favour of the station. This indicates that Miss

MacIntyre is not fraudulently acquiring the money from her family or employer.'

He cleared his throat and continued, 'When advice was sought regarding the possibility of George Thaler and Jane Ransom being one and the same person, the opinion was that they were not. But I suspect that this information and this evidence throws doubt on the testimony of Ms Sarah Cronin.'

Seton then turned to Jessie and indicated that they were ready to begin the proceedings. He commenced with the usual first question, 'Would you please state your name?'

'Jessie MacIntyre,' she announced in a soft and reverential manner.

'That is your full name?'

There was a short delay in her reply. Then in a soft and cultured voice she replied, 'Yes, that is my full name – not Jessica – not Jezebel – just plain Jessie.'

'Are you known by any other names, Miss MacIntyre?'

She gave him a piercing stare of disapproval and pondered her reply with another delay before answering, 'Of course not!'

There was already a buzz in the room.

'Louder!' shouted someone up the back, accompanied by shushing and murmuring.

'Yes, Miss MacIntyre,' echoed the judge, 'you'll need to speak up.'

She turned to face him and shared her intense stare with him. In a deliberate and quiet tone, she announced, 'This is how I speak.' And with a hint of defiance, added, 'If you want to hear me you will have to listen better.'

There was a louder murmuring through the room. The judge showed his annoyance by turning his disapproving glare onto an unsuspecting Seton, who flinched and shrugged his shoulders. He looked pleadingly towards Jess, as if to say, 'Please don't make this worse for yourself.'

Seton tried to restore some dignity to the morning and recommenced his questioning. Caxton and Seton both agreed that the first issue to be addressed, apart from the initial comment regarding the finances raised last afternoon, was that of the incident on the Gibb River Road involving Sergeant Moore. It had boiled down to his word against hers and Mookargey's, and who appeared to be the more likely to be truthful.

Seton recommenced after all the initial disturbance by asking Jess, 'Do you recall the altercation that occurred on the Gibb River Road between yourself and Sergeant Moore?'

There was a long and deliberate pause, then Jess slowly and softly answered, 'Yes, very clearly.'

'Can you please recount that for us.'

Another pause, then a softly spoken reply, 'We were travelling along the Gibb heading back to Milbark when I spotted Moore's car in the mirror. He sailed past and stopped in the middle of the road ahead of me. Well, 'Jimmy' doesn't just pull up on a sixpence.'

'Who is 'Jimmy?"' asked Seton.

The court was now becoming used to the customary deliberate pause before every answer from Jess. "Jimmy' is my truck,' she announced, slightly surprised.

'I see, you call it 'Jimmy'?'

A pause. 'Yes, of course. It's a GMC 1943 model six by six deuce and a half. What else would you call it?'

'I see,' said Seton. 'Please go on.'

Slowly and softly, she continued, 'Two men, cops, got out of the car and walked over to 'Jimmy'. Sergeant Moore walked up to the normal driver's side but Mookargey sat there.'

'You mean he was driving?'

'No. Of course not. I drive. It's a left-hand drive, as manufactured,' she said with a hint of annoyance.

'I see,' said Seton, not really seeing at all.

'When he realised that I was on the other side they swapped over and Moore came around to me. He shouted some profanities at Mooky and then rudely ordered me out of the cab.'

'You mean he swore at you?'

'Both of us. Most offensive it was.'

'Exactly what did he say?'

There was an unusually longer pause; the courtroom was hushed as all strained to hear the quietly spoken witness recount her story.

'I'm not going to repeat that.'

'Such prudery is unbecoming of a street walker, Your Honour. We all need to know exactly what was said,' interjected Ivan Sebeski.

The court erupted into a muffled pandemonium with the judge banging his gavel and trying to regain some decorum.

Chapter Ten

After silence returned to the room, Seton again asked Jess what was said.

After another pause, she replied, 'I'm sorry, I do not use that sort of language. Not under any circumstances. It is most offensive to me and disrespectful. I refuse to lower myself to that level.'

'I gather it was unpleasant for you?'

'Yes indeed. I'm not sure what kind of circles Sebeski moves in, but I'm not accustomed to that sort of language, and won't repeat what Moore said to me.'

'I can vouch for that,' interjected Stuart from the floor. There were more murmurs in the room.

'Quiet!' exclaimed the judge.

Caxton sat spellbound and inwardly smug with delight, as he felt that this unexpected turn lifted the character of his client in the eyes of those who considered Jess a woman of low repute.

'Very well. What happened next?' asked Seton.

'He dragged me out of the cab and frog-marched me over to the car. By now, Worner was yelping and very agitated.'

'Moore slung me against the bonnet of the Toyota facing the car and kicked my legs apart. Wornor leapt off the truck and ran at him. Moore shot him dead at my feet. When I tried to go to him, he grabbed my arms and flung me back against the bonnet. He was mumbling crudities and obscenities at me all the time and began to search me for something. He ripped my blouse open, pulled it back and fondled me. I was petrified. Then he began to undo my belt and that is when it happened.'

'What happened, Miss MacIntyre?'

There was another pause and then an answer, 'It was a case of now or never. If he got my moleskins below my knees, I would not be able to defend myself.'

'What happened next?' asked Seton with a tone of anticipation.

'His face was right next to mine. I could smell his foul breath. It smelt of alcohol.'

'You mean he had been drinking?'

'Objection!' shouted Ivan. Seton stole a glance at the judge.

'Strike that from the record,' announced the judge. Jess looked confused and wondered what that meant.

'Continue,' requested Seton.

'I performed a double milton, which immediately rendered him into a dazed state.'

'Please explain?' quizzed Seton.

Jess looked at him slightly puzzled. Clasping her manacled hands in front of her and swinging them in a certain fashion, she demonstrated the movement and said slowly, 'One of these.'

'And you connected with him?'

Another now customary pause. 'Yes. That sent him stunned and reeling backwards. As he slid back, I turned and clobbered him with a sharp jab from my left foot, which connected with his right elbow. Then I repeated the manoeuvre to his right knee and then, as he fell, I smashed one into the side of his head.'

'Was he badly injured?' asked Seton, a hint of concern being evident.

There was a long pause. 'He was out. He should have had a ruptured cruciate ligament to the knee. A lateral and side twist would have rendered it inoperable. I heard his elbow shatter and his jaw was probably broken. I stunned him with a maccliff manoeuvre to the back. He would trouble me no more that day,' she said in a direct matter-of-fact manner, disarmingly indicating she would be safe.

Seton was momentarily silenced at the brutal and calm manner in which the action had been described in such a detached way. 'What about his partner?'

'He just stood there gaping the whole time. I tried to do up my trousers and clasp my torn blouse around me as I walked over to him. He went for his holster but was really in a daze of confusion. I struck him one swift left kick to his right elbow too. That fixed his cart. I said to him, "that's for just standing there and watching." Then I turned to check on Wornor. He was dead. Mooky was by him by then and together we picked him up and placed him on the truck. Their car was in the way so I shoved it to the side with the bull bar and drove off.'

'What about the two injured policemen?'

'What about them?' she asked coldly.

'You just left them there?'

'They were going to assault me, Mr Tennex. It was not a picnic for me, mate. Besides, their vehicle was operable and there was plenty of traffic. They would soon be found. A short time alone might allow them time to contemplate their behaviour.'

'What did you do next?'

'We drove back to the river crossing. I was still in a state of nerves so I stopped at the river and cleaned myself up and stayed there about two hours. I asked Mooky not to tell anyone at all. He agreed to that.'

'Why would you not report it?'

A small delay. 'Come off the grass,' she said slowly. 'With half New South Wales looking for me for the murder of two policemen. I had Buckley's, mate. If I was not charged with their murder, I was the only witness to a crime committed by a cop. He wasn't going to let me off. How do I know if these two weren't after me for that?'

There was an audible gasp that went around the room.

Seton indicated he had finished his first interrogation and walked back to his seat to prepare for her cross-examination. Ivan rose and strode demonstrably over to stand before her in the box. He stared at her menacingly and she returned in kind, not flinching an inch. He began by asking, 'Is it customary in your part of the world, Ms MacIntyre, to assault officers performing their lawful duty?'

'No,' she said defiantly.

'Well, that is exactly what you did.'

'No. I defended myself against a despicable individual who was molesting me in the name of the law.'

There was a pause and then she went to continue but Ivan interrupted her. He had noticed, as had everybody else, that she always answered a question preceded by a short, deliberate pause. He was unsure whether this was a clever ploy to indicate thought and intelligence or whether she was just a bit slow. Her demeanour and replies tended to abrogate that latter theory.

She presented as a sane and credible individual with this slightly quirkish habit of deliberating over her replies. But Ivan noted that she was edgy and jumped at any noise; be it a cough or a pencil dropping; doors opening or anybody entering or leaving the room; in fact, any interruption caused her to cease mid-sentence. He found that he could control her responses if he strategically interrupted her. This he was now doing.

Caxton observed that these continual blatant interruptions of Jessie's evidence by Sebeski were beginning to annoy some of the jury.

Seton Tennex, not quite as astute as his father, let the interruptions continue because he was not entirely sure how best to approach this ticklish issue.

'You cannot just go about the country assaulting policemen, Ms MacIntyre.'

Jess just stared at Ivan in silence.

'Sergeant Moore observed that you had unlicenced firearms on the truck. He was frisking you for concealed weapons, no?'

'He certainly was not. He was molesting me in a very deliberate manner, with altogether an ulterior motive.'

'He had a right to suspect you of possession.'

'No. He had never seen me before. And he was drunk.'

'Ms MacIntyre, you have been warned already about making false statements about witnesses,' stated Ivan. 'Have you not?' he continued in a sarcastic way.

There was a long pause before she replied. 'I see Sebeski. It's all right for you to fabricate stories about Donald and myself, but if I try to fulfil my second oath, I am forbidden repeatedly.'

There was a murmur again about the courtroom. The judge leaned over to face Jess and announced, 'Ms MacIntyre, it is customary for defendants to address council as Mr.'

Jess turned to face the scowling old judge. She knitted her brow slightly and, through piercing and rather disdainful eyes, said in a low but menacing tone to him, 'I will address someone with a respectful epithet when and if they earn that respect, Judge.'

There were more gasps and shuffling in the courtroom.

'Silence!' shouted the judge with rising annoyance. 'Mr Tennex, please advise your client that I will not tolerate disrespect for this court and I will hold the defendant in contempt if it continues.'

This unexpected episode had caught Seton off guard. The judge was determined to indicate to all who was in command and who made the rules.

'Yes, sir. I will,' spluttered a surprised Seton.

'Thank you, Your Honour,' gushed Ivan. 'Now, please answer the question.'

Jess stared in complete silence at her interrogator.

'Well, Ms MacIntyre?'

There was another long pregnant pause.

'What is the point? I swore to fulfil three things and I am continually prevented from doing so.'

Chapter Ten

'And how is that so?'

'I swore to tell the truth, the whole truth, and nothing but the truth. You continually prevent my fulfilling the second, to wit, the whole truth.'

'There is a difference between telling the truth, Ms MacIntyre, and fabricating a story.'

'And you would know the difference, would you?'

There was more pandemonium. The judge was getting exasperated. He looked over at Seton again and raised his eyebrows, warning that he would hold Jess in contempt if it continued.

'Thank you,' said the judge. 'Now continue.' The judge then turned to stare down at Jess who was now facing the front of the court. She returned her gaze back to the judge and responded, 'Contempt indeed! Contempt would be an appropriate description for the distain in which I hold this farce of a system.'

'Mr Tennex, I will not warn you again.'

By now the court had descended into a mild form of hysteria as the totally unexpected banter erupted. Caxton sat at his bench open-mouthed at the turn of events.

The judge addressed the courtroom. 'If this continues you will all be in contempt.'

There was a momentary delay before Jess, turning to the judge, asked, 'And what? You'll jail me, will you? I guess I should really fear that outcome.'

'Enough!' shouted the judge.

Silence slowly descended back over the court with only

the occasional giggle as proceedings recommenced.

Ivan decided he had extracted enough damage in this exchange and indicated that he had no further questions at this stage. Seton resumed his place in the centre of the floor to continue.

'Now, turning to the real purpose of this trial, Miss MacIntyre, can you recall the events of the evening in question?'

'Yes,' she stated softly again.

'Please tell us what happened.'

'I returned from the gym, which was five doors down, about ten-thirty in the evening. I normally enter through the back door from the alley. I knew from Don that there was a meeting occurring in the front of the workshop so I normally come in as quietly as possible and go straight up the stairs to my room. This night, there were two men standing in the half light coming from the workshop talking between themselves. I could not hear what they were saying.'

'Who were these two men, Miss MacIntyre?'

'They were two men whom I later discovered were working for Knuckles.'

'Who is Knuckles?'

'Inspector Knuckey.'

'Did you know this Inspector Knuckey?'

'No. I never met him.'

'Go on.'

'Suddenly, two more men came in the back door and almost closed it. The first two men turned and one said,

"What are you doing here, sir?" To which Stolt replied...'

Ivan Sebeski interrupted, objecting to the naming of his client. Jess stopped, startled at the interruption, and looked at the interrupter.

'Carry on Miss MacIntyre,' asked Seton.

'Thank you ... Stolt replied, "I thought I told you this was off tonight, Sergeant," in a menacing manner. Then the first man said, "This is the final night, sir. We will be making arrests tonight." Then Stolt pulled out a gun from his coat and fired two shots, one at each of the first two. They fell like dead weights to the floor.'

There was a large gasp within the room.

'Objection!' demanded Sebeski, amid the mayhem.

When Jess was eventually able to continue, she said, 'The other man with Stolt asked, "Miko, what did you do that for?" or words to that effect. Stolt replied with something like, "Shut up, Hindie. Get back to the station and plant all that stuff on Knuckey as we arranged. Be quick about it. Now man!" The other man had not yet left, he stood there in shock, I suppose. Stolt walked up to the two on the floor.'

'Were they moving?' asked Seton.

'No. There was no movement. He shot them both again in the head.' Jess was getting a little shaky at recalling that horrible night.

'What happened next?'

'I was so scared, I hopped up quickly while he was standing up the hall and ran for the back door. He must have heard me as his torch light flashed at the door and as I opened it to run out, he shot two more times at me and luckily missed and hit the door frame, or the wall.'

'Then what happened?'

'I waited outside hiding in the dark. Stolt came out almost immediately and looked around with the torch then ran off down the alley. I raced inside and told Don. That's when he told me to get some things and we drove off to the airport.'

'And the shots, Miss MacIntyre, were they loud or not?'

'No. Not at all. They sounded like *phoot*. Very quiet.'

'Did you see the gun at all?'

'Yes, briefly when he was up the hall. It was very long in the barrel and quite large in his hand.'

The court adjourned for lunch. On returning, rather than continuing on with questioning about the other issues raised by the prosecution, it was agreed that they could cross-examine Jessie on this revelation first. Ivan Sebeski rose with an air of supreme confidence and haughtiness to begin his questioning.

'Ms MacIntyre,' he began, 'you say the lighting in the hallway was dim?'

'Yes.'

'Then it was impossible for you to distinguish faces in such poor light?'

'Yes, mostly.'

'Then how can you identify Deputy Commissioner Stolt in such poor light?'

'I knew it was him, not only from his face and voice, but also from his name being called by his offsider.'

'But you said the man was called Miko.'

'Yes, that's his name.'

'His name is Mick, Ms MacIntyre.'

'Yes. As well.'

'Mick Stolt had never been there before as we all know, so how could you possibly recognise him?'

'No. He had been there at least half a dozen times before.'

'Ms MacIntyre, you know that is not true.'

There was an awkward pause, then she replied, 'No. I know it is true. He appears in my diary at least that many times.'

'Now we have a diary, do we?'

'Yes.'

'And you kept a diary just to record all these events in case you needed it later?' said Sebeski sarcastically.

'No, of course not. I once kept a small diary of what was happening in my life as a young girl. It was peripheral and tangential events such as these meetings that interfered in my behaviour that I may have recourse to record. That is all.'

'And where is this diary? I suppose it's conveniently available?'

'No. Not really.'

'I thought as much. I think we'll all find there is really no diary is there?'

'Possibly,' she replied indifferently. Jess did not intend to reveal the existence of her treasured tomes, and assumed their mention would be glossed over, she had not bargained on them being scrutinised. To that end, she began to play down their existence.

'Apart from the non-existent fictitious diary, Ms MacIntyre, it may have escaped your notice, but Deputy Commissioner Stolt happens to be of German descent.'

'Yes?' she replied with an air of confusion.

'His partner on that evening was also German, Ms MacIntyre, and they conversed together in German the whole time they were there. And unless you speak German, Ms MacIntyre, you were totally unable to understand a single word spoken. Agreed? Do you speak German, Ms MacIntyre?'

Jess looked over at Stuart with the hint of a knitted brow. Stuart was gazing disbelievingly at her with his eyes wide open and a quizzical look about his face.

The silence was palpable and then, above the muffled shuffling in the gallery, Sebeski asked again, 'Well, Ms MacIntyre? We are waiting.'

'Ja. Natürlich. Ich spreche sehr gut Deutsch. Die deutsche Sprache ist nicht schwierig für mich. Ich spreche es fließend,' she said, staring intently at Mr Stolt, who suddenly sat up straighter, and in amazement, stared back at her.

Suddenly, the judge, who was taking all this in with increasing intensity, banged his gavel and demanded, 'I will have only English spoken in this court Mr Tennex, if you please. Now, what did you just say then?' he said peering down at Jessie.

'I said, "Yes, of course. I speak excellent German. The German language is not difficult for me. I speak it fluently".'

Ivan Sebeski was obviously taken completely by surprise.

'Back to the events of that evening, Ms MacIntyre. If it

Chapter Ten

was the first visit to the premises of the deputy commissioner, I say again you had no way of recognising him.'

'I knew him well from the photographs.'

'What photographs would that be then? The ones in the newspapers?' he asked sneeringly.

'Donald always had photographs taken of every meeting and all those that attended. His insurance, he called them.'

'First it was a diary, now we have a picture gallery?'

'We had one, yes. Vern was an expert photographer and took wonderful full-colour pictures from the landing overlooking the workshop. Then he developed them in the dark room and Don stored them in a secret place just in case. I was told by Don to pass them onto Knuckles if anything happened.'

'And who is Vern? For that matter, who is Knuckles? And where are all these photos now, then?'

'Werner. He was our mechanic. Photography was his hobby. He was very good at it. As I have already indicated, Knuckles was Inspector Knuckey. He was the only honest cop among the lot of you. I don't know where all the photos went, but I certainly saw pictures of Stolt and many others.'

'By Inspector Knuckey, you mean disgraced former Detective Ian Knuckey? Are you sure you want to be associated with that dishonourable and corrupt former officer?'

There was a much louder disturbance, as this torrent of information came cascading out from the slim, blonde woman trussed up in manacles in the box.

'You say you don't know where these photos are?' asked the judge, once the disturbance had subsided.

'No,' she replied.

'And what sort of people were the others that you mentioned?' he continued.

'Oh, there were a lot of cops, some solicitors and...,' she turned to peer at the judge and continued disdainfully, 'a couple of judges.'

Uproar ensued in the courtroom as the judge tried to regain control by banging his gavel.

Jess snarled meekly at him and whispered, 'The whole lot of you are below contempt.'

The judge looked at his watch and announced that the court would adjourn for the day.

Caxton and Seton Tennex gathered together with Stuart and Jessie before she was removed from the courtroom and earnestly began to talk. Caxton was brimming with happiness.

'This is wonderful, Jess my girl, just wonderful. Now listen, we need to discuss this German stuff. It is wonderful. Also, what is this about a diary? You never mentioned anything about a diary.'

'It's irrelevant, Mr Tennex.'

'Indeed, it is not. Can we get hold of it? I mean is it still around?'

'Well technically, yes. But I refuse to even consider it. It is all girl talk and written when I was quite young. I don't want anybody else to see it.'

'We'll see. More importantly, what is this about photographs? Would they also be available?'

'I doubt it. They were all hidden years ago in the shop. I

would be surprised if they were still there.'

'Let's have dinner and talk some more,' said Caxton to Stuart, Seton and Philippa, still beaming as Jessie was about to be led away by the court guards.

Caxton Tennex turned to Jessie, 'Any chance at all of getting hold of that diary? It might really put the kybosh on their case and bring it all to a quick end.'

'You got Buckley's, mister,' was Jessie's stern reply.

Caxton looked at Stuart quizzically, but he just shrugged his shoulders and said, 'Don't look at me, mate, I didn't even know there was a diary.'

'Look,' continued Caxton, leaning over to talk more to Seton, 'I think we should ask for an adjournment in order to sought out some of this detail. What do you think?'

'You think old judge will grant one?'

'No harm in trying.'

Jess was removed from the room and Stuart tapped her on the shoulder for reassurance. He gave her a long look of sympathy and wished her a safe return tomorrow.

Caxton, in the meantime, approached His Honour and sounded him out about an adjournment. The judge was less than enthusiastic, and due to the circumstances of the previous day's evidence, disallowed the request, declining on the grounds that not enough information was forthcoming to persuade his opinion. It also would have given the prosecution a chance to prepare for the devastating allegations that were presented that morning.

Judge Shippard returned to his room and removed his

robes. He slumped exhausted into his large and comforting leather chair. He regarded himself as a good judge of people and character, but he was finding this woman an enigma still at this point in the trial. He had seen them all; the thorough crooks, the con men, the shady, the innocent and the crafty. This woman was still baffling him. He could not decide whether she was clever, cunning or just plainly a criminal. *Trouble is, she exuded class and culture, but refused to acknowledge it. She was one minute a perplexed and shy individual, yet she could turn on a vicious look that resonated disgust at the state of affairs in which she found herself. And what was all that talk about Stolt killing those two policemen?*

Shippard recalled the telephone call he'd received from retired Judge Hensley, advising him to disqualify himself from this case with all speed. *What was that all about?* He had warned him not to take on this case as there was no way of telling where it might lead. *Is this what he was on about?*

Caxton and his team returned to his chambers in the evening after dinner. He sat in his old chair contemplating the events so far. They had managed to convince the jury, he was sure, that Jess was a child when these atrocities were perpetrated. He had a major win over her being left-handed and Stolt convincingly insisting she had committed it using her right hand. He deflected the unexpected blow over the large sum of money in her name thanks to the efforts of Anna Delaney.

In fact, this might be the ace up our sleeve. If Jess happened to be this famous author, it will tilt the whole thing.

Chapter Ten

Caxton was less sure about the Sergeant Moore incident on the Gibb River Road. That had the potential to injure her case. *It all depended on how convinced they were about her story. The revelations about her incredible childhood will enlist all the sympathy votes, so that's a winner.* The clincher, as far as he could see, would be if this diary really existed and how incriminating it really was. The pictures he dismissed as a fantasy too brilliant to exist, as that would end it there and then. *No, the diary would clinch it if I could only convince her to deliver it.*

He thought about the best ways to achieve that aim. It was obvious that she was not going to budge for her own sake. She had already paid a huge price so far with the revelation that she was not Stuart's biological niece. She was also hiding something over these authorship claims. *What was so wrong with revealing that identity?*

Caxton sat quietly for some time while Seton and his wife worked on in the other office. Slowly a plan was developing. If he could convince her to release the diary, not for her sake but for either Donald's or Stuart's or someone else's, she might be persuaded. He wondered if Ian Knuckey held the key.

Caxton had had many failures in his career as a barrister, but none rankled more than his failure to clear Ian Knuckey of the fraud, corruption and drugs charges that had ended his illustrious police career all those years ago. Caxton was tempted into this seemingly impossible case of Jessie MacIntyre when he saw the glimmer of a chance to gain retribution for Knuckey and to get one over his victorious nemesis in that notorious case. It had totally destroyed Ian

Knuckey and he faded away to live a demoralised existence with his faithful and long-suffering wife on the central NSW coast. He picked up the telephone and dialled Knuckey's number. Mrs Knuckey answered and she went and found her husband. Caxton spoke to Ian Knuckey for many minutes.

CHAPTER ELEVEN

The court was scheduled to recommence next morning at nine-thirty, but unusually, none of the defence or the judiciary arrived on time. There was an expectant buzz all around the packed room as, after yesterday's startling revelations, no one knew what would occur today. One and a half hours late, the judge and his clerks, and the defence team, swept into the court room and sat down amidst much display. The judge apologised to all and then proceeded to announce that the court would forthwith be adjourning for one week. He explained that there had been a disturbing event the previous night that impacted substantially on the bearing of the case.

The room was now noisily reacting, wondering what it could possibly have been. The judge went on to briefly state that during the small hours of the morning, a building in

Australia Street was destroyed by fire following an explosion that was deliberately and callously set by persons unknown. It was, however, a major fire that totally destroyed the building and several others nearby.

The court erupted into a frenzy of conversations. Everybody had heard the news of the devastating fire in Newtown but no one associated it with the trial. When the judge revealed that it was the former address of Donald MacIntyre and the defendant Jessie MacIntyre, the implications suddenly became very clear. Questions were being asked about the diaries and photographs, which may have been hidden in the building that could have implicated not only Stolt but other criminals. Suddenly the potential seriousness of this case began to rise from the mire. Now there appeared to be some truth in Jessie's fears.

Caxton returned to his office and called Ian Knuckey again to ask him if he would be able to come down to Sydney for a consultation. Ian had certainly been following the case but he had been disappointed so many times before that he never got his hopes up. He wondered why the evil seemed to prosper and the righteous be punished incessantly all their miserable lives. Nevertheless, he agreed to come down on the train the next morning about ten.

Ian Knuckey arrived in Caxton's office before lunch and together they sat down to review the case. He advised Ian that he was hoping to persuade Jessie to release her diary and thought that Ian might be able to aid him in that desire. Ian knew nothing of a diary let alone the existence of any photographs. Caxton had arranged a meeting with Seton, Jessie and Stuart for that afternoon, as time was critical.

Jess and Stuart were waiting in the interview room for the arrival of their team. Jess was a little nervous as she had never actually met Ian before but had heard a lot about him from Donald. When they entered the room, Jess stood up and greeted him with a reticent nod and sat down again. She eyed him thoroughly. She knew this was a critical point in their case, otherwise why else would Caxton introduce this man into the scenario, given his reputation as a cop gone bad.

Before her sat a haggard old man with grey-white thinning hair and a wrinkled and burdensome countenance. He was thin and wiry, slightly hunched, and his clothes were showing signs of wear. He reminded her of an old stockman or drover who had spent too much time in the long paddock. He was humble, self-effacing and poignant, almost miserable. She liked him instantly.

They reviewed the case briefly, especially in relation to its effect on the MacIntyres and Ian Knuckey. At Caxton's bidding, Stuart again raised the issue of the diary in a general way as they were all aware that their conversations were probably bugged, especially now. Jess simply said she would think about it. They remained for more than an hour when all departed except Stuart.

Later that afternoon, Stuart returned to the Tennex office to see the team again. He had an offer to present to the group. Jess would agree to the release of the two diaries on strict conditions. Only Ian Knuckey was to read them;

Stuart was to promise not to read them and they were to be returned to her immediately they had taken copies of the relevant passages. She recommended that the arresting officer from Western Australia be engaged to guard them, as she expected everything would be done to destroy them before they got here. They were her only remaining contact with her past life and she did not want anybody to see them or destroy them.

Jess suggested the officer from Western Australia because, apart from anything else, something he had said to her in the heat of her arrest and transport back to Derby convinced her that he was at least honest and trustworthy. She certainly would not trust a single cop in NSW.

Caxton was delighted. He enthused about the possibilities and potential outcome from such an item. He went straight around to the hotel where Ian was staying to pass on the request. Ian rang his wife in Woy Woy to ask if she would be alright if he stayed away for a few more days. Stuart arranged a direct charter flight to Derby from Sydney and booked two seats. Caxton said he would try to arrange the secondment of the Western Australian officer to accompany them on their return. Jessie described where in the workshop she had secreted her prize and in what kind of container she had placed them. She managed to describe the hiding place in a quiet moment while the two of them were together. She had no doubts that their interviews were being bugged. She trusted Stuart, and so far, had no reason to mistrust Ian Knuckey.

The two men, Stuart and Ian Knuckey, departed

from Bankstown Airport for Derby at daybreak the next day. It was a small charter and there were only three other passengers on board, businessmen doing the rounds in the northwest. Stuart had arranged for George to retrieve the ammunition box from its hiding place and have it transported by Ravymoota helicopter to Derby. There he was waiting for them when they touched down about midday. Also waiting at the airport was the sergeant in charge of Jessie's arresting detail. He had no real idea why he had been seconded at such short notice but was told it was highly sensitive and secretive work that needed the utmost discretion. He would be armed during the entire process. He was to wait at the airport until he was met by two men who were described to him. The sergeant observed the charter arrive from Sydney and also the two men as described alight from the aeroplane.

Stuart and Ian made straight for George who was already there with the still-intact ammunition box wrapped in its plastic protection. Stuart cut the plastic away with George's knife and unclipped the two side clips holding the wooden lid in place. Inside were two well-wrapped and large folios just as Jess had described. Stuart could see that from the outside at least they still looked in order and as they had been packed away by her all those years ago. He placed them in the briefcase he had for that express purpose and bade farewell to George.

Stuart and Ian searched the lounge for the officer they hoped would be there to escort them with their treasure. The lounge was empty, but standing quietly in an unobtrusive corner was a large man in non-descript overalls carrying a small port and watching them intently. Stuart looked at Ian and indicated that that was probably the man. Together they walked over and asked if he was here for the consignment of cargo to be transported to Caxton. He said he was, and that his name was Sergeant James Musgrave. He was as much as Jessie described him, given the nature of their last encounter.

Stuart asked Sergeant Musgrave if he was ready to accompany them back to Sydney as they wished to leave immediately. James was taken aback at that news. He had no idea he would be travelling interstate. After a short break for refuelling, the three men boarded the jet and prepared for take-off back to Bankstown.

Once they were airborne, Ian could not wait to begin his search through the dairies of Jessie. He removed the last of the protective coverings and without ceremony began the long task of reading through them. Stuart let the plane get safely under way and then went and sat next to James. He introduced himself as Stuart only as he still was not certain that this man was going to understand his mission or be in any way sympathetic to its aims, given that last time he had anything to do with this topic, several of his mates ended up in hospital. Ian was furiously jotting down notes and muttering to himself, often very excitedly, at least initially.

Stuart then broached the subject in earnest. He looked nervously at the face of the rugged young officer and said, 'Do you know what Ian is reading over there?'

'No, I'm sorry. I was told nothing at all about this assignment except that it was highly sensitive.'

Chapter Eleven

'That is the diary of Jessie MacIntyre.'

James looked a little nonplussed. Then he blurted, 'You mean that woman I arrested and is on trial right now?'

Stuart nodded slowly.

'You don't say...' was all James could respond.

Stuart then explained the purpose of the assignment and James's role in it. He pointed out that Jessie had specifically requested James for this job and explained why. James was a little shocked at this revelation. He had been following the trial with great interest as it developed, but assumed that was the last he would ever be involved with it again. He was also informed about the occurrences back in Sydney, the dangers, and his expected part in the safe delivery of the precious diaries.

The plane landed safely just after dark in Bankstown. There was a hire car awaiting their arrival driven by Seton, and he quickly whisked them all back to his office in the city. There they were met by Caxton and Philippa as Ian still flicked through the diaries.

'Anything yet?' asked Caxton eagerly.

'My word,' enthused Ian. 'This is a gold mine. But gawd, she don't half write bucketloads of stuff. No wonder she can write novels.'

'Excellent!' replied Caxton.

The next day, armed with a massive note pad full of jottings, Ian Knuckey, accompanied by Caxton Tennex paid a visit to Jessie. She was sheepish about her private thoughts being scrutinised by strangers and greeted them with reserve.

Ian had a pile of questions to ask her and got her to write down the answers in his pad so no one could overhear them. Then she ventured a strange question, 'Do you recall the workshop, Mr Knuckey?'

'Sure, I still remember it quite well.'

'Here, I'll draw you a plan from the front. If the photographs still exist, they will be inside that pillar in an iron box. Don always allowed for the event of fire, so you never know your luck in the big city, some might have survived the fire.'

Ian held out no hope of that eventuality, but agreed to find out when he could.

Next morning, Ian went to the location in Australia Street, which now resembled a bomb site with its burnt mangled mass of debris. He was granted access to the site that had been constantly guarded since the night of the fire and its connection to the MacIntyre case became evident. Ian picked his way about the site turning things over and kicking pieces of wood and iron. He indirectly sauntered over to the pillar he thought was the one indicated by Jessie.

As she had described, there was a hatch in the pillar that required a special technique to remove. It was located about knee height and if one was not aware of its existence it would never be found. He searched around for a suitable tool and prised off the cover. Inside, to his complete amazement, was a black box about twice the size of a house brick. He gently removed it and placed it in his small square suitcase. He replaced the removed cover and discarded the tool. He casually wandered around for about half an hour more and

Chapter Eleven

then returned to the car where Seton was waiting, passing the guards and indicating that there was nothing there of interest.

Ian Knuckey could hardly contain his excitement. If this black box contained anything like the treasure Jess intimated it might, then it would be even better than her diaries. He headed straight back to Seton's office in eager anticipation.

Mr Knuckey was not disappointed. The contents of the box included one-hundred-and-sixty-eight photographs, most in superb colour and all annotated on the back with names, dates and times. Ian either knew all the people, or knew of them, and just as Jess had hinted in the courtroom, there were crooks, cops, solicitors and two judges. This would be dynamite.

Caxton was very pleased, both for himself, for Jessie, and in particular for Ian Knuckey. He gathered his team around him and set out two rules. Firstly, absolute silence must be maintained about these discoveries. Secondly, they must prepare a strategy to reveal the relevant contents without warning when the proceedings recommenced next Monday. Neither Stuart nor Jess was informed that the pictures had been successfully retrieved.

The trial reopened on Monday morning at nine-thirty. The judge had barely sat down when he pointed at Jessie and demanded with a loud and officious command, 'Get those things off her for a start!' waving his hand to indicate that Jessie's shackles should be removed.

'Damn silly rule that those are required. Anyone can see this woman is no threat to this court.' The guard obeyed the command and removed the clinking manacles from Jessie's arms and feet. There was an air of smugness about the prosecution, who now firmly believed that neither diaries nor photographs were found; indeed, they may not have ever existed.

Ivan Sebeski had had over a week to prepare a withering attack on the hopefully vulnerable defendant. The judge had been alerted that the defence may wish to submit some further evidence resulting from information gathered in the adjournment but gave no details. Mr Knuckey had spent the entire time collating Jessie's half-dozen diary entries that pertained directly to this case and aligning seven photographs specifically showing Stolt at the premises on previous dates.

The day was to open with Jess resuming her seat in the witness box preparatory to questions beginning.

Ivan Sebeski arose to begin his tirade and hoping to end the defence's case quickly. He wanted to know, as indeed did the gallery and most of the public, whether Jessie MacIntyre was actually George Norman Thaler and/or Jane Ransom. He proffered she was not, and on that assumption rested most of the prosecution's case for conviction, because of the large sums of money still not officially accounted for.

Ivan began by reiterating the points raised before the adjournment. He finally asked in an exaggerated gesture that he eagerly awaited the presentation of the diary entries supposedly made by the defendant as a child. At this point, Caxton nodded to Seton and he rose to address the bench.

'Your Honour, in response to that request, may we take

leave to present some further evidence uncovered during the adjournment?'

The judge looked at the prosecution and they shrugged their shoulders in silent agreement. Seton turned to the bench and began. 'Contrary to rumours and the beliefs of the prosecution, the defence team has managed to locate and retrieve not only one, but two, yes two, substantial tomes that constitute the aforesaid and hitherto hidden writings of the defendant.'

At this point Seton was standing by his desk and picked up two foolscap-sized royal-purple, cloth-covered and bound journals that he waved above his head to the assembled court.

He replaced them on the desk in front of him, then continued, 'Also, contrary to the hopes of the prosecution, and as you all can see, they are far from the girlie jottings of a mere child. They feature in minute detail the happenings and visits to the workshop. We have prepared for the court copies of extracts that indicate times, dates and in some cases reasons for at least six meetings that involve Deputy Commissioner Stolt and that date from at least two years prior to the deaths of the officers.'

There was a noisy shuffling within the room accompanied by murmuring. A set of copies was passed up to the judge amid whispering among the prosecution. The judge scanned them intently and then perused the photographs. He stared at the diary entries again then at length at the pictures. He placed them on his bench and turned to Seton still standing to one side of the bench.

'These are remarkable, Mr Tennex,' he said sedately. 'What else have you got?'

'Well, Your Honour, we have uncovered a multitude of evidence that will reverberate well beyond this case,' Seton said, patting the diaries again on the desk. 'It seems Miss MacIntyre was telling the truth that the web of connections stretches to many boundaries within the judiciary. May I respectfully suggest that in light of this new information that the charges brought against my client now be dropped.'

'For the benefit of the jury, Mr Tennex, please summarise the reasons for that suggestion.'

'Certainly, Your Honour. Members of the jury, I have endeavoured to prove to you that the defendant, Miss MacIntyre, not only did not commit this heinous crime, but was not in a position to have done so. I think you will all agree that she was proven to have been only a child of thirteen when the crime was committed. Yes, certainly she was there, but as a witness, not the perpetrator. An unwitting but critical witness as it turns out. I have conclusively proven that the defendant is habitually and strongly left-handed. Yet the only other known witness defiantly and consistently insists that the crime was carried out by a person using his or her right hand. Being ambidextrous is all very well, members of the jury, but such a premeditated and deliberate act would lead one to assume the perpetrator would always use his or her favoured hand.'

'Furthermore, members of the jury, in light of the evidence here provided, it becomes understandable that the defendant reacted to being sexually and verbally assaulted by a member of the very organisation that she had come to detest and fear for that very sort of behaviour. It is evident that Sergeant Moore was in the habit of engaging in this sort of activity and had a reputation for it in the past. It was unfortunate for him this time that he chose a victim who was unusually more than capable of defending herself. I think in light of the circumstances, this was a justifiable reaction.

'To the issue of the character assassination by the witnesses, I think we can all agree that their statements can all be dismissed as totally unreliable and almost fabrications, indeed, we may be pursuing further action over some of the more blatant falsehoods. The last issue to resolve is that of the large sums of money in the account name of the defendant. I think we have accounted for that situation satisfactorily. It is of no consequence to the facts of this case whether or not Miss MacIntyre is or is not using a *nom de plume* to follow another interest that has no bearing on this case.

'Might I conclude by asking you, members of the jury, does this woman look and sound like the sort of person who would commit any crime, let alone the despicable one with which she was maliciously charged? Was she charged in order to direct the gaze of the law away from the real perpetrators?'

The judge sent the jury to deliberate with words of advice, but requested that they unanimously agree on the verdict. They deliberated for only four hours which, after such a long and high-profile trial, was relatively brief. Their uncompromising verdict was a resounding 'innocent'. The court erupted into pandemonium. Loudest of all was the scream of the widow of one of the murdered officers. She had spent years befriended by Stolt, and more than friendship had eventuated. She realised that this man was possibly responsible for orchestrating, if not actually committing, the crime that led to the demise of her husband.

The verdict was not all that unexpected, but it left many questions unanswered. Firstly, if Jess was innocent, who then was the perpetrator? The evidence was pointing directly at another person already well known in police circles.

Unfortunately for Jess, she was not free. She would now have to be retained in custody while awaiting extradition back to Western Australia to face the charges arising from the assaults associated with her arrest, plus the outstanding issues of the assault on Sergeant Moore and the traffic offences.

Most devastating to Jess was the fact that Stuart now knew she was not related to him, and the unapproved usage of the Ravymoota Station name as her domicile.

The attorney general from Western Australia had been following the case closely, especially as it began to deepen his state's involvement in Jessie's appalling encounters with police forces and the misuse or abuse of power.

To this end, he had on standby an inexperienced, but very personable, female police officer assigned to fly to Sydney and accompany Jessie back to Derby in a much more civilised and respectful manner than her original exit.

The police escort arrived the next day and, in order to expedite this potential public relations nightmare, immediately arranged for Jess and Stuart to be flown back the following day. There was a large crowd at the normally quiet Derby airport and Jess was whisked away to the local lockup as quickly as possible. The attorney general had specifically requested of the rostered travelling duty magistrate that the case be conducted as expeditiously and surreptitiously as possible. There was already consternation enough regarding police brutality and corruption, especially in remoter parts of Western Australia.

Unfortunately for the attorney general, the magistrate was a controversial young woman who had been selected amid much controversy and disquiet because she was almost straight from university and had little practical experience in the legal system, let alone life itself. In fact, it was rumoured that she was appointed for ideological reasons to fulfil quota obligations for minorities, as she was a female and of sub-continental descent.

Some of her rulings had caused consternation. It was deemed, however, too obvious and contentious to replace her with another magistrate so, after considerable briefing, she was allowed to conduct the case.

She was, nevertheless, unable to resist her moment in the spotlight and castigated Jessie severely for her antics on the lonely and isolated Gibb River Road. She also announced that while she could use her discretion about that issue, she was not at liberty to do so regarding the traffic and firearms infringements that she had accumulated that day. She fined her for her misdemeanours, but worse still, issued her with a three-year, good-behaviour bond. The crowd in attendance was vocal in their annoyance, but more irritated was the attorney general. The outcry added to the newly appointed magistrate's controversy and calls for her dismissal were rife. That would be difficult as magistrates were appointed for life.

All through the hearing, the magistrate had appeared officious and rigid in her findings. She continually referred to Jess as Ms MacIntyre, dragging out and emphasising the z sound in Ms and disdainfully peering over her black-rimmed glasses. On the issue of the resist-arrest charges, the self-important young magistrate again berated Jess for her unacceptable behaviour and lectured her at length about civic responsibility. Jess was furious, and barely able to contain her anger. Stuart was stunned that such a performance was allowed to occur.

The attorney general, amid much disquiet within his government and the local population, was forced to fly to Derby in an attempt to assuage public opinion and ease the pressure on his ailing government's standing. He arrived next morning and immediately arranged to meet with Jess and Stuart, along with the now-embroiled local member for the Kimberley district. He proffered his sincerest apologies and strongly advised Jess to appeal, more or less assuring her of a favourable outcome this time. She declined the offer with contemptuous dismissal, informing them with crystal clarity of her opinion of the judicial system yet again.

The attorney general reiterated, 'But Ms MacIntyre, I can assure you that any appeal will be given the most favourable treatment. And again, I must apologise on behalf of the Government for this total misunderstanding.'

The local member nodded demonstrably in agreement. Jess sat unmoved and emotionless as she had all through the ordeal in Sydney. She cast a loathsome glare at the two men seated uncomfortably across from her and, after her now customary delay in speaking, said to them in a soft and severe voice, 'No thank you.'

The attorney general and the local member began to discuss other possibilities between themselves, occasionally including Stuart, more by looking at him rather than actually engaging him. Meantime, while all this was going on, Jess was getting more annoyed at the circus that surrounded her. Finally, after much chatter, which excluded Jess, there was a most uncharacteristic occurrence emanating from Jess herself.

Mid-sentence and while the two officials were excitedly discussing several possibilities, Jess brought her left arm down with a loud thud as she hit the desk with the open palm of her hand. The noise was shattering.

Stuart had never seen Jess get angry in all their years together. He had never heard her raise her voice, not even during the recent distress of the trial in Sydney, or indeed throughout the dismal charade that was the recent hearing in Derby. She was normally a placid and inoffensive person, at least within his confines. He looked at her in partial shock, and wondered what was going to happen next. The two officials turned to face her with a startled look on their pallid faces.

Jess stared at them with a withering countenance, unblinking. After a long, difficult silence with no one knowing what to do or say, Jess said in a soft, but menacing voice, 'Enough! You lot. Just listen to yourselves.' She stared harder, knitting her brow noticeably. 'No amount of chatter will convince me ever to go through that farce you call a court system. Haven't you noticed that each time I go anywhere near them, I cop it? You can all go and suffer all the embarrassment possible over the whole sorry saga.'

There was another long silence. Finally, the attorney general, with a sheepish look, said, 'Look Ms MacIntyre, we all realise that this whole episode has been most unfortunate and rather badly handled all round. But I'm sure we can come to some understanding in order to ease some of the wrongs done to you. If you would only consider an appeal, I'm sure we can promise you a much more sympathetic hearing.'

'Don't come the raw prawn with me, cobber! The cops can molest me, taunt my friends, kill my dog, shoot at me, arrest me at any moment, and ... get away with it for years. I know how the system works. I don't give a rat's how embarrassed you are. I'm not going near any courts for any reason. I'll wear this bond and you can stick your offer. I hope I can remind you every day about it. This world is about inequity and injustice, discrimination and prejudice. Offering me a cheat's way out is about all I would expect you to understand.'

The two men just looked at her in silence. Then the local member, whose electoral constituency covered a huge area of the West Kimberley, said to Jess, 'Look, I understand your feelings and accept that this is not quite how we hoped it would be, but please, if there is ever anything I can do to be of assistance in the future, don't hesitate to contact me.'

He handed over his card to Jess and she looked at it carefully.

'All right then. Just to prove you can be useful, arrange for me to get a licence and to get my truck registered.'

The attorney general looked at the local member and said, 'Bob, can we arrange for Ms MacIntyre to have a licence issued from here?'

There was some chatter between the two men, but Jess determined that it appeared possible for this to be arranged, at least her licence, if not the immediate registration of her vehicle. Jess asked for the licence to be arranged immediately and for a road train, and a permit to be issued for her to legally drive 'Jimmy' into town in order to have the necessary inspections and modifications carried out to comply with all the rules.

Jess and Stuart departed the office that the local member used when in Derby and returned to the motel. Jess sat on the bed in the pokey and drab room and looked up at Stuart.

'Stuart, are you sure you want me to come back with you?'

'What do you mean?' he asked, feigning surprise. He knew exactly what she meant and why.

'Well, after all I've done to you, I would understand perfectly if you told me to go.'

'Look Jess,' he said, 'I know you've been through the wringer, we both have. I won't say I'm not a little sad that you're not really my niece in a family way, but I love you like a daughter, in spite of everything and I guess I always will now. I admire you tremendously and can't believe what pride and pleasure you have brought into my life. Things I thought I'd never have. You'll never know how much Norm and Peter, and especially George, admired and respected you too.'

Jess could feel the sad, bitter tears slowly trickle down her cheeks. At the mention of their names, she realised that she had let all of them down too, the people she admired the most.

'Don't cry Jess, it'll be all right. You'll be fine as soon as we can get back home.' With that, Stuart walked up to where she was seated on the edge of the bed and pulled her up by the arm. He gave her the most affectionate hug that he was capable of. Jess embraced him momentarily then, still sobbing softly, released herself from his embrace and resumed her seat on the bed.

'I'm so sorry,' she whispered to him.

Next morning, Jess and Stuart went to the post office to try to collect what she expected to be quite a lot of mail. Jess went up to the counter and requested if it was possible to clear all her mail, even though she had no identification or the keys. She was right about the quantity of mail. There were bags of it. Jess was still dressed in the garb that the prison had provided but she just wanted to get home, so Stuart loaded up the ute and left as soon as she was ready.

By the time Stuart reached the turnoff to Milbark, Jess was calm. She was a little unsure how George would react to her after all the revelations from the trial, let alone the other station hands or the clan down by the billabong.

Stuart drove up to the ramshackle homestead in the late afternoon light. Jess sat in the car and peered at the decrepit, unpainted hovel and another tear arose in her eyes. She realised how much she had missed this haven of serenity and isolation over the last eight months.

Here she would find her soul restored and people who respected her and treated her with dignity. Here were all her triumphs and tragedies and the source of many of her troubles: her novels. She reminded herself that she had the near-completed draft of her fifth book still sitting on her computer hidden in the shed. There suddenly arose in her a conflicting sensation momentarily overwhelming her as she contemplated the huge draft that awaited her command for release. She was undecided whether to destroy it, or to pass it on to the eagerly awaiting world. She would decide later, right now she just wanted to see George and settle back into her old life as much as she could after all the traumatic events.

CHAPTER TWELVE

George was waiting in the house for Stuart to return. On hearing the motor arrive, he wandered out to the veranda to watch as the vehicle stopped and Stuart got out to unload. George watched as Jess sat in a daze for many minutes. Then she turned and looked at him and opened the door to jump out. She closed the door with a hard push and turned to approach him gingerly.

George descended the few steps to the gravel and said, 'Yessie, Yessie, mine Fräulein.' He gave her a big bear hug and looked down into her moist eyes as he continued, 'How you are now Yessie?'

Jess just looked at him in silence, nothing needed to be said. She gave him a slight hug back, which he knew was all powerful.

That evening, Jess asked Stuart if she could telephone

Edna, as she wanted to pay her a visit as soon as possible. She rang, and a man, who was not Ralph, answered the telephone. Jess asked Edna if she could see her tomorrow if possible. Edna was delighted.

Next morning, Jess spent most of the time preparing 'Jimmy' for the short trip over to Ravymoota. She cared not that the permits for her to drive the vehicle on public roads had not yet been arranged, she cared even less that she still had no licence. She was just so pleased to be able to drive her old truck along the dusty bush track that passed for their entrance road. She stopped a couple of times to ensure she did not arrive too early. She was invited for lunch and Hubert was to prepare a sumptuous fare for the occasion.

Jess drove the lumbering truck into the manicured grounds of the extensive station complex and brought it to a stop not far from the front fence. She hopped out and gingerly looked about for the Conistons. They were all eagerly standing on their wide veranda and waved merrily for her to enter, some walking briskly over to meet her. Edna gave Jess a huge hug, and as was Jessie's custom, she stood there with arms by her side, tolerating the embarrassing show of affection. Then Edna clasped both her hands as she spoke fondly to her. Edna could feel that Jessie's hands had softened during her long and forced stay away from cattle work. She looked down at them and noticed that her fingers were clearer and her nails were manicured and unchipped. They went inside to be greeted by Hubert and one of Edna's sons, who had returned to help out in the business.

After some preliminary chatter, Jess said in a soft apologetic voice, 'I wonder if I may have a quick word to you and Ralph in private first?'

'Sure, of course my dear,' enthused Edna. 'Come through to the small lounge. It's so good to see you back here again after all…' Edna stopped mid-sentence at the unsavoury reminder of so recent an event. Jess sheepishly dropped her eyes and forgave the foray into the realm of unease.

Once the three of them were all seated in the lounge, Jess began, still speaking in a low and deferential manner, 'I really want to apologise sincerely to you both for such a rude and impolite thing I did to you over the address of the boxes in Derby.'

'Not at all,' exclaimed Edna. 'Don't think another thing about it. It is quite an honour that such prestigious things come our way.'

'Well, it was very wrong of me to do so without your permission and I'm deeply sorry.'

Both Edna and Ralph were a little non-plussed as to Jessie's embarrassment and rushed to assure her that all was well. It did, however, confirm the rumours that Jessie MacIntyre was also George Thaler and probably Jane Ransom as well.

'So,' began Edna rather tentatively, 'it is true then. You are who they say you are?'

Jess looked ashamedly at them then averted her eyes to gaze at the floor some distance ahead. *So, this is what it's going to be like now everywhere I go I suppose*, she thought to herself.

Chapter Twelve

They sat momentarily in silent reflection. Then Edna said brightly that they should all adjourn to the dining room where Hubert had prepared lunch for them.

There were a few strangers at the table. One of the Coniston's sons joined them and there was a dapper and well-educated guest who also joined them. Jess only stayed about three hours as she wanted to be alone and to return to Milbark. She took her leave and expressed her gratitude for the support that they had all shown her during her ordeal. As usual, Edna loaded Jess up with all sorts of goodies prepared lovingly by Hubert.

There was one other task Jess regarded as essential, and that was to assuage her guilt for the despicable things she had pronounced to the man who was probably most responsible for her present position; and that was Caxton Tennex. In the late evening of her second day home, she sat down to write him a letter. She began,

'I have many regrets in my life, to which I have added another. I wish to thank you for your perseverance and ability in achieving the seemingly impossible. Mr Knuckey esteems you very highly and I can but concur; he is a man of trustworthy assessment. But for me, I ask that if you cannot forget, then at least please forgive my totally unworthy and inappropriate outburst of insulting and harsh words uttered to you and about you in that close little room. I deeply regret that occurrence and wish I could retract it all. While it may have been heartfelt and reflected my perceptions at that moment, the opposite is now the case and I sincerely apologise for that ungrateful and unforgivable performance. Please respond at your leisure in order that I may truly retain your much desired and ongoing friendship, undeserved as that may be.'

Jess felt at least that went someway to righting the wrong she had done to the man whose eccentricities it took her some time to learn to accept and finally appreciate. She still occasionally compared his flowery and illuminating outbursts to those she so fondly recalled coming from Norman.

Jess now found it even more difficult to attain good sleep and often had disturbed nights merging all her horrors from her childhood to the night at Don's, to assaults on the Gibb and now her violent arrest and torturous trial. She once found consolation in her writings but as these had resulted in more traumas, she was ambivalent in that direction. She found inspiration was slow in coming and the desire to create dissipated. She sat on the draft of her fifth novel and thought about the things that that enterprise had brought upon her. She had difficulty in attending to her mail, which was now piling up. She received several letters from her publisher urgently requesting if there was a new novel and could it be sent on to them. More disturbing to her, however, were the constant mutterings and requests for her hitherto secret diaries to be released as a series once the investigations into the items alluded to in them had been attended to.

The diaries had by now attained huge popular mythology and there was a constant clamour for them to be released. She feared that outcome enormously and was most downcast at the prospect. She had learnt that passages of relevant text had been released regarding criminal activity and some pertaining to some of the occurrences in the Kimberley, all against her wishes. Disturbingly, she had received several offers for huge sums of money, reputedly over ten million dollars, for the exclusive rights for them when the police investigations were finally completed. She had no interest at all in releasing them, not for any money. Worse than all this, however, was the prospect that they were to be extensively utilised and indeed form the basis of a new commission of inquiry into police corruption and the now generally recognised false dismissal of Inspector Knuckey.

In fact, he was to be instrumental in the conduct of that inquiry and had thus been re-appointed as a temporary officer in the Police Conduct and Integrity Bureau, or PCIB, to root out crooked cops, some dating back to his days. There were rumours that she would be required to attend as a chief witness, against all her wishes.

Jess finally relented and succumbed to the demands of her exuberant publishers. She sent the final draft of her fifth novel without checking it and left them to it. She still had not produced anything as Jane Ransom, despite Romantis's heavy lobbying.

She slowly regained her composure and the desire to return to Derby to attend to her mail played on her. After she had been home many months and the new Dry was under way, Jess approached Stuart and asked him if he would mind accompanying her into Derby as support in her effort to obtain registration for the truck. She had finally been issued her driving licence thanks primarily to the efforts of the local member. She was now officially in existence. As she had no other documentation at all, not even a birth certificate, she thought that it could be difficult to arrange. She remembered the words of the harassed local member at their last unpleasant meeting offering to be of assistance, so she decided to make use of that offer in registering old 'Jimmy'.

Once in town, Jess, with Stuart by her side, entered what passed for the traffic authority building and asked for the manager. It appeared to them that he had some warning of her appearance as, after a couple of telephone calls, he announced that they would be able to assist with the issuing of the truck registration. This was unusual, as that normally required considerable testing. Jess looked at the manager with a slight knit in her brow and asked, 'Will that cover my truck and the trailers I tow?'

The manager made another telephone call. After hanging up, he looked at Jess and announced that he would be able to arrange for the engineering works required to gain registration for the truck. Jess greeted that news with mixed feelings. Maybe the altercations with the local member had paid off in this rather pleasing result. It also meant, however, that she was now definitely in 'the system' and no longer anonymous to the world. She asked what was involved in getting the truck registered and was informed of the complicated and bothersome rigmarole that that entailed, but decided to follow it all in order to comply fully with all the laws, as she was still on her good-behaviour bond. It took her six months to comply with all the requirements and modifications that were required in order to bring the GMC up to roadworthiness and get it registered.

The other outstanding matter that needed her attention was that of the taxation office. They were very understanding, but frowned on the use of false names and identities; in fact, it was illegal. After several meetings with a representative who flew up from Perth, Jess was able to satisfy their requirements and pay outstanding taxes incurred with some small penalties and fines. They appreciated her position, given her extenuating circumstances. She was warned to keep her affairs in order from now on, however. She was allowed to keep her own account as well as one in the name of Jane Ransom and George Norman Thaler, provided she fully explained her position annually through her returns.

Jessie had returned to Milbark Station just before the Wet set in. It was early summer in Sydney and the ripples emanating widely from the fallout from her trial were spreading into some most unexpected corners.

The disgraced former detective Ian Knuckey found he was suddenly more acceptable to his once reticent neighbours. It had been about fifteen years since he was unceremoniously and publicly dumped from the police force and stripped of all his entitlements. He had lost everything, except his long-suffering and loyal wife. Ian was now about sixty. When he was working with Donald, he was about forty-five but he looked about sixty-five. He had spent most of those fifteen years embittered and disillusioned, eking out an uncomfortable existence for himself and his selfless wife, surviving on a reluctantly given government pension.

He was unemployable and suited to little else. His wife, Beryl, a thin and gaunt lady of rather tallish frame, had only one dream, and that was to end up living with her husband in a house by the sea. That dream had long since disappeared and they lived a desolate life in a dingy rented unit in the Central Coast village of Woy Woy, having forsaken their rather spacious house in the inner-city area not that far from Newtown. The cramped and dilapidated building overlooked a neglected bushy reserve in an airless little hollow, though it was reasonably close to the water.

Beryl knew that her misery would now be as it began, endless. She had watched her husband slide into melancholia and waste away, smoking his roll-your-owns and having the occasional tipple. He walked for miles about the water and bays, deep in black thoughts about the injustices of this world.

Suddenly all was reversed. He sat at their tiny dining table surrounded by cheap note books, scribbling interminably and furiously in this one then that one and rubbing out this line then adding to that one; on and on. He was congenitally messy and untidy, but this enterprise seemed to bring out the apogee of that characteristic. Beryl had never seen him so animated and engaged. He smoked frequently, sometimes so engrossed in his activities that he let the cigarettes burn themselves out in one of several heavy glass ashtrays he had

Chapter Twelve

stolen from numerous local hotels that he attended without taking one puff. He plotted his long overdue revenge and savoured the possibilities that presented themselves.

He arranged lists of accomplices by profession: judges, police, solicitors, cronies and other assorted hangers-on. Some of the chief culprits were now dead, so he allowed himself some poetic licence to embellish their faults and crimes to assuage his pent-up anger.

Ian Knuckey sat in the splendid and imposing office of the newly appointed commissioner. He was a recently retired judge from the Supreme Court of Queensland, a man with a fearsome reputation and a recognised stickler for protocol and honesty. He was appointed because of his renowned independence and prodigious output and because he was deemed to be fiercely independent of the tainted New South Wales police force and legal system; the system which he was about to tear asunder with a probing investigation over the MacIntyre case revelations that centred on corruption.

Judge Trimble sat officiously at his large desk dictating memos and issuing instructions. He was not a man to be crossed.

'What do you mean, she can't be contacted,' he snapped at Knuckey. 'I want this person here and if I issue a subpoena, by gum, she'll be here. Or there'll be hell to pay. Now get her.'

Ian Knuckey could sense his revenge slipping away, or at least being slightly threatened. He was not, under any circumstances having that. He felt his hackles rising. Uncharacteristically for him, he was about to chide a superior.

'Now look here, Judge,' he said rather apologetically, 'this is not the sort of woman we can just order about.'

Trimble scowled at him and was about to interject, when Ian said to him, before he could speak, 'This is not one of your usual scummy low-life criminals you are dealing with here.'

Ian saw the judge close his mouth so he continued, 'Have you any idea where this person lives? She is almost uncontactable. She doesn't just live around the corner, you know. It will take her days to get here.'

Ian watched as Trimble, stunned into temporary silence by this unaccustomed affront, slowly leaned forward in his chair.

Without hesitation, Ian continued, 'I have waited fifteen years, hoping beyond hope to be in this position, and crikey, no one's gonna threaten it for me now. You better get a grip on who we are dealing with and where she lives, and the information we need from her. And what's more, Judge, I'll go straight to the premier if I feel this commission is put in jeopardy by the wrong people being in charge. I've already put too much work into this to have it threatened.'

The old judge looked fiercely at the inwardly cringing old man seated before him. He was still slowly leaning forward to emphasise and impose his authority when he was cut short by this unexpected tirade from the man who was to be his main aid and chief source of information. He was so inwardly startled that he instantly stopped his forward motion and remained momentarily stationary, then he slowly reversed his movement to glide effortlessly backwards into the depths of the huge leather chair.

Chapter Twelve

Ian stared unflinchingly at him, his determination showing through in his steadfast composure. There was a long and awkward moment of silence. Trimble was quickly summing up his position. He was very grateful and appreciative of the New South Wales authorities for giving him this rather prestigious appointment and opportunity to continue in his chosen field. The man mainly responsible for his fortuitous position was seated meekly before him now. He realised that this was not his usual domain and procedures might have to be altered to accomplish this delicate and controversial duty.

The judge relaxed a little in his seat then replied in a calm and deep voice resonating with authority. 'Very well, Mr Knuckey,' he said, stroking his chin with the thumb and fingers of his right hand, 'I'll remember that.'

Ian was unsure what he meant. *Did he mean he would remember that in order to get even later, or did he mean he would remember that as good advice and act on it accordingly?*

While Ian was contemplating all the ramifications of this exchange, the judge interrupted his thoughts to say, 'Mr Knuckey ...' There was a pause. Ian prepared for more confrontation, then Trimble continued, 'Where do you live?'

'Woy Woy, Your Honour.' The words came out automatically. He regretted addressing him so, as it implied some differentiation in their status that was, nonetheless, real, but not really how Knuckey saw it; or wanted it to be seen. There was another break while the old judge peered at him over his heavy glasses.

'Is there any reason why this inquiry cannot take place in Woy Woy, Mr Knuckey?'

Ian was dumbstruck. He was not expecting that question. He stammered awkwardly in reply, 'Not in Woy Woy, Your Honour, but maybe in Gosford.'

'Why not there then?' asked Judge Trimble, motionless in his chair.

'Why not indeed?' responded Ian with a slight grin and an easier tone. 'It would probably be much cheaper to conduct it there and also more convenient for witnesses to attend.'

'Arrange it, Mr Knuckey. Then advise me about Ms MacIntyre.'

Ian was totally confused. He had commenced this meeting with trepidation and a hope of enlightening the judge on some critical matters, instead, he had not only achieved his former aim but the judge had suggested they move the inquiry nearer to his home. *Maybe it was going to work out satisfactorily after all. At least the immediate threat had been removed, for now.*

The move to Gosford certainly made life much easier for the Knuckeys. For a start, it reduced Ian's travelling time to almost nil and it also reduced the separation from his lonely wife. Beryl was reluctant to renew friendships that had died as a result of the adverse publicity following the original trial. At the time, this framing of Knuckey was not entirely known to anybody, but Caxton Tennex for one, strongly suspected that Knuckey was innocent of the crimes of which he had been accused.

Beryl had been a strong supporter of the Church. She was

a practicing Catholic, having been born into a small country community where that faith was strong. However, any support for her withered away under the unsustainable strain and weight of accusations emanating from the evidence presented at several trials following the assassinations at Donald MacIntyre's workshop. Now, after years of lonely isolation and being ostracised from her most cherished organisation, she was finding it difficult to forgive them their outcasting of her and her husband. Despite several tentative overtures from former acquaintances, Beryl Knuckey was going to hold her head up as the injured party and retain the high ground in dignified silence. Even their two children had limited contact nowadays, as having a notoriously infamous father was not conducive to advancement, socially or professionally.

Ian Knuckey had been assigned as a reinstated government appointee to the eagerly awaited commission. In this role, he had been allocated a full-time probationary constable, Sharon McBride. She was young and untainted by the controversies surrounding the corruption allegations involving the New South Wales police and as such hoped to further her career by a significant contribution to this inquiry.

When Jessie MacIntyre was reluctantly convinced to agree to attend the commission, Ian Knuckey eagerly volunteered to pick her up at the Sydney airport and transport her in his ancient vehicle back to the commission hearings in Gosford. He casually mentioned to his wife that he would be collecting her on Wednesday; he assumed she did not wish to accompany him there on the long drive from Woy Woy.

He was starkly alerted that that assumption was incorrect. Not only did she enthusiastically insist that she would be accompanying him, but added that she would be preparing refreshments on a slightly grander scale than she normally would for their own meagre tripping around.

She sternly advised him that, after all those years of desolation, she would not miss the chance to meet and return with the sole cause of the sudden and unexpected alleviation of that affliction. Ian was unsure about this. He had never had his wife associated with any of his professional work before. However, he agreed that she could accompany him as it was way past her time for some recompense, and if meeting Jessie MacIntyre went some way to aid that, he could at least provide that satisfaction for her.

Jessie's attendance was to remain a secret as much as possible, but that would probably be difficult, given her status and fame as an author. Ian hoped to interview her informally for several days, going over numerous entries in her diaries and then eliciting from her any other information she held. She had hinted at her trial that she held within her memory much more information. Her diaries, as she incessantly pointed out, were only about her life and events that impacted directly on her were entered. That did not mean that she did not have a lot more knowledge, however.

Ian Knuckey knew it was going to be difficult to contact Jess. He asked Sharon McBride to begin by trying to contact Edna Coniston, her neighbour on Ravymoota. Edna advised that it would indeed be difficult to contact Jess as, during the

Wet, most communications with some of the more remote cattle stations were often cut for many weeks. Edna told Sharon that she would attempt contact and return a call when such was achieved.

It took several days, but finally Jess was ferried over to Ravymoota by chopper and contact was made with Sharon. Jess required several days to finally arrive in the confines of the Gosford building from where the PCIB was going to operate. Ian Knuckey took full advantage of every moment with his reticent witness by compiling voluminous notes in several different books.

Jess was resigned to the buffeting that life on the Kimberley cattle station might hand out. It was now over seventeen years since she first arrived there as a young girl. She had lost Norm and Peter, but still had Stuart and George. That was now about to change. George had hinted a few times to her that he was considering leaving Milbark while he was still capable of making that decision. For some reason, he did not fancy dying and being buried there along with his mates. He had always indicated that he would like to move to Darwin where it was still warm but where there were more amenities than here. He was now well into his seventies and decided to make the move before any more disruptions and interference to the running of these isolated cattle stations made it too difficult to manage them.

It was now late 1998, and George took Jess aside as the Dry was drawing to a close and said to her, 'Yess, mien Linkisch,' a term he had endearingly called her with reference to her left-handedness, 'I decide to go to Darwin soon and vish to tell you first.'

There was a slight delay as Jess turned to face him and then replied, 'Oh?' she queried with uninhibited disappointment. 'I am very sad to hear that, George.'

'Ja Yessie, me too. But I like to give you small gift to remember me by.' He pulled out a small package from his overalls and handed it to Jess.

'What is it, George?' she said, staring at the small paper bag roughly crumpled about something he had placed in her hand.

'Open, please. You see.'

Jess unwrapped the paper bag until a small cloth-covered item was revealed. She unwrapped the rag slowly and revealed one of the large silver thalers, a coin that she knew meant a huge amount to this lonely Austrian emigrant. She handled it carefully, turning it back and forth in embarrassed silence and reading the inscription on both sides. She looked up into his dark eyes and with a hint of a tear just returned his gaze. No words could express her feelings and the overwhelming sadness welling up inside her. George understood. He placed a huge craggy hand on her slight shoulder and smiled contentedly.

Jess composed herself and placed the coin in her pocket. She would examine it properly later.

'What will you do?' she asked, wiping the moisture from her cheeks.

'I have plenty things to do,' he announced. 'I buy new truck and travel a bit about tropics.'

Chapter Twelve

They had the semblance of a meaningful conversation but Jess was in no mood to make small talk. She excused herself and went to a quiet corner of the workshop and extracted the coin. She peered at it again. It was large for a coin and made of solid silver. It carried an inscription of 'M THERESIA D.G. 1780'. Jess knew how much it had meant to him. She was doubly pleased that she had used the name 'Thaler' as her pseudonym. Within a few weeks, George was gone.

Jess was involved on several occasions with the investigations into the police corruption revealed by her court case. She had gone down to Gosford and to Sydney and met up again with an enormously grateful Ian Knuckey. Ian insisted that Jess meet Beryl several more times. Beryl had spent her childhood in the country, which helped her associate with Jess. She was so appreciative and indebted to Jess that it was almost embarrassing for Jess to be near them. They never tired of informing her how much they owed to her for restoring their dignity and social acceptance once more. Despite this minor difficulty, Jess was rather fond of the aging country couple that doted on her. It was a minor consolation to Jess that they were now so rewarded.

An imposition resulted from the fallout of the case. The trial had received widespread coverage both nationally and internationally, but particularly in Britain. This only resulted in enhancing the reputation of George Norman Thaler. However, one of the unexpected outcomes was that her fourth novel, the one that dealt primarily with Norm and his early life in England, had aroused much speculation.

The British police were making tentative enquiries regarding the fourteenth Earl of Bromley and public interest in that matter was causing consternation among the royal watchers. Jess received a telephone call late one evening from an agent of the BBC requesting the possibility of an interview to discuss the issue of Mr Woods or du Bois or whoever he was.

Jess refused every attempt to get her to comply. Finally, the BBC sent a representative to Australia in an attempt to get her to change her mind. He even travelled all the way up to Ravymoota to meet her. The upshot was that she would agree to a brief interview provided certain conditions were met. These conditions were: the interview was definitely not to be screened in Australia and it was to take place at Ravymoota, with the Coniston's agreement, of course. Last, the good name of Norm was to be sacrosanct. She finally agreed because the BBC had convinced her that it was actually in the interests of Norman's memory that his disappearance be cleared up, not only for himself but also for those left behind wondering. It would also be a way of revealing actually who killed his beloved. She insisted that assurances be given that it would definitely not be shown in Australia. All these conditions were agreed to.

Edna was enthralled that the world-famous author would conduct an interview at her property and could barely contain herself. All was arranged for the following late Dry season by which time the BBC would be able to finalise all their own research that end.

The interview would be conducted by a suave young presenter who was just beginning his interviewing career in

Chapter Twelve

the industry, but who was held in high esteem. His name was Patrick Main and he already had a reputation for some probing interviews. Jess hoped she knew what she was doing, agreeing to this arrangement.

On the day arranged for the interview, Jess decided to ride over to Ravymoota via the shortest route, which would be more enjoyable for her than driving the long way around via the Gibb. She departed Milbark at daybreak and hoped to arrive well before eleven. She carried with her the mourning locket, the two rings, and a couple of the books that Norman had left to her. All these she deposited securely into two saddlebags that sat either side of the horse.

The BBC was ecstatic, not only at her arrival, but the method of that arrival. It added some authenticity to the drama and the cameras were buzzing madly as she arrived. She dismounted at the front fence and asked one of the boys to attend to her horse, a huge and flighty bay animal with a striking white patch along his nose. She disconnected the saddlebags and walked to the front door. Here she was greeted by Edna and Ralph, who in turn introduced her to the crew and Mr Main.

Edna had arranged for the entire crew to have lunch in the main dining room along with Jess and themselves. Edna was abuzz with uncontrollable excitement. The interview was arranged to take place in the small lounge where it had been set up. About two o'clock, Patrick departed to prepare for the interview.

Patrick was struck by the dramatic, heavy and ominous

sound of Jess's riding boots as she walked up the timber hallway towards the room. It sent a slight shiver up Patrick's back.

Patrick commenced the interview with a preamble that ended with, 'I guess first of all we should establish that you are indeed George Norman Thaler.'

Jess hesitated before answering and then said softly, 'It's pronounced Tarler.'

'I beg your pardon?' asked Patrick in a quizzical tone.

There was a pause from Jess before she continued. 'I said, it's pronounced Tarler,' she reiterated softly. 'The name is pronounced Tarler.'

'I see,' replied Patrick, not really seeing at all.

Jess, noting his confusion, added, 'The name is taken from the Austrian coin, the Thaler, and is pronounced Tarler, same as the coin.'

'Well, I'm glad we got that all cleared up,' he responded with a sly grin. 'I guess that answers my question.' Jess looked at him without emotion.

'Does that also mean that you produced the novels by the person known as Jane Ransom as well?'

Jess set a steely stare at an uneasy Patrick and said after a long pause, 'I thought we were here to discuss Norman Woods.'

'Yes, you're right. It does have a bearing on the subject though to establish that you are those persons and that will ensure we are dealing with an authority.'

She again stared at him. 'Well, you know I am. Now let that be an end to it.'

'Yes,' agreed a chastened Patrick. 'If that is the case then we can move onto the crux of the discussion. As far as you know, was Norman Woods also known as Norman Melville Redveres du Bois?'

'No.'

'You mean he wasn't Norman du Bois?'

'No. I did not say that.' There was another slight pause, which Patrick found disconcerting. He was as yet unaware that this trait was peculiar to Jess.

'You mean, he was not Norman Melville Redveres du Bois?'

'No,' said Jess firmly. 'I said he was not *known* as Norman Melville Redveres du Bois.' After another pause accompanied by a piercing stare from Jess, she continued with, 'In fact, I am the only person he ever told that secret. I failed him badly by revealing that information to the world by my ill-advised actions.'

Patrick was becoming slightly uneasy.

'Can you describe him for us, Jess?'

Jess went on at some length to describe her friend and mentor, giving an astute and deeply moving sketch of the man who had meant so much to her. Patrick was finally into safer territory. Jess proved herself a worthy wordsmith as she moved into familiar territory and unfolded the description of her great friend. She seemed to relax a lot more as they got onto safer ground.

'Before we go on Jess, could you please look at these four pictures and tell me if you can recognise him in any of them.' Patrick handed her four old and faded photographs. Jess looked at each thoroughly in turn and then repeated the process. Then she announced, 'This could be him as a young man.' Looking at the second, she said, 'That also could be him.' She handed Patrick the third and said, 'I have no idea, but I doubt that is he.' Then she looked at the fourth again, and handing it over to Patrick, announced, 'I'd almost swear that this is a picture of Norman as a young man, from what I know of him. Is that Charlotte with him?'

Patrick placed the four photos beside him without saying a word. Then he looked back up at Jess and asked, 'Did he mention her much or the accident?'

There was a slight pause again before she responded, 'It was no accident.'

'What do you mean?'

'I mean it was no accident. Not according to Norman. Charlotte was killed at the instructions of Catherine du Bois, his own mother, but by the hand of their butler Roderick Palmer, who severed the girth strap on her horse to kill her in a fall.'

'You don't say?' said Patrick in surprise. Finally, the interview was progressing.

'In your novel, you mention that Mr du Pont, the main character in that novel and the fourteenth earl, after many years, married a station owner's daughter and had children. I'm sure you understand the significance of that revelation?'

Jess gave a longer than normal pause and then said in a soft but determined voice, dripping with emotion and pain,

'Norman Woods never married in real life. He remained eternally faithful to his lost love for all his years. I only hope they are together now. He only ever spoke of her in the most reverential manner and with true love. Your usurping earls have no fear in that quarter.'

Patrick looked down at his pad to prepare for the next point. He could feel the tension in the air. Behind those enormous blue eyes was a sharp mind that would brook no servile accusations.

'What have you brought with you, Jess?' he asked.

Jess leaned over and retrieved several well-wrapped items from within the saddlebags. She commenced with the books she had brought showing the inscriptions within. Then she displayed the two rings and finally the mourning locket. The ring that held the most value to the interviewer was the one that contained the symbol of the earls of Bromley. Jess had inadvertently alluded to it in the novel as she assumed it was a common character widely utilised in such matters, as Norm had referred to it as 'familiar'. Jess assumed this meant familiar to everybody; she did not know that he meant familiar only to himself and his family. She was totally unaware that it was uniquely du Bois.

It was a strange device, or 'charge', as Norm had called it, that looked a bit like a 'T'-topped five in stark red. Norm called it 'gules', a strange name Jess had thought, but correct according to Norm. It lay on a completely white shield with no other markings. It had given Jess quite a turn at its mystery and potence when Norm had first shown her. She felt it possessed sinister or mysterious powers and was fascinated by it.

There followed an intensive, though very pleasant, discussion on any and all matters pertaining to Norman that Jess cared to recall.

Patrick concluded the interview with two questions, 'May we take some of these items for further investigation?' He fully expected a complying answer. He did not receive one. Instead, Jess replied softly but firmly, 'No, definitely not. You may take the locket on promise to return it. I was supposed to put it into his grave with him, but again I failed him,' she said sadly. 'But you are certainly not getting the ring or the Bible.'

'Fair enough,' responded Patrick, a little taken aback.

The last question pertained to receiving permission to fly over to Milbark tomorrow and see the grave of Norman du Bois. Jess reluctantly agreed on condition they land nearby to that spot and then depart, as all the men will be at one of the cattle camps.

The interview ended there. Jess again asked that the interview was not to be shown in Australia, to which she received assurances to that effect. She was to learn to her sorrow years later that that undertaking was soon forgotten in the name of public interest and demand, not to mention mercenary considerations. Jess had a few pleasant moments with all the visitors and then departed for Milbark.

The next day, the Ravymoota chopper brought over the camera crew and Patrick to take some footage of the sad little graveyard in the dry grassy plain that housed, besides a few others, the grave of Norman Woods. They took a few shots of the house and its surrounds as they left and that was the end of that episode for Jess, she hoped.

Jess was now approaching thirty-one. She had managed to arrange most of her life into some semblance of order. She had finally succumbed to the relentless pressure of the publishing world and allowed the release of her precious diaries, a few years after the Bureau investigation had completed its work and they were no longer required for that job. She had received a tidy sum for them, nothing like she could have received, for she decided to publish them with Advent, the publisher of George Norman Thaler, and at a reduced fee as a sign of appreciation for getting her started. She even relented and recommenced some tentative Jane Ransom novels as payment for their initial support of her first writing endeavours.

The writing of the Jane Ransom novels was a simple matter for Jess. She had the formula down pat and instigating it was an effortless pastime that she found very undemanding. Her biggest problem with this format was to keep her ideas in check in order to maintain the rigid length boundaries of such undemanding output. It was from this frustration that the germ of the idea of Kimberley West originated. That became the outlet for her dissatisfaction at having to curtail so much of her creation in the short Ransom novels.

In time, Jess, as Kimberley West, began to encroach more onto the territory she had previously covered in a cursory manner in her Ransom novels. Despite altering names and places, even dates, in expanding and developing the characters and the settings, there was a distinct appearance of similarity in some of the two different types of works for the discerning and exploratory reader. It was highly unlikely that a Jane Ransom reader would venture into the extended works of Kimberley West, let alone George Norman Thaler. It never occurred to Jess that the expanded and embroidered output of the former two would ever be compared. It came to pass, however, that the publishers at Romantis were alerted on occasion by discerning readers that some of the work of Kimberley West bore an uncanny resemblance to the earlier works of Jane Ransom.

Closer inspection led Romantis to thoroughly investigate and compare all the works of both authors to check for plagiarism. Each successive release of a book by Kimberley West was carefully scrutinised by Romantis to ascertain its originality. The similarities were often rather minor and could have been coincidental, but as they occurred rather too often to be by chance, Romantis began to suspect, if not plagiarism, then certainly free and considerable use of some of Jane Ransom's earlier themes in such a way as to indicate possible access to the source of the stories.

Romantis novels were printed in great quantities but released for only a very short time onto the market, so it was not always possible to obtain back copies once they were withdrawn from release. It was noted that the stories of concern from Kimberley West were nearly always similar to those of Jane Ransom from her earliest work, those that would be the most difficult to find in the marketplace.

Chapter Twelve

This was of scant concern to Jess; in fact, she was totally unaware of the issue. It was of no concern at all to her if it ever arose as it never occurred to her that such a comparison would ever be made. The only reason she became aware of the fact was that her publisher's lawyers in Melbourne notified her by mail that they were investigating the issue and legal action was being contemplated to protect their interests and also her own. It came as a shock to Jess, who had been ploughing on in all her efforts and producing copious amounts of literature.

In the end, the threats and implications became such that, reluctantly, Jess decided she might have to journey down to Melbourne to sort out all the problems. She was considerably embarrassed within herself to have caused so much trauma, and also feared she may be placing in jeopardy not only Kimberley West but also her other two beings.

Jess rang the Melbourne company and discussed at length the problem and intimated strongly that she was not interested in any form of legal proceedings no matter who was supposedly doing what to whom. The legal people in Melbourne refuted this argument and dismissed it as irrelevant. She finally arranged a meeting with them in their Melbourne office for the third week in January to give herself plenty of time to make all the arrangements.

Jess departed Milbark between showers and was ferried by courtesy of the Ravymoota chopper to Derby where she had booked a flight to Melbourne via Perth. She would have a few days in Melbourne before the meeting, giving her plenty of time to allow for hold-ups, of which there was ample opportunity for them to occur from such a distance, given the time of year.

Jess chose the Wet as the most suitable time as there was little work able to be done and she would be the least missed at this time. Jess took this rare opportunity to purchase for herself some new clothes from the bush outfitters. She bought herself a pair of brown elastic-sided boots with a block heel and chisel square toe and leather sole. She also bought new moleskins with mid-rise and boot-cut legs as well as new shirts in white and sky-blue, and an expensive dress coat with light-grey checks and fashionable pockets. She hoped that would create the right impression on her arrival.

Melbourne was an eye-opener to the unsophisticated and unworldly country woman that Jess had become after so much of her life in the outback. She wandered about the city in amazement at the lifestyle and the differences in living circumstances of other people.

The meeting was arranged for ten-thirty on Wednesday morning in the tower block that was the headquarters of the Advent Publishing Company, as they had better facilities and more legal expertise; plus their prime client, George Norman Thaler, was deserving of total service as they wished to protect one of their greatest assets. The Sydney publishers, Kramer's, sent their top lawyer and her Sydney literary agent was in attendance as well. Romantis was represented by a lawyer and a woman who was Jessie's contact in that company. As none of the attendees had ever actually met Jane Ransom, George Norman Thaler or, for that matter Kimberley West, let alone Jessie MacIntyre, there was an expectant buzz about the room as they eagerly awaited her arrival. Kimberley West had indicated that, as she was still overseas, she would be unable to attend but her agent could work in her best interests. That would be simple as their interests coincided completely.

The word on the street was that Jessie MacIntyre was thoroughly annoyed with this whole episode, but the real reason for that annoyance was not forthcoming, at least not from Jessie herself. It was assumed that she would be very cross at another author stealing her ideas and creations for her own benefit. It was still totally unknown and not in the least suspected that Jessie MacIntyre was also Kimberley West. The meeting was expected to be lively.

Jess was definitely not looking forward to this gathering. For one thing, she was very fearful of having to reveal herself as being Kimberley West for several reasons. She feared that she might alienate her first two publishers by her deviousness, or incur their wrath at not having pursued her dreams through them exclusively. She was also fearful of the repercussions of this revelation on her already tattered reputation for her scheming and the effects it might have on her enterprises. She hoped to get through it all without revealing her identity, but would have to play that one by ear. She was resigned within herself that her deceitful little schemes must one day end, but she hoped not just yet.

Unusually for Jess, as she was so disappointed that it had all come to this, she was actually late for the meeting, she normally being a stickler for punctuality. The meeting was scheduled to commence at ten-thirty, but by ten-forty, she still had not arrived. Ten minutes late, Jess entered the grandiose foyer of the lavishly decorated headquarters of the famous Advent Publishing house. The receptionist was serenely calm and professional. There were inquisitive personnel lingering in the foyer, and Jess suspected they were not all awaiting someone else's arrival.

An elegantly dressed young woman was beckoned over to the counter to take charge of Jessie. She introduced herself as Deborah Campbell and ushered a nervous Jess into the waiting lift. The woman chattered convivially to an almost mute and somewhat awestruck Jess as they ascended the many flights to arrive on the nineteenth floor.

As Jess entered the room, she was met by a sea of expectant faces that was initially slightly daunting for her. Her escort headed straight for the woman already advancing from the throng and began the introductions. As she was led one by one around the room, noting the sartorial qualities of those attending, for the first time she was suddenly aware that the practical bushman's provisioner, R M Williams, was possibly not the most appropriate formal wear when attending city gatherings surrounded by so much glamour.

Jess was finally ushered to the end of the boardroom table and shown an impressive cloth-covered chair into which she was directed to sit. She sat nervously for many minutes trying to take in the barrage of information that descended upon her. The woman whom she first met on entering the room took charge and acted as the chairwoman of the meeting.

The meeting commenced officially with some more formal introductions and an indication of who was responsible for what aspect of this fiasco. Jess was able to make a much better fist of sorting out everybody once they were all seated and stationary. Jess was slightly overawed by all the seemingly high-powered presentations that were offered initially by way of a preamble. She sat in mute amazement at the toing and froing that proceeded before her. She was, however, slowly regaining her composure and self-worth and decided that she should attempt to take control of this affair before it advanced too far.

There was a lull in the chatter as all faces turned to Jess on the raising of some point that she found totally irrelevant. She seized that opportunity to espouse her ideas. After a long, almost embarrassing pause, during which she deliberately looked at each of those attending, she said softly but firmly, 'I thought I made it perfectly clear that I did not wish this issue to be pursued any further.' There was another long pause. Then the lawyer for Advent, Bill Miller, an elegantly dressed and well-spoken middle-aged man responded, 'With all due respect to yourself, Ms MacIntyre, I don't think you fully grasp the seriousness of the issues involved here. As the representative of Advent and in association with my colleague Mr Gho from Romantis, I have an obligation to both protect your interests as well as our own and an obligation to do that under the Publications Act. We view with great seriousness the incidents of alleged plagiarism apparent in the work of Ms West. You must agree it is serious?'

There was another long delay before Jess answered, saying, 'No, I do not.'

There was a slight flicker of a smile on the face of Granville Alexander, the literary agent who was the sole defender of Kimberley West. Jess observed that change but did not acknowledge it.

'I say again, I do not wish for this to proceed any further. Surely my wishes are important?'

'Yes indeed, Ms MacIntyre, but there are other issues at stake.'

'I think not, Mr Miller. I think not.' Jessie's tone was beginning to gain a more ominous note and her disdain of the legal profession was beginning to raise her ire again. She was quite dismissive of his arguments.

He was about to speak again, when the chair of the meeting interrupted, saying in a conciliatory tone, 'Maybe we could just move onto another point for the moment.'

Jess gave her a slightly searing look and responded, 'No, indeed not. After all, this is the crux of why I have been dragged down here at considerable inconvenience. I say again, I wish for this issue to be dropped, and that should be an end to it.'

There was a long and nervous silence in the room. Mr Miller spoke again, 'Do you not concede that Ms West is responsible for copying and utilising many of your own ideas and storylines?'

'What if Jane Ransom and Kimberley West were acquaintances, Mr Miller? Quite good ones at that and that

Chapter Twelve

Jane Ransom held lengthy discussions with her friend and acquiesced to her restricted Romantis output to be expanded into something different and more appealing? Is that a crime, Mr Miller?'

'I understood,' said Bill Miller, 'that you are Jane Ransom.'

'And what has that got to do with the price of eggs?' asked an annoyed Jessie.

Bill Miller smiled slightly at the turn of phrase, then asked, 'Are you saying that you have an understanding with Ms West then?'

'I wish this topic to be ended Mr Miller. That is my wish.'

'Be that as it may Ms MacIntyre, that may not abrogate the problem in a strict legal sense unless an agreement is struck that is binding and mutually agreed.'

There was a long pause. Jess stared at Miller for many seconds, then responded, 'You mean between some set of lawyers, not between the creators of the art?' Her tone was a little more scathing.

He looked at the chairwoman for guidance. Mr Gho, the young solicitor from Romantis looked at Jess and added, 'You are saying that Jane Ransom, you, knows Ms West?'

'Is that relevant?' asked Jess again.

'Possibly. In this context.' Mr Gho then turned to Granville Alexander and asked him, 'Where is Ms West now?'

'She called me a day or so ago from London.'

'Does she know Ms MacIntyre?'

'I'm not aware of that,' he said, turning his gaze to Jess. She did not respond. The room descended into silence.

Finally, Jess announced, 'Good, that's all settled then. We'll have no more talk about any legal actions by anybody.'

Once the gathering realised that Jess was intractable about this issue, the discussion deteriorated into small groups of chit-chat that finally resolved to postpone the entire issue indefinitely. Jess had only one aim of this meeting and she had achieved it. But she wondered if it was possible to plagiarise oneself, even using another name. She was not prepared to venture down that path.

Once back home after that deflection of trouble, Jess could see, however, that the writing was on the wall, so to speak. She missed Norm's intellect and stimulation enormously. She also missed the knowledge and sympathetic attitude of George, as well as the honing of her language skills. When Peter died, she lost an endless source of information and understanding about the industry in which she had found herself. She still had Stuart, but he was by now getting quite elderly and much less capable of the hard work he used to do.

Jess had found the few trips she had made to Sydney and especially Gosford had stirred up long-dead thoughts of her lost childhood and teenage years. She especially found the early morning walks around the water and jetties of the Gosford and Woy Woy areas stirring, and the sunrises out of the Pacific stimulating.

She had seen plenty of sunsets over the azure-blue Indian Ocean while on fishing trips with George or Stuart to the capes around the Kimberley, but these southern waters held a familiar fascination for her tortured mind. Maybe it was the fact of more people being around her that aroused her interest. Anyway, it certainly confused her mind as to where her life was heading, especially as those treasured souls from Milbark fell one by one.

All these people had not been replaced with any inspiring individuals at all. In fact, the younger replacements were decidedly uncouth and much less amenable to intellectual pastimes. She began to feel out of place there and the dim and distant call of the unknown was slowly increasing within her as the eventful years trudged by in rhythmic seasonal change.

The young part-Aboriginal man that George had trained up to operate the grader for the station and be the mechanic was quite an intelligent and energetic man but he had none of the drive and inquisitiveness of his mentor. There were several other rough young men who joined the crew but again Jess found them wanting. She never did decide whether that was just the result of her own inner weakness when it came to socialising or whether they were really of a lower standard than she had previously known.

Once George had departed, Jess found it difficult to find suitable companions to accompany her on her long trips to Derby or Broome. It was also becoming more difficult to scrounge a decent vehicle to perform that task. In the end, she advised Stuart that she wished to purchase for herself her own four-wheel drive vehicle from Broome. She got a lift into town with Ravymoota people and arranged to buy a new Toyota Land Cruiser station wagon with all the bells and whistles for rugged outback driving. She included long-range fuel tanks, upgraded suspension, heavy-duty bull bar and a full-length roof rack. She was very pleased with her new vehicle and thoroughly enjoyed driving something that was much more comfortable than her old GMC.

The inevitable demise of Stuart played heavily on Jessie's mind. She was totally unsure what she was going to do with the arrival of that event. Stuart viewed his approaching passing with resigned stoicism, but was not prepared to formulate a will in any form, especially following the disappointment of the discovery that Jess was not his blood relative. There was no one to leave his few worldly goods to, and the lease of Milbark was solely in his name, so it could be transferred to the person who most wanted it.

Deep down he knew that person was not Jess. She proclaimed undying love for the property and its environment but made it clear to him that she did not see herself capable or willing to take on that difficult responsibility. This was the product of several influences on Jess, not the least being Norman's advice, nay warning, not to bury herself in this dream world of isolation and mystic influences. Jess felt she had already disobeyed his warning for too long and was now only awaiting the inevitable before departing.

Towards the end, Stuart received many visits from his neighbours at Bingarini Station because they were very keen to secure the lease for themselves and to prevent others acquiring that pocket of very desirable land. They also wished to avoid any possibility of a native title being proclaimed over it as that might lead to the eventual loss of their own lease and family property that they had built up over a couple of generations. Jess had no strong view either way and was accepting of any outcome. She befriended as best she could the young family that would probably take over Milbark Station on Stuart's death as there were a lot of boys in the family.

Stuart finally died one afternoon in early January, 2008. The weather was especially cyclonic and the Wet had dumped much rainfall over the region. Jess arranged a small funeral in the graveyard with a few of the locals able to reach the property, mostly by helicopter between squalls. Edna and Ralph came with a small band of his acquaintances from there, as well as most of the family from Bingarini Station. Those of the Aboriginal clan that were still close by came wailing loudly as they knew their circumstances might be changing as well as the sadness of the loss of the Boss.

It took some time, before Jess was able to organise for the lease arrangements to be altered and re-leased into the new names. The Jennings family were very understanding and allowed Jess to stay as long as she required to arrange her departure. She would have to rationalise her meagre possessions for them to fit into the wagon and leave anything behind that she did not need as she felt that her departure would be final and complete. She did, as one small favour, ask if sometime in the future she had the facilities, that she might wish to return to retrieve her old mate, the GMC truck that had played such a huge part in her life at Milbark. Jess found it difficult to rouse herself with the same enthusiasm to attend to the station cattle work. She was able to direct the men to see to the mustering but increasingly relied on the Jennings boys coming over and supervising activities. She gathered her few possessions and began to pack them into her station wagon. The bulk of the space, especially on the roof rack was taken up with the copies of her extensive range of publications that she had accumulated over the last twenty-two years or more.

The station was worth quite a sum of money, as it included all the land, some improvements and all the cattle. Jess paid out all the staff who deserved any extra and the remainder was left to her as the only remaining original of the crew. All she could do was to invest the surplus in yet more term deposits. During her last full Dry season at Milbark, Jess drove extensively over the property in her old truck and often camped well away from the homestead. This was her last reward and parting gift to herself, because she knew she was leaving something that was familiar and heading into the totally unfamiliar, something she had not done since she was thirteen, when she first arrived at Milbark.

The last few nights that Jess spent in the workshop that had been her productive office, she studied intently the maps she had bought while in Sydney. She wished to visit her publishers in Melbourne after what had been a few neglectful years. There were many ways that she could travel from Milbark to Melbourne, all were difficult, some treacherous and some much longer than others. In the end, for some reason, she decided to travel via Queensland and see some of the rugged outback tracks that Peter had mentioned in his late-night campfire stories.

Chapter Twelve

Jess drove out along the long slow road that led to the river and onto the Gibb. She was in no hurry to take her last leave of what had been so much a part of her life. She was now forty-three years old and she knew that whatever awaited her in her new life, the chance of meeting a nice young man had long passed. She would approach the end alone. She crossed the river in her heavily laden Land Cruiser and slid out of the gravel bed and onto the firm dirt road. There she stopped the car and got out for one last walk back to the spot where she had first crossed the river into the unknown when she was only thirteen.

So much had happened since then; and as then, she came alone and would leave alone. She sadly contemplated the gently gurgling isolation, and with a hint of a tear, turned and went back to the vehicle. She stopped momentarily at the Gibb turn off and then set off in the direction of Ravymoota Station.

Edna Coniston in particular was very sad at the leaving of Jess and she did cry a little at the prospect of never seeing this strange and remarkable young woman again.

Jess said her farewells to the station people there and returned to the Gibb River Road. For the first time in her life, Jess turned left towards Kununurra instead of right, and headed off into only God knew what. Jess had been cast unwillingly and begrudgingly into this enigmatic country, now she was departing of her own choice. She hoped she knew what she was doing.

www.ingramcontent.com/pod-product-compliance
Lightning Source LLC
Chambersburg PA
CBHW030252010526
44107CB00053B/1674